**China and
Southeast Asia —
The Politics of
Survival**

China and Southeast Asia — The Politics of Survival

A Study of Foreign Policy Interaction

Melvin Gurtov
University of California, Riverside

Heath Lexington Books
D.C. Heath and Company
Lexington, Massachusetts
Toronto   London

To Ellene Lien-hua, and to Gertrude and
Eugene Farkas, with deep affection

Table of Contents

List of Tables and Figures

Tables

Figures

List of Abbreviations

AFPFL — Anti-Fascist People's Freedom League (Burma)
ASA — Association of Southeast Asia
ASEAN — Association of Southeast Asian Nations
ASPAC — Asian and Pacific Council
BSPP — Burma Socialist Program Party
BWP — Burma Workers Party
BWPP — Burma Workers and Peasants Party
CCP — Chinese Communist Party
CPB — Communist Party of Burma (White Flags)
CPR — Chinese People's Republic
CPT — Communist Party of Thailand
DRV — Democratic Republic of Vietnam (North Vietnam)
GUB — Government of the Union of Burma
GVN — Government of Vietnam (South Vietnam)
ICC — International Control Commission (also, and more officially, the International Commission for Supervision and Control)
IPC — Indochinese People's Conference
KCFA — Khmer-China Friendship Association
KIA — Kachin Independence Army
KMT — Kuomintang
KNDO — Karen National Defense Organization
KNUP — Karen National United Party
NCNA — New China News Agency
NDUF — National Democratic United Front (Burmese Communists)
NLFSV — National Liberation Front of South Vietnam
NUF — National United Front (Burmese Communists)
NUFK — National United Front of Kampuchea
PKI — Communist Party of Indonesia
PLA — (Chinese) People's Liberation Army
RLG — Royal Laotian Government
RTG — Royal Thai Government
SEATO — Southeast Asia Treaty Organization
TIM — Thai Independence Movement
TPF — Thai Patriotic Front
UWPB — United Workers' Party of Burma
VNA — (North) Vietnam News Agency
VTP — Voice of the Thai People

Preface

In this book, I hope to broaden our understanding of foreign policy in Asia by examining, case-by-case and comparatively, the relations of the Chinese People's Republic with Thailand, Cambodia and Burma. The study looks at both sides of these relations: it is concerned not only with China's foreign policy instruments and objectives, but also with the place of China in the foreign and domestic policies of the three Southeast Asian states. China's relationship to dissident movements in these countries is of special interest. Conclusions and hypotheses are offered about policy motivations and goals that bear on the much-disputed question of the dimensions and substance of the "Chinese threat" to, and American security interests in, Southeast Asia.

I would like to draw attention here to one theme of the book, not because it is the dominant theme but because it often receives inadequate attention in American studies of international relations in Asia. Key developments in China's relations with Southeast Asia—events that seem decisively to determine whether and to what extent relations will be friendly or hostile—rarely can be fully understood unless account is taken of the role of the United States. This may seem almost a truism and yet it is surprising how often relations between China and Southeast Asian countries are evaluated in a narrow, bilateral context, as though American actions and declarations had only marginal and tentative impact on the quality of those relations. As will be described in the case studies, China's policy choices concerning relations with governments and antigovernment movements in the three countries have been heavily influenced by American policy in the Indochina area and by the support given or denied it by the Southeast Asian governments.

In addition to the official publications and broadcast and newspaper reports of the countries under study, I also cite from interviews with Thai and Cambodian officials that were conducted during a research trip in the summer of 1968. At their request, I have not identified them in the citations. But I take this opportunity to thank them and the Ministry of Foreign Affairs of the royal governments of Thailand and Cambodia for their hospitality and cooperation during my stay.

I also want to thank Robert L. Solomon of Rand, Allen S. Whiting of the University of Michigan, and David A. Wilson of the University of California, Los Angeles, each of whom gave the manuscript a careful reading and made numerous invaluable suggestions to improve it. Richard Baum and David Farquhar of the University of California, Los Angeles, and Paul F. Langer of Rand also provided helpful comments. I am grateful to Mrs. Jo Sloan, who drew the maps. Miss Lilita Dzirkals kindly translated the Russian materials, Mrs. Anna Sun Ford helped bring together the Chinese newspaper accounts, and Mrs. Marie Hoeppner typed the many drafts, from first to last, with her usual grace and efficiency. My wife, Rochelle, deserves special thanks for tolerating this book long enough to do the index. I am responsible for translations from Chinese and French, as well as for any errors or omissions in the book as a whole.

**China and
Southeast Asia —
The Politics of
Survival**

1   China in Southeast Asia: Some Problems for Analysis

While debate continues over the motivations and objectives of Communist China's foreign policy, remarkably few detailed studies have appeared to substantiate generalizations about it. Typically, the nonpolemical literature on the foreign policy of the Chinese People's Republic (CPR) has taken one of two forms: the comprehensive overview or the single-case study. The weaknesses common to both have been the lack of a comparative perspective and a Sinocentric orientation. This book aspires to fill these gaps by assessing China's foreign policy in Southeast Asia (mainly since 1964) on the basis of three case studies—Peking's relations with Thailand, Cambodia, and Burma—and by identifying the place China has had in the policies of these three nations. In this manner, we should be able to offer some conclusions or hypotheses concerning how China deals with nearby countries and what the Chinese "presence" in Asia means for the political decisions of their governments.

China's Foreign Policy

An analysis of China's relations with three countries is particularly important for the implications it may have about the *pattern* and the *actuation* of Chinese foreign policy in general. One of the main purposes of this book is to deal with the question of the confirmation and definition of patterns in Peking's external relations. Is China's policy toward a given country part of and determined by a basic set of policy guidelines? Does the policy toward one country depart from an overall policy line? Perhaps there are fundamental policy aims and tactics, but considerable flexibility in their application, depending on the country and the circumstances, local and international.

The ways in which ideology, as it is expressed in foreign policy doctrine, and practicality ("realistic" judgment of alternatives) interact is, consequently, an important theme to trace in the case studies. As is widely accepted, China's policy toward a single state or on a particular situation may be only partially reflected in a general doctrinal pronouncement. Doctrine and policy (intentions) simply cannot be equated; but neither can doctrine be dismissed as irrelevant to understanding policy.

By way of illustration, a theoretical Chinese statement concerning "national liberation movements" may have important bearing on the Sino-Soviet dispute— by projecting China's revolutionary image, establishing China's independent ideological position in the international Communist movement, and distinguish-

1

ing (and thus isolating) Soviet from Chinese Communism. But that same statement may not denote *the* Chinese policy toward all left-leaning dissident movements abroad. To determine China's policy requires investigations not only of Chinese statements but also of related actions regarding specific countries in which dissidence or a revolutionary potential exists.[a]

In attempting to correlate Chinese statements and actions, we need to accept two notions about China's foreign policy that have long been accepted in discussing Western diplomacy. The first is that foreign policy may as often proceed from unpremeditated circumstances as from carefully conceived plans. A foreign policy can be not only initiatory but in reaction to such conditions as local crises or disturbances, or perceived external security threats, as in Chinese actions designed to outflank or depressurize externally initiated actions. Chinese intervention in Korea was a specific instance of a reactive foreign policy.

Secondly, a foreign policy may be highly ambiguous and uncertain as well as decisive and calculative. For example, after the Tonkin Gulf incidents of August 1964, statements from Peking asserted that "aggression against North Vietnam is aggression against China." These statements were designed to deter the United States from further military action against the North. But what was Chinese policy to deal with subsequent instances of American attacks, if deterrence failed? Here, Chinese policy probably was as ambivalent as the Chinese statements, since Peking's choice of response depended on a wide range of possible United States actions and perceived intentions.

A principal aim of this book, then, is to elucidate the flexibility and spontaneity of Chinese foreign policy no less than the functions of ideology in it. Having done that, some propositions can be offered about the aims and calculations that lie behind China's external behavior.

China in Southeast Asian Politics

In this book we also look at China's actions and statements from the standpoint of the interests, goals, and politics of three Southeast Asian states. China's impact is judged by examining the foreign policies and foreign relations of Thailand, Cambodia, and Burma in three aspects: as discrete units (i.e., as both nation-states and political systems), as members of a region called Southeast Asia with which they identify, and as actors in the international community. These countries were chosen because of their proximity to China, the difference in

---

[a]Even then, of course, alternative Chinese methods for implementing a policy need to be kept in mind. When the Chinese call for "struggle," they are signaling their hostility; but which tactics they are advocating (armed struggle, political organization, diplomatic pressure, united front) and which role in the struggle they intend to play (vocal encouragement or opposition, material support of the antagonist's enemy)—not to mention how they will play it and under what conditions they entered and may withdraw—cannot always be inferred from public statements alone.

their foreign policy style and management, and their similarity in having to deal with Communist and other dissident internal forces.

Among the questions that arise when the focus is on China in the context of Southeast Asian politics are: How has China's power and influence affected the structures and pattern of these countries' bilateral, regional, and international associations; their definitions of national policy; and their degree of independent choice internally as well as externally? What means have been available in the Southeast Asian countries to deflect or moderate Chinese influence? What have been the effects of indigenous political phenomena such as rebellion, nationalism, ethnic heterogeneity, and cultural pride on the foreign policy choices of Southeast Asian governments and of Peking? Finally, what difference has the level of governmental stability and authority in Southeast Asian countries made for Peking's assessment of foreign policy opportunities?

When we talk about China's "place" or "impact" in Southeast Asia, the implication is that China is an influential but by no means dominant actor in that region's politics. The analysis that will follow in the case studies is designed to bring out this distinction by noting the variety in the foreign policies of Southeast Asian governments, including those professing to be neutralist but often depicted as "leaning toward" or "accommodating to" China. Put in theoretical terms, whereas the "dominant system" of major-bloc relations profoundly affects the foreign policy of Southeast Asian nations in their "subordinate system," there is much more to international politics in Southeast Asia than the behavior of China, the Soviet Union, or the United States.[1] Southeast Asian governments have not merely been objects of the foreign policies of the major powers. This study will show that they have adopted policies independent of, and with motivations different from, those of their big-power allies. It will further seek to demonstrate that relations between and among these governments may be more salient to understanding politics in Southeast Asia than the actions and declarations of the major powers. The fixation in much of the literature on Southeast Asia on the behavior of the "dominant system" members has obscured the maneuverability, changeability, and manipulative power of the region's governments, perhaps because power has been equated too much with military punch and has not taken sufficient account of diplomatic cleverness and ideological pliancy.

Some light may be shed on the ways in which power is used, channeled, and diffused as Southeast Asian governments have confronted China and other large nations. At the same time, the study shall take issue with two common notions about power in Asia. The first is that Southeast Asia, because it consists of militarily weak, economically impoverished, and politically unstable and unintegrated states, is a power vacuum that is vulnerable to external penetration, especially by Communist China.[2] The case studies may enable us to assess whether and to what extent the term "power vacuum" is appropriate, and how and under what conditions China has actually penetrated it. Second is the notion of an Asian "balance of power," a term that has sometimes been applied to describe an existing condition, sometimes to prescribe the policies states are pursuing, and sometimes to indicate the systemic result of balance policies.[3] In view of the special conditions that seem necessary to the functioning of a power balance, it should be asked whether they exist in present-day Southeast Asia; whether national leaders there have acted in order to establish or preserve a balance of power; and whether national interests and priorities are conducive to a regional consensus about which major power should play the balancer, and when. Insofar as the answers to these questions may be revealed, they should be able to inform us about the state of and the prospects for security in Southeast Asia.

2

Thailand and China: The Politics of Confrontation

In the fall of 1964, the Communist Party of Thailand (CPT), about which little had been heard for several years, and which had been outlawed and a politically inactive force in Thailand for much longer, suddenly received publicity from Peking with publication of a message from its "central committee" to the Central Committee of the Chinese Communist Party (CCP). In quick succession, two Thai Communist front organizations also made their appearance, issued revolutionary programs that were published in the Chinese news media, and, by the second half of 1965, assertedly were leading a growing insurgent movement. To portray China's policy toward Thailand and China's place in Thai policy, the motivating forces behind the emergence of the CPT and its front organizations need to be closely examined. To do that, in turn, requires investigation of the development of the Communist movement in Thailand, China's relationship to it, and the Thai Government's attitude toward Communism within and outside Thailand.

Communism in Thailand

Marxism, whether as a class-based ideology, an organizational tool, or an economic doctrine, has enjoyed far less success in Thailand than perhaps in any other country in Southeast Asia. Among the many reasons for this[1] is that political organization is based on personal allegiances, because of which politics has featured the maneuverings of bureaucratic groups and factions rather than produced disciplined, ideological mass parties. Second, the stress in Buddhism on individual merit has influenced a general societal interest in upward mobility, self-reliance, and profit. Marxism's rigid class distinctions have thus not appealed to Thai peasants or intellectuals, especially in the absence of widespread economic discontent. The combination of diplomatic ingenuity and plain good luck that enabled Thailand to avoid a colonial experience is a third factor. As a result, Western influences were adapted without displacing tradition or becoming the catalyst of nationalist resentment. Finally, the Thai ruling class has been a stable social group that has generally been successful in preserving Thai national interests.

The inability of Marxism to take root in Thailand helps explain the scarcity of data concerning the origins and early development of a Communist movement there. Like leftist groups that began to form elsewhere in Southeast Asia, the one in Thailand seems to have first emerged in the late 1920s and to have had at

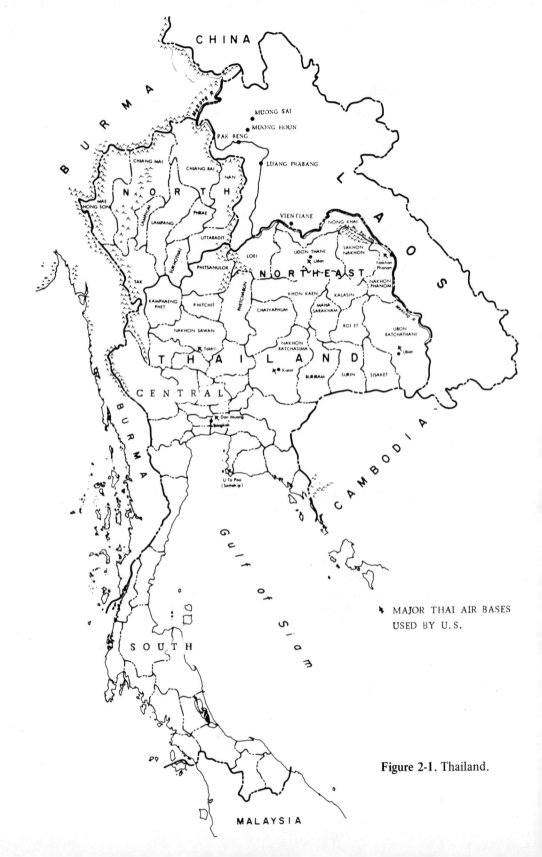

Figure 2-1. Thailand.

least a tenuous connection with the Soviet Comintern's Far Eastern Bureau. A Siamese Communist Party may have existed by 1935, although the present CPT dates itself from December 1942.[2] The composition of the Siamese Party, such as it was, is equally obscure. It appears to have been an organization of overseas Chinese;[a] but it is possible that there were actually two separate Communist groups, one composed exclusively of Chinese, the other of ethnic Thai.[3]

These shaky beginnings were doubtless due as much to the on-again off-again anti-Communist activities of the Royal Thai Government (RTG) as to Marxism's limited appeal. From 1946 on, the Communist Party or parties underwent alternating periods of government leniency and crackdown. The Communist movement was able to carry out propaganda and recruitment activities during 1946, for instance, when the law banning them was lifted as a condition for Soviet acceptance of Thai membership in the United Nations. Moreover, the radical socialist regime of Pridi Phanomyong (March-August 1946) proved more amenable to the development of political parties than did its successors. Finally, the establishment of diplomatic relations between Thailand and the Chinese Nationalist government in 1946 led to a brief period of relaxed pressures against the overseas Chinese community that may have enabled left-leaning Chinese to join the Communist movement. This situation changed radically following the military coup that emplaced Phibun Songkhram as prime minister in April 1948. From then until September 1955, the Chinese were the object of government restrictions (deportation, press censorship, school closings, etc.), martial law was imposed, and anti-Communism became the order of the day.[4]

Although the Thai Communist Party no doubt profited from brief periods of relaxation such as occurred in 1946, overall, the party's movements were considerably more hesitant than was the government's determination to expunge it. While underground in 1952, the party held its second national conference (the first was held in 1942) and elected a new central committee.[5] During Thailand's "hundred flowers" (Hyde Park) period (roughly, September 1955-September 1957) of fairly open political debate, the party apparently remained clandestine, with most of its leaders in Peking. It was in fact probably from Peking that the CPT greeted the Eighth Congress of the Chinese Communist Party in September 1956[6]—one of the rare overt communications with Peking until October 1964.

Programmatically, there were two CPT documents of significance in these early years, a ten-point statement of aims published in 1945 (entitled "What the Thai Communists Will Do Now") and a presentation of party tactics in 1957. In

---

[a]Skinner has estimated the Chinese population of Thailand in 1942, including local-born and China-born Chinese, at 1,876,000 or 11.7 percent of the total population. (*Chinese Society in Thailand: An Analytical History*, Cornell University Press, Ithaca, N.Y., 1957, table 8, p. 183.) No more than about 5,000 were probably Communist party members, however. (Ibid., p. 323.) As Skinner's discussion points out, Thailand's Chinese Communists were active in a number of legal associations in the postwar period but, until 1948 and the start of the Communists' final drive to victory on the mainland, the pro-Kuomintang Chinese formed a clear majority.

the former document, the party, reflecting Mao Tse-tung's theses in "On the New Democracy," announced its support of a series of political, economic, and social reforms, socialist in nature, that would make the country "truly democratic and independent." The party called for a united front of all progressive elements internally and, externally, cooperation with the wartime allied governments.[7] By 1957, when a number of Thai leftists had availed themselves of the Phibun government's relaxation of restrictions on visits to China, the united-front theme was given added emphasis. In a "New Year Message to the Thai People,"[8] the party advocated an antiimperialist alliance of all political parties—the "united front from above" tactic—aimed at formation of a coalition government. Yet, the party explicitly opposed overthrowing the Bangkok government; instead, the united front seems to have been intended to bring about a broadening of the Thai government's composition and a permanent liberalization of its policies.

The Northeast

The post-1957 history of the CPT and other radical groups is intimately connected with the northeast region of Thailand. A small increase of antigovernment violence (political assassinations and clashes between rebellious elements and authorities) had occurred in this region of fifteen provinces beginning about 1959. Although this development coincided with the rise to prominence of Field Marshal Sarit Thanarat,[b] the northeast had been the setting for discontent and antigovernment activity long before Sarit came to power. Yet, it may be more than coincidental that once the Sarit regime stepped up its hunt for Communist sympathizers in the northeast in 1960, certain antigovernment groups there forged closer relations with Communist forces in Laos than ever before and the first reports were heard of Thai Communist organizational activity.

Thailand's northeast has recently been the subject of intensive interest, and some dispute, by American specialists. On two points relevant to this study, however, there seems to be general agreement. In the first place, the northeast has historically been a distinct region of Thailand, different from the other regions (north, south, and center) even if not unique in any of its specific

---

[b]Prior to having assumed the prime ministership in February 1959, Sarit, as head of the armed forces, had led a successful coup against Phibun Songkhram in September 1957. General Thanom Kittikachon was installed as prime minister in January 1958, but Sarit took over as head of a Revolutionary Council in October 1958.

characteristics.[c] Secondly, opposition to the Thai government has been a political tradition that has, however, taken many forms, of which Communist-supported rebellion is only the most recent and by no means the most prominent.

The northeast first gained national political significance during World War II in the Free Thai movement. Led by Pridi Phanomyong, the Free Thai movement was originally an allied-supported intelligence gathering force based in the northeast. In the years immediately after the war, the movement was either supported or at least left alone by Bangkok. As prime minister, Pridi's ambition that Thailand play a prominent role in an anticolonialist Southeast Asia League led to the northeast's becoming a sanctuary for pro-Viet Minh rebels. With his resignation in 1946 and the failure of his coup attempt in 1949, northeastern dissidents were faced with constant government harassment. Bangkok was suspicious of their involvement with Communist forces across the Mekong.[9]

The issue of separatism, which has been a matter of concern to Thai governments down to the present, seems to have been based on Bangkok's belief that northeastern dissidents, because of their presumed ethnic similarity to the Lao,[d] hoped to link up with the Viet Minh, and later the Pathet Lao, in order to realize the goal of union with Laos. When a former Free Thai named Khrong Chandawong, once a member of Thailand's National Assembly, reportedly cooperated with Laotian rebels to build up a Thai Exiles' Association of about 4,000 men, the government, between 1960 and 1961, broke it up and executed Khrong.[10] Nevertheless, some Thai-Lao as well as Vietnamese of the northeast evidently served with the Pathet Lao during the conflict in Laos from 1959 to 1962.[11] It is by no means clear, however, that these dissident Thai in fact wanted to amalgamate the northeast with Laos, though they may well have wanted

---

[c]There is a growing body of literature on the northeast, the most careful study being that by Charles F. Keyes, *Isan: Regionalism in Northeast Thailand*, Cornell University Press, Ithaca, N.Y., 1967. See, in addition, the symposia in *Asian Survey*, Vol. VI, No. 7, July 1966, and *Asia*, No. 6, Autumn 1966; Donald E. Nuechterlein, "Thailand: Another Vietnam?" *Asian Survey*, Vol. VII, No. 2, February 1967, pp. 126-130; Willard A. Hanna, "Thailand's Strategic Northeast: Defense and Development," American Universities Field Staff Reports, Southeast Asia Series, Vol. XIV, No. 1, January 1966.

Among the "special" characteristics usually attributed to the northeast are its geographic and physical isolation from the center, its poverty, its vulnerability to hostile penetration, its history of political opposition and dissidence, and (see below) the ethnic distinctiveness of the majority population.

[d]The so-called Thai-Lao people, who are the majority (6.9 million in 1960) in a region of roughly 8 million, are ethnically Thai and culturally closer to the populations of western and southern Laos than to the Thai of central Thailand. But, as Charles F. Keyes points out, most of the northeastern peoples do not identify with the state of Laos, but they do distinguish themselves from the central Thai by a localist ethnic affiliation called Isan-Lao (or Northeast-Lao). See his essay, "Ethnic Identity and Loyalty," *Asian Survey*, Vol. VI, No. 7, July 1966, pp. 362-369.

greater autonomy from central Thailand. Nor is it clear that they had any connection with the CPT or were meant to return to Thailand to continue their insurgent activity after service in Laos. To judge from circumstances at that time, the Pathet Lao and their North Vietnamese backers were primarily interested in gaining recruits for the war in Laos.

As noted, beginning roughly in 1959, there was a slight increase in armed incidents in the northeast and in extremely limited crypto-Communist organizational activity. But these developments seem not to have involved Thailand's Communist party. According to Pierre Fistié,[12] some incidents probably stemmed from autonomist plotting abetted by the Pathet Lao, while others may have been prompted by arrests and executions of villagers suspected of Communist affiliations by the Thai police. Actually, from 1959 through the end of 1964, such rebellious activities as did occur tended to be carried out by a variety of dissident bands, organizations, and individuals having separate aims, leaderships, and base areas. Several, perhaps most, of them were less subversive or autonomist than simply antigovernment; they were more concerned with maintaining their supply lines (to Laos) and assuring a stable manpower supply than in building a mass base, developing a political apparatus, forming structured fighting units, or coordinating among all the small groups that were operating in the region. Prior to the reemergence of the CPT in late 1964, in short, there is little evidence that a Thai Communist organization had managed to recruit widely or attract allies in the northeast or anywhere else.[e]

The activities of Vietnamese who have resided in the northeast are another matter. In the late 1920s, Ho Chi Minh sought to gain adherents from the scattered Vietnamese communities of Sakhon Nakhon and Udon provinces. As a security problem for the Thai government, the Vietnamese did not become a concern until the late 1950s, after sizable migrations had occurred in the years between the return of the French to Vietnam (1945) and the end of the Indochina conflict (1954). In 1959, the Red Cross societies of Thailand and North Vietnam reached agreement in Rangoon to begin the repatriation of these Vietnamese, whom the RTG suspected of being largely pro-Viet Minh. Of some 70,000 Vietnamese registered with the Thai government, about 40,000 were sent home between January 1960 and July 1964. (In addition, about 1000 refugees were repatriated to South Vietnam between 1953 and 1963. According to North Vietnam, the number of Vietnamese repatriated from Thailand between 1959

---

[e]From interviews conducted by the author with province and district officials of Chiangmai and Chiangrai provinces in northern Thailand, it was learned that while terrorist incidents—murders, indoctrination meetings, arms smuggling, and the like—had been encountered by government authorities in the early 1960s, the CPT itself was not heard of until 1965 and 1966. A Thai intelligence source interviewed by the author asserted that a Volunteer Liberation Organization (VLO) loyal to Pridi, then in China, had been active from a base in Laos and had sought out Peking's support in 1963 or 1964. But the VLO, he said, was separate from the CPT in organization, membership, and leadership—and China and North Vietnam indicated as much by recognizing the party-led Thai Communists rather than the primarily military VLO.

and 1965 is 45,025.)[13] As the result of population growth and illegal immigration to Thailand, the remaining number of Vietnamese has always been uncertain. One informed estimate, drawing from official Thai sources and reasoned speculation, puts the total at about 75,000 in all of Thailand, of whom some 27,300 live in eight towns in the northeast.[14]

While the Thai government was seeking to repatriate the Vietnamese—an effort that collapsed in mid-1964 at the time of the Tonkin Gulf incidents and did not resume until the fall of 1970[f]—it also adopted various control measures to keep tight surveillance over them. Moreover, the Thai police many times after 1959 arrested alleged Vietnamese Communist sympathizers and agents, drawing warnings from Hanoi. Nevertheless, it appears that those Vietnamese who were and are Communists have been able to establish and maintain a number of front organizations in the northeast, the most prominent of which is the Vietnamese Mutual Aid Association of Thailand. According to Peter A. Poole, the association and the other fronts form part of an elaborate hierarchical arrangement that is ultimately responsible to the Lao Dong Party of North Vietnam. Assertedly, the Vietnamese Communists have their own area and district committees in heavily Vietnamese communities to control the front organizations, the school system, and the youth.[15] With all this, there is no firm indication that either before or after 1964 have Thai Communists established ties to the Vietnamese Communist structures in the northeast. The North Vietnamese have chosen to rely on the Pathet Lao and their own training facilities to sustain the present rebellion in the northeast, and seem to have avoided seeking support for the CPT from among the Vietnamese communities.

Developments in the Communist Party, 1959-1965. The few reported activities of the CPT until October 1964 are understandable against the background of small-scale, organizationally disparate violence that was occurring in the northeast. Only one additional communication was published between the party and Peking: a congratulatory message to the CCP on October 1, 1959, the CPR's official founding day. As published by the New China News Agency (NCNA), the message contained no reference to revolutionary activity taking place or in preparation by the Thai Communists.[16]

According to Thai Communist sources, the CPT held a third meeting in 1961 at which a decision was taken to form an armed group and to abandon the "parliamentary road" of political struggle.[17] In September 1961, an unnamed Thai delegate to a Communist party congress in East Germany reportedly declared that the CPT was aiming "for the establishment of a patriotic, democratic united front for driving out U.S. imperialism from Thailand,

---

[f]After negotiations between the Red Cross organizations of the two countries had begun in Bangkok in September 1970, a Thai official announced that a preliminary agreement had been reached to repatriate 37,000 Vietnamese beginning in January 1971. *Bangkok Post*, October 25, 1970. The relevance of these negotiations to Thai policy in Indochina is commented on in the concluding part of this chapter.

overthrowing the treacherous, dictatorial Sarit government, and for independence, neutrality, peace and democracy. It will put up an unyielding struggle by relying upon the popular masses and organizing and mobilizing them."[18] What is important about this statement is that the Thai delegate did not claim the existence of a revolutionary movement, armed struggle, or external support for either from China or North Vietnam.

Although the Thai delegate's failure to mention Chinese and North Vietnamese support for armed struggle against the Royal Thai Government was only partially a reflection of reality, it did suggest Peking's unwillingness then to announce its support of a weak party at a time when a commitment was probably not deemed necessary. As late as January 1965, Chinese commentaries on the world-wide development of revolution against so-called reactionary regimes either omitted Thailand from the list or assigned the Thai situation an importance well below that of insurgencies in South Vietnam, Laos, and elsewhere. (In fact, between 1960 and the fall of 1964 news commentaries and analyses in Chinese Communist sources referred to Thailand almost exclusively in connection with the volatile Laotian situation.)[19] It was in keeping with Peking's quietness that when a delegation "representing" Thailand appeared at the Second Asian Economic Conference in Pyongyang (North Korea) in mid-1964, the Communist spokesman attacked Thailand's alleged subservience to United States policy, for the first time criticized the "incorrect position" of modern revisionism, but made no allusion to a revolutionary movement in his country.[20]

The first indication of a changing Chinese position on the Thai Communist movement came when Peking published the National Day congratulatory message of the CPT. In its message, the Thai party stated that the cornerstones of its policy were self-reliance, antiimperialism, and antireactionism. Revolution, the message said, had been betrayed by revisionist forces (the Soviet Union was not specified and would not be for some time). China's spirit of internationalism, on the other hand, far exceeded that of other socialist nations, and as Thailand's revolution developed, it was promised, "the relationships between the peoples of our two countries will grow closer and closer." Describing the events that had led up to "the present situation," the message stressed Thailand's transformation into "a new type of colony and a most important military base of U.S. imperialism," the reduction of the government of Thanom Kittikachon to a "slavish tool" of the United States, the impoverishment of the country by the RTG, and the RTG's "hostile policy toward China."

The message called for the overthrow of the royal government by the combined force of a "patriotic, democratic united front" composed of "any groups or individuals that are against the U.S. imperialists and their lackeys. . ."[21] Armed struggle to achieve the ends of "independence, neutrality, peace and democracy" was still not specifically urged, perhaps reflecting Peking's hesitancy to support a rebellion.

Compared to the CPT's New Year Message of 1957, the October 1964 message was far more focused and uncompromising. The appeal in 1964 was for the formation of a united front "from below" rather than "from above," a change necessitated by the absence of contending political parties in Thailand. The aim in 1964 was to overthrow the government, not to bargain with it; but neutrality was still preached as the appropriate foreign policy for Thailand. Finally, the party had clearly chosen to align with Communist China and to make the United States-Thailand alliance a major target of its propaganda.

Precisely one month after publication of the CPT's message, on November 1, 1964, the party's appeal for a united front was said to have received its first response. According to the Voice of the Thai People (VTP), a clandestine broadcasting station probably located in south China,[22] a Thai Independence Movement (TIM) was launched on November 1 with the issuance of a proclamation to the Thai people. The proclamation took special notice of alleged American control over the Thai armed forces. The United States was said to have "dispatched over 10,000 troops to occupy our territory" and to have transformed Thai military bases into aggressive instruments of American policy in Vietnam and Laos. Describing itself as a political organization open to all regardless of background or social stratum, the TIM announced its program: (1) "Chase the American imperialist aggressors from Thai soil"; (2) "Overthrow the Thanom traitorous dictatorial government, establish a government formed by patriotic, democracy-loving political parties and personalities which carries out neutral, peaceful policies"; (3) "Struggle to save and preserve the true democratic rights of the people"; (4) "Struggle for the policies of neutrality, peace, democracy, prosperity, and the people's happiness." Once again, the advantages of China's friendship were stressed.[23] The TIM's program was thus clearly designed to be compatible with that of the CPT.

The trio of organizations that would take up the fight against Bangkok was completed in January 1965 when the VTP broadcast the program of the Thai Patriotic Front (TPF), said to have been formed on the first of the year. Like the other two groups, the TPF leveled its attack on United States-Thai military cooperation, demanded the removal of all American troops and the overthrow of the government, and espoused a six-point program of "peace and neutrality" in a new government run by "patriots and democrats."[24] The fact that the Front merged with and became paramount to the TIM in December 1965[25] may indicate that the appearance of the TIM was merely a ruse to create the appearance of an ever-growing united front. The two organizations were programmatically indistinguishable, so that the subordination of the TIM to the TPF lost nothing ideologically and supposedly accomplished the Communists' purpose of demonstrating unity against a common enemy.

The next step in this seemingly contrived sequence of developments[g] was the founding of additional front organizations that would give the Communist

---

[g]The stages in the appearance of the party-front apparatus were strongly reminiscent of what had occurred in the South Vietnam Communist movement. In September 1960, Lê Duan, at the Lao Dong Party's Third Congress, called for formation of a National United Front in South Vietnam. The National Liberation Front (NLFSV) appeared on December 20, 1960, followed by announcement one year later that a People's Revolutionary Party had been established. As would be the case in the Thai Communist movement, the PRP's supremacy within the Front was also claimed.

movement international standing and seek to prove that the Front's appeal for nationwide support had been answered by a variety of "democratic elements." Between March and June 1965, several Thai "delegations"—in fact, appendages of the TPF—appeared at Communist-sponsored gatherings: a Thailand Federation of Patriotic Workers; a Thai Afro-Asian Solidarity Committee, which took part in the fourth session of the Afro-Asian People's Solidarity Conference in Ghana during May 1965; and a Thailand Federation of Trade Unions. Other "patriotic" organizations were referred to as having been organized in Thailand for teachers, monks, "combatants," and lawyers.[26] Later in 1965 and in succeeding years, still other front groups were introduced by the Communist media.

Along with the appearance of the CPT and its front groups came the emergence in Peking of several Thai exiles from obscurity. Once the TIM and TPF had been set up, two men—Monkon Nonakon and Phayom Chulanond—emerged as their leaders. Monkon Nonakon, imprisoned for subversion by Thai authorities in the mid-1950s, became head of the TIM until its merger with the TPF and thereafter assumed the title of assistant permanent representative of the TPF. He is said to have been born in 1912 in Trang province, southern Thailand.[27] Phayom, apparently considered more an opportunist than a leftist by Thai government leaders,[h] was a member of the Thai parliament from Phet Buri province (south-central Thailand) from 1948 to 1950, when he failed to gain reelection. He held the rank of lieutenant-colonel in the Thai army until stripped of it by the RTG in 1964.[28] Phayom is now described as a member of the TPF central committee and its "overseas representative."[29] A third Thai exile who has been linked to the Communist movement is Kulab Saipradit, a writer and member of the Free Thai Movement. Like Monkon Nonakon, Kulab has served time in Thai prisons.[30] He has usually been mentioned as a Thai Communist delegate to various Communist-sponsored international front meetings.

Foremost among the Thai in exile is former prime minister Pridi.[31] Until his sudden departure for France in the spring of 1970, Pridi had made China his home. But he has associated his name with Communist causes on only a few occasions,[i] and his precise role in the Communist movement has never been

[h]Interviewed by *Newsweek* magazine in January 1966, Thai Foreign Minister Thanat Khoman described Phayom as "an insignificant man who tried to win a certain reputation for himself. He was once elected representative to the National Assembly, but afterwards he consistently failed to win subsequent elections. That may explain why he became frustrated and thought he could carve a place for himself by going to the Chinese Communists, since he could not do it on his own here in Thailand." Quoted in *Foreign Affairs Bulletin* (published by the Ministry of Foreign Affairs of Thailand), Vol. V, No. 3, December 1965-January 1966, p. 308.

[i]For instance, in 1954 Pridi authored an article in *Jen-min jih-pao* (July 20) that supported the five principles of peaceful coexistence and urged struggle against the Thai government and American imperialism. Following the appearance of the TPF, Pridi reportedly met with the consul general of North Vietnam in Canton and expressed his support of the anti-American effort in South Vietnam. *Jen-min jih-pao*, February 12, 1965, p. 4.

defined. He has not been appointed to or accepted any official position in the hierarchy of either the party or the fronts; nor has he endorsed these groups. Having been implicated in the mysterious death of the young King Ananda (Rama VIII) in 1946, Pridi cannot return to Thailand without having to face trial. But his credentials as a Communist and a partisan of the Chinese are extremely doubtful, and these have assuredly been factors in his aloofness from the Thai exile groups. One explanation for his quietness while in China, and perhaps also for his departure, may be that Pridi was regarded by the Chinese as ideologically questionable and by his Thai Communist counterparts as more neutralist than Communist, antiparty, and lukewarm toward the rebellion.

By mid-1965, the Thai Communists assertedly had reestablished a party and forged the semblance of a united front. Yet, the fact that the party had no announced leadership (which is the case to the present), that the heads of the TPF were little known in Thailand, and that the only well-known Thai exile in China (Pridi) was not identified with the Communist political movement could only have hampered the party's appeal and undermined its claim to respectability. Beyond these circumstances, the Thai Communists' talk of resistance to the RTG was belied by the continued low level of violence in the northeast and elsewhere. During the first half of 1965, reports of Communist propaganda and recruitment activities in the northeast and of contact between "CTs" (Communist Terrorists) and government authorities were more frequent than in 1964. But not until August 1965 did the Communists themselves claim that their rebellion was indeed underway.j

Conceivably, the Chinese had decided to give propaganda attention to the Thai Communists' revolution prematurely, that is, well before the rebels had actually begun to set up a functioning party headquarters, united front groups, and military organizations in Thailand.[32] To determine whether and, if so, why this was the case requires examining the nature and extent of China's role in the Thai Communist movement and China's changing attitude toward the Thai government.

China and the Rebellion in Thailand

The fact that Peking waited until late 1964 to give prominence to the Thai Communist movement—the party, the front organizations, and their leaders—should not obscure the support Peking had rendered Thai exiles in earlier years. An important distinction shall be suggested, however, between the extent and motivations of Peking's assistance to the Thai Communists prior to and after the fall of 1964.

Peking's Role, to 1964

During the 1950s and early 1960s, Communist China's attitude toward Thailand, at the diplomatic level, changed from attraction to hostility whereas, at the

---

jThe Thai Communists consistently refer to August 1965 (in Nakhon Phanom province) as the month when the first armed incident was initiated by Communist guerrillas.

covert level, it remained constant in terms of very low-level training and propaganda support of Thai Communist exiles. In the middle 1950s, after the Bandung Conference, Sino-Thai relations seemed to be moving toward a limited rapprochement through trade relations and the RTG's reduction of restrictions on travel to the mainland. In part, this trend had been promoted by assurances Premier Chou En-lai had given Prince Wan, Thailand's delegate to Bandung, concerning such matters as Pridi's role in the Free Thai movement, the dual nationality of the overseas Chinese, the removal of Vietnamese to North Vietnam, and the external significance of a Thai Nationality Autonomous Area in Yünnan province that the Chinese government had announced in January 1953.[33] Once the honeymoon ended, any possibility of a genuine reconciliation between Peking and Bangkok on the basis of Chou's assurances was eliminated. Nevertheless, little was heard from Pridi, the overseas Chinese were by and large effectively assimilated into the Thai culture, Thailand reached agreement with North Vietnam on the Vietnamese immigrants, and no threat emerged from the autonomous nationality area in Yünnan.

What limited information on China's early involvement with the Thai Communists exists provides little evidence of a meaningful Chinese effort to foment trouble in Thailand. Apparently, beginning in the early 1950s, the Chinese accepted a small number of Thai leftists for political indoctrination at the Marxist-Leninist Institute in Peking and at a cadre training school in K'un-ming, Yünnan province. It is also generally believed, though again on the basis of fragmentary evidence, that at one point in the early 1950s the Chinese Communists were in contact with a Chinese Communist Party of Thailand (CCPT). If this organization of ethnic Chinese in Bangkok ever existed, it has since either gone deep underground, been abolished, or taken on more the activities of a businessmen's club than a political party.[k]

In China, aside from its own infrequent broadcasts on conditions in Thailand, Radio Peking gave some broadcast time to Thai-language programs—according to a Thai source, 14 hours a week until October 1964, 21 hours thereafter.[34] And, of course, China was home to Thai exile leaders such as Pridi and Kulab Saipradit. In this connection, the ethnic composition of the Thai Communists in

---

[k]This circumstance has not, however, kept the Thai government from maintaining a close watch on the activities of Bangkok's Chinese, who today account for an overwhelming proportion of Thailand's total Chinese population of roughly 3 million. Once the rebellion in the northeast began in earnest late in 1965, several measures were adopted to reduce the potential of the Chinese to assist the Communists' cause. In April 1966, for example, Chinese-language broadcasts were banned in the belief coded messages were being transmitted. Inspection procedures for Chinese schools were regularized in the fall of 1967 out of fear that Communism was being preached. Interestingly enough, the RTG even opposed a proposal that overseas Chinese join or set up their own *anti*-Communist, anti-China organization, evidently because of concern about any political organization among the Chinese. (*Bangkok Post*, October 21 and 22, 1968.) But the Thai government has used carrots as well as sticks. In May 1967, for instance, it lifted a twenty-year-old ban on Chinese-language instruction in secondary schools. *New York Times*, July 11, 1967, p. 11.

Peking, to the extent it can be determined, may be predominantly Sino-Thai, that is, ethnically Chinese, but Thai in nationality.[1] If true, this might further explain the aloofness of Pridi, a Thai, from the Chinese Thai involved in the party and the fronts. It might also help explain the long-standing adherence of Thai Communists in China to Chinese ideological and policy positions.

Besides this rather limited Chinese Communist association with the Thai Communist movement, mention should also be made of North Vietnam's role. Whereas the Chinese undertook responsibility for training a small number of relatively senior Thai cadres, North Vietnam, apparently beginning about 1962, "graduated" a number of Thai (probably Thai-Lao) from its Hoa Binh (Peace) School outside Hanoi. According to Girling, 68 Thai received training at Hoa Binh in 1962 and 130 in 1965.[35] What remains open to speculation is how many of this handful were placed into Pathet Lao units rather than returned to Thailand's northeast. There is evidence that at least some Thai-Lao were indeed sent back to the northeast,[36] and certainly the intimate ties between the North Vietnamese and the Pathet Lao, together with the Pathet Lao's control of strategic Mekong River access routes into the northeast, facilitated the process of recruitment, training, and reintroduction. But prior to late 1964, it does not seem that Hanoi, concerned preeminently with maintaining a strong Communist position in eastern Laos, made any substantial effort to return Thai-Lao to the northeast.

Peking's Role since 1964. The division of labor that Peking and Hanoi evidently established during the early 1960s—the Chinese indoctrinating and training higher ranking Thai Communists, the North Vietnamese training and probably equipping ordinary soldiers and low-level cadres—seems to have persisted after the reemergence of the CPT. China provides the Thai Communist spokesmen with a propaganda forum and seeks to embellish their credibility as representatives of an authentic nationalist movement. The CPT and its front organizations are also given ideological and strategic guidance by their counterparts in the Chinese bureaucracy, in return for which the Thai groups have consistently espoused the Chinese position on international events while handling their own tactical problems.

In south China, the Chinese reportedly increased the training of CPT cadres in 1965.[37] But based on one of the few figures available concerning Chinese-trained Thai Communist personnel—about 700 from 1952 to 1969[38]—it would appear that either the CPT has not recruited many Thai with leadership potential

---

[1]The frequent mixture of Thai and Chinese blood makes accurate ethnic distinction extremely difficult. Chinese in Thailand who are informed about the exile leaders consider them ethnic Chinese and can usually identify them as such by their surnames. (The author is grateful to Professor Frederick W. Mote of Princeton University for communicating this point to me.)

or that Peking has shown no haste to prepare cadres for duty in Thailand.[m] Other forms of assistance to the Thai Communists have also been much less than China is undoubtedly capable of providing. Chinese propaganda materials have appeared much more frequently than arms and equipment in the north and northeast. The few Chinese weapons and hand grenades that have been taken from the insurgents suggest that the flow from China is probably very small, since the insurgents' weapons may be part of North Vietnamese aid to the Pathet Lao, or may have been purchased in Laos on the black market. In terms of financial aid, too, there were reports in 1965 that Chinese agents in Hong Kong had purchased $1 million in Thai *baht*;[39] but no reports have appeared since to indicate that Chinese financing has continued despite opportunities for doing so by sending funds directly to the insurgents or employing sympathetic Chinese in Bangkok as middlemen.

From the standpoint of close-hand involvement in the rebellion, North Vietnam's activity has been much more significant than China's, although still not of a magnitude to indicate that a Communist revolution in Thailand is a priority matter for the DRV leadership. As noted, the training of Thai guerrillas at the Hoa Binh School about doubled in 1965 over 1962. It seems fairly certain that the North Vietnamese, advantaged by geography, also increased the number of guerrillas infiltrated from training bases in central and northwestern Laos beginning in 1965, though it is practically impossible to determine how many men have been returned to Thailand.[n] What is clear is that North Vietnamese and Pathet Lao cadres have avoided direct involvement in the Thai insurgency, despite occasional reports from Thailand to the contrary.[40]

This breakdown of Chinese and North Vietnamese aid affords a basis for two propositions about the Thai Communist movement and its relationship to external powers. First, China aimed at becoming the dominant foreign influence over the Thai Communist movement. But the nature and amount of aid and comfort given the Thai Communists up to the fall of 1964 suggest that China only intended, with collateral assistance from North Vietnam, to sustain their revolutionary enthusiasm, not to equip them with the tools for a serious insurgency. Second, the apparent limited increases in tangible external support of the Thai Communists between the fall of 1964 and the spring of 1965, when placed beside the rudimentary character of their indigenous organization at that time, imply a certain tentativeness about the commitment of Peking and Hanoi to a revolution in Thailand. We are therefore brought back to the suggestion made earlier concerning possibly significant differences between Peking's

[m]If the Chinese are not returning to Thailand as many Thai and Sino-Thai recruits as are available or have been trained, the explanation may be that Peking has not considered the Communist movement sufficiently advanced to be able to absorb many cadres. This explanation fits with the suggestion later in this chapter that by mid-1967, Peking's confidence in the capabilities of the Thai had declined sharply.

[n]In the *Senate Hearings on Thailand*, the rough estimates given are 600 Thai Communists trained in North Vietnam and 1000 in Laos. As with the figures for Chinese-trained insurgents, however, these cover the period since 1952 and do not indicate how many trained guerrillas returned to Thailand or remain active in the Communists' ranks.

motivations before and after October 1964. Can we simply conclude that the division of labor that seems to have been achieved, tacitly or explicitly, between China and North Vietnam was all along designed gradually to strengthen the Thai Communist movement to the point where it was prudent to publicize the CPT and its fronts?[o] Or was that publicity geared less to the character of the revolutionary environment in Thailand than to broader Chinese considerations, especially with regard to developments in Laos and Vietnam and Thailand's role in them?

The Motivations of Chinese Involvement. It would seem that only by looking at the context of events in Southeast Asia during 1964—as they took place and as they may have been perceived from Peking—can we hope to explain China's interest in supporting a rebellion in Thailand. For by the end of the summer of 1964, several developments of concern to Communist China (and equally to North Vietnam) had occurred: the involvement of American and Thai personnel in the Laotian conflict; the use of Thai bases for bombing runs in Laos; and the first direct American air attacks on North Vietnam.

Thailand's role in the Laotian conflict in 1964, as before and since, was a direct outgrowth of an historic relationship between Laotian stability and Thai security. Particularly since the nineteenth century, when most of what is now Laos was under Thai suzerainty, Thai governments have always been conscious of the nation's vulnerability to external penetration from the north and northeast. Linguistic, religious, and cultural similarities between the peoples of Thailand and Laos have contributed to a longstanding concern on the part of Thai leaders over developments in Laos, particularly those that have involved the major powers.[p] This concern was registered most emphatically when Laos,

---

[o]This line of argument is frequently supported by citation of CPR Foreign Minister Ch'en Yi's supposed remark at a cocktail party in early 1965 that "we will have a guerrilla war going in Thailand before the year is out." For one thing, Ch'en's remark, if it ever was made and if it was accurately reported, may be taken less as evidence that the Chinese manufacture insurgencies at will than as an off-hand expression of hope that revolutionary violence will erupt. For another, quotation of that remark can be misleading by turning attention from efforts to explain the reasons why it may have been made. The comment has been reported in Marshall Green's speech, cited previously; *Newsweek*, January 31, 1966, p. 29; *Far Eastern Economic Review*, February 10, 1966, p. 235; and Maynard Parker, "The Americans in Thailand," *The Atlantic*, Vol. CCXVIII, No. 6, December 1966, p. 51.

[p]In a speech to the Geneva conferees on May 23, 1964, for instance, Thanat Khoman said: "... Thailand in more than one respect is the closest neighbour of Laos. It has a more than one-thousand kilometer long border with that country, and the Mekong River which serves as border links the Lao and the Thai peoples rather than separating them. Laos and Thais originally came from the same racial stock. Their languages and culture are similar. The two peoples also share the same Buddhist faith.... Our sole desire has been to see a free, united and independent Laos, because on those conditions alone can Thailand feel secure from any threat to her own freedom and independence from that direction...." Quoted in *Thailand at the Geneva Conference on Laos*, Information Department, Ministry of Foreign Affairs, Bangkok, 1961, p. 607. See also Thanat's interview with Seymour Topping of the *New York Times*, in *Foreign Affairs Bulletin*, Vol. III, No. 5, April-May 1964, p. 543.

beginning late in the 1950s, nearly devoured itself in a civil war during which the terms of the 1954 Geneva accords were expressly violated by all sides. The crisis of confidence of the Thai government during 1961 and 1962, when the United States failed to take forceful action under SEATO in support of the Laotian right wing, has been documented fully elsewhere.[41] To Bangkok, the hesitant American response that culminated at Geneva in agreement to maintain Laotian neutrality reinforced the conviction that Thai national interests will always be subordinated to the interests and convenience of Thailand's allies.[q] This reduced faith in the American commitment to Thailand's security was somewhat offset by the statement issued by Foreign Minister Thanat Khoman and Secretary of State Dean Rusk on March 6, 1962, under which the United States became committed to Thailand's defense independent of obligations under SEATO. But neither that communiqué nor the dispatch of U.S. Marines to Udon in May completely erased Thai uncertainty about the United States response to future security threats to Thailand from Laos.

Against this background, it was hardly surprising that the RTG should have expressed satisfaction at the right-wing coup that a group loyal to General Phoumi Nosavan carried out in Vientiane on April 19, 1964. But on May 1, Bangkok's satisfaction turned to sharp displeasure when the United Kingdom and the Soviet Union, the co-chairmen of the Geneva Conference, joined in condemning the coup as a violation of the agreements reached in 1962 establishing the neutralist Prince Souvanna Phouma at the head of a coalition Government of National Union.[42] In a note to the UK and USSR ambassadors on May 7, 1964, Bangkok expressed concern that the Pathet Lao, who (convinced that Souvanna had thrown himself into the rightists' camp) had launched an offensive in the Plain of Jars following the coup, were posing "an imminent threat to the security of the Kingdom of Thailand." "Should the highly dangerous situation in Laos be allowed to continue," the note went on, "Thailand might be obliged to reassess her position as a party to the [Geneva] Agreements of July 1962."[43]

The response to the renewed fighting in Laos by Thailand, the United States, and Communist China provides important keys to China's changing perception of Thailand. The United States refused to throw its support to the Vientiane clique. In view of the Pathet Lao's quick advances, however, Washington authorized American aircraft to be used in May on reconnaissance missions for the neutralist forces of Prince Souvanna Phouma. When two of these jets were

---

qFor critical comments on the West's response to the Laotian crisis, see those by Thanat Khoman, "Which Road for Southeast Asia?," *Foreign Affairs*, Vol. XLII, No. 4, July 1964, p. 634, and in *Foreign Affairs Bulletin*, Vol. III, No. 5, April-May 1964, p. 544.

Nuechterlein's conclusion on Thai policy is instructive: "The major flaw in Thailand's policy was the assumption that the United States would support a pro-Western government in Laos under all circumstances, and that it considered the defense of Laos identical with the defense of Thailand." *Thailand and the Struggle for Southeast Asia*, p. 219.

shot down, the United States retaliated by dispatching fighter-bombers to attack Pathet Lao installations, an action that Souvanna, who had undoubtedly condoned the reconnaissance flights, sharply protested. Once Pathet Lao and North Vietnamese forces continued their offensive in the Plain of Jars, however, Souvanna asked that the flights be resumed.[r]

As the situation worsened for Souvanna's forces, Thailand's role in the fighting became more important. On June 11, Laotian aircraft, some of which were later revealed to have been piloted by Thai nationals, attacked Khang Khay, the site of the CPR cultural and economic mission to Laos. One Chinese official was killed and five others were wounded.[44] Then, beginning in August and September, American jets taking off from bases in northeast (Udon) and central (Korat) Thailand bombed portions of the Ho Chi Minh Trail in Laos in an attempt to interdict the flow of supplies into Laos from North Vietnam. These aircraft were reportedly flown by "civilian" pilots of various nationalities, including Thai and American, under the pay of the Central Intelligence Agency.[45] By this time, it should be added, the Tonkin Gulf incidents had just passed and American personnel, mostly Air Force, in Thailand were in the process of increasing from 4,000 to 6,500 by the end of 1964 and 18,000 by the end of 1965.[46]

The events between April and September 1964 in Laos, not to mention the Tonkin incidents, were viewed with apprehension from Peking. The right-wing coup in Vientiane came only a few weeks after Prince Souvanna had completed an apparently successful visit to the mainland.[47] Despite American disavowals, Peking's leaders regarded the right wing's challenge of the coalition government as a premediated American plan to manipulate Souvanna and take another stab at building a Western stronghold in Laos. Chinese comments on the Laos situation further charged that the Vientiane coup was linked to broader United States designs in Indochina.[48] Although Thailand was not specifically indicated in the coup, Peking quickly asserted Bangkok's direct involvement in behalf of the United States and the Laotian right wing.[49] From Peking's vantage point, it may be surmised, the North Vietnamese-backed Pathet Lao advances were a necessary counterplay to keep Souvanna "honest," i.e., away from Phoumi, the Americans, and the Thai.

The Khang Khay incident added oil to the smouldering fire. Coming only two days after Peking (on June 9) had for the second time in two weeks voiced

---

[r]Actually, United States photographic reconnaissance jets had been flying over Laos since the summer of 1962 in response, it was said, to North Vietnamese contraventions of the just-concluded Geneva agreements. The reconnaissance flights of May 1964 were confirmed by the State Department. See Arthur J. Dommen, *Conflict in Laos: The Politics of Neutralization*, Pall Mall Press, London, 1964, pp. 238, 255-256, 258-259.

Laotian Communist sources usually refer to May 17, 1964, as the starting date of United States aerial intervention in Laos. E.g., the comments of a Laotian Communist party member at a Havana news conference, reported by *Granma*, January 9, 1969; Radio Pathet Lao, February 5, 1969; Radio Pathet Lao, February 12, 1969, quoting a letter of Prince Souphanouvong, the Laotian Communist leader.

approval of Cambodian and French proposals to reconvene the 14-nation Geneva Conference on Laos, the incident was said by *Jen-min jih-pao* to have demonstrated the readiness of the United States to enter "a phase of direct and open armed aggression in Laos whereas previously it had been instigating and making use of local reactionaries to undermine peace there." [50] Since the air raid had occurred after Souvanna had requested the cessation of overflights, the prince was undoubtedly "a mere tool of the U.S. government and the Laotian Rightist coup d'etat clique."[51] The Thai government was accused of massing forces across the Mekong from Vientiane[52] and engaging in provocative actions not only along the Cambodia border but even on Cambodian territory.[53]

That the Peking press did not pay greater attention to Thailand's role in Laos may have been due to China's more immediate concern over events in Vietnam. In 1962, when American marines landed in Thailand, Peking became worried that the United States was preparing for direct intervention in Laos with its own and Thai forces.[s] In 1964, with escalation in North Vietnam a sudden new possibility after the August clashes in the Tonkin Gulf, Peking's attention may temporarily have had to turn to the Vietnam theater. Nevertheless, United States sorties into Laos from bases in Thailand, the American training program for the Thai armed forces, and increased American deliveries of war material to Thailand after the Tonkin incidents were all duly noted in Chinese commentaries as indicative of Thailand's conversion from an independent state to a United States military bastion.[54]

What, then, may we surmise about China's intentions in having helped resurrect the Thai Communist movement later in 1964? Viewed in the context of the conflicts in Laos and Vietnam, Peking's principal interest may have been to give Bangkok a preliminary signal that further Thai involvement in support of American objectives in Indochina risked an expansion of the Communist effort in Thailand from primarily political to military action. Peking may have decided that the best way it had to warn Thailand against permitting her bases to be used by American planes and to be manned by United States personnel was to hint at the possibilities inherent in Chinese support of a Communist insurgency in Thailand. From Peking's perspective, it was not simply that Thailand was accepting American military and economic assistance, politically supporting U.S.

---

[s]In May 1962, an initial force of 1,800 marines landed in Thailand and was reinforced by additional troops from the United States (for a total of 5,000), Britain, Australia, and New Zealand. (Nuechterlein, *Thailand and the Struggle for Southeast Asia*, pp. 239-240.) On May 19, a page-one editorial in *Jen-min jih-pao* charged that the United States was prepared for direct intervention in Laos if necessary to the setting up of a "pro-American coalition government in Laos" under the pretext of the Communist threat. The editorial further stated that the "Chinese people cannot be indifferent" to the United States move, "firmly oppose armed intervention in Laos by United States imperialism, and even more, absolutely cannot tolerate United States imperialism's establishing a new military bridgehead pointed at our country from an area contiguous to China." The United States was warned that it was "playing with fire." No further such statements followed, apparently because Peking became convinced that American intervention in Laos was unlikely. Cf. the editorial and the comments of an unidentified NCNA reporter in *Jen-min jih-pao*, May 23, 1962, p. 3.

policy in Vietnam,[t] or even maintaining ties to SEATO. Rather, it appears from the specifically anti-American focus of the Thai Communist programs that were enunciated in Peking, from the fact that the Chinese news media made no references (and Thai Communist spokesmen only one) to a potential revolutionary situation in Thailand before October 1964, and from the possibly premature Chinese association with the Thai Communists' cause that what mainly disturbed Peking was Thailand's cooperation in the American buildup for the sake of the Laotian and Vietnam conflicts. Perhaps sensing also—and if so, quite rightly—that the United States was preparing to increase still further its use of Thai facilities for Vietnam,[u] the CPR may have sought to rein in the RTG before it became irrevocably tied to the so-called "U.S. war chariot."[v]

[t]Thailand's consistent position, as expressed by its eloquent foreign minister, Thanat Khoman, has been that the Vietnam conflict, having become a veritable testing ground of the American commitment to Southeast Asia's security by virtue of the scale of the American presence, requires consistent Asian support. He has stopped short of considering Vietnam a domino by saying that whereas the fall of Vietnam to Communism would seriously endanger the security of nearby countries, it would not automatically ensure their downfall. Thailand was a firm supporter of such steps as the bombing campaign over North Vietnam that began during February and March 1965. For typical comments, see Thanat's address to the National Press Club, Washington, D.C., May 11, 1965, Press Release of the Permanent Mission of Thailand to the United Nations; his televised statements on "Meet the Press," May 9, 1965 (National Broadcasting Company transcript, Vol. 9, No. 17); his remarks on the domino principle in a talk with U.S. Senate staffers in Washington, D.C., on May 10, 1968 (Press Release of the Permanent Mission No. 44, May 31, 1967); and his address before the Bangkok South Rotary Club on January 27, 1967, in *Collected Statements of Foreign Minister Thanat Khoman*, Department of Information, Ministry of Foreign Affairs, Bangkok, Vol. III, November-December 1967, p. 10.

[u]Aside from the increase in American Air Force personnel in Thailand following the Tonkin Gulf incidents, the number of Thai bases used by the United States also increased as United States jets attacked targets in North Vietnam as well as in Laos. Although the RTG for many months issued repeated denials, it was an open secret that, beginning with the United States air strike of February 7, 1965, against North Vietnam in retaliation for the Viet Cong attack on the Pleiku barracks (see Parker, p. 54), roughly 80 percent of the sorties flown over North Vietnam originated from bases in Thailand. Initially, the bases used were those at Udon, Korat, and Takhli, all of which had been operational when United States troops landed in 1962. The other Thai facilities that were expanded or newly built for Vietnam purposes are Don Muang (Bangkok), Ubon, Nakhon Phanom, Sattahip (naval base), and U Ta Pao. For background discussion, see *New York Times*, May 20, 1962, p. 3; April 9, 1965, p. 13; December 12, 1965, p. 1; January 23, 1966, p. 1; May 8, 1966, p. 2; July 1, 1966, p. 3; August 11, 1966, p. 2.

[v]Among the alternative hypotheses that have been advanced to explain Communist China's objectives in Thailand in 1964 is that Peking hoped to divert American military resources from South Vietnam by in effect threatening to open a second front in the northeast. The hypothesis would stand up better were it not for the fact that the Viet Cong, far from needing a respite, were by that time well on their way toward mastery of the military situation in South Vietnam. Moreover, it is difficult to imagine that Peking was counting on the United States, which had still not made a substantial ground or air investment in Vietnam, to divert significant resources to Thailand merely because a few Thai Communist groups had issued propaganda statements.

A second alternative explanation is that, in view of the rapid advances made by the Viet Cong in 1964, the Chinese decided that in Laos and Thailand they could take advantage of

If the timing of China's identification with the Thai Communist political fronts related primarily to the growing role of Thailand in the Indochina conflicts, a correlary is that China's interest in a Communist rebellion in Thailand actually took second place to China's concern over Vietnam and Laos. Had Peking wished to discourage a Thai-American alliance of the limited kind that existed prior to 1964, it could presumably have tried to do so at any time by reference to the CPT. The delay until 1964, when the threat of a wider war involving countries bordering on the CPR had become substantial, may indicate that China actually had less of an interest in a Communist revolution *per se* in Thailand than in using the *potentiality* for one as a lever against Thailand's strategic support of the United States.

The Evolution of Chinese Policy Toward the Thai Rebellion

Beginning in the spring of 1965, commensurate with the establishment of the TPF and various other front organizations, the CPR accompanied its limited additional aid to the insurgents with a carefully phased application of propaganda pressure on the Thai government. In several ways—including a gradual scaling upward of warnings to Bangkok, an apparent withholding of direct support of the CPT, and a delay in identifying the rebellion as a "people's war"—Communist China seemed to be trying to communicate to the RTG that the opportunity remained for it to back off from involvement in Laos and Vietnam.

Verbal Escalation

Comments in the Chinese press on the situation in Thailand and on Thai policy were at first confined to quotations of VTP broadcasts, reports from Western

---

the Viet Cong's momentum. But this hypothesis seems no more convincing than the first. To begin with, if the Chinese (and the North Vietnamese) were confident of a Viet-Cong victory, stirring up trouble in Laos and Thailand would have seemed an unnecessarily risky venture. It would have created the appearance of a multifront Communist offensive and thereby increased the likelihood of direct United States intervention in the area. Second, it should be remembered that fighting in Laos began anew in 1964 because of the Vientiane coup, not because of Chinese instigation; and that from May until August, the consistent Chinese position was that a high-level Geneva Conference on Laos ought to be reconvened. When Peking's stance toughened in August and the line on negotiations was dropped, it was probably in order not to appear weak in the face of United States military pressure against North Vietnam. (See the discussion in Chae Jin Lee, "Chinese Communist Policy in Laos: 1954-1965," unpublished Ph.D. dissertation, University of California, Los Angeles, 1966, pp. 268-271.) Finally, the hypothesis assumes a very offense-minded Chinese leadership in 1964, whereas the available evidence—which is limited to Chinese statements—strongly suggests that by the summer, China's preoccupation was with her own security because of the United States air attacks on North Vietnam. (See the documentation and interpretation in Harold C. Hinton, *Communist China in World Politics*, Houghton Mifflin Co., Boston, Mass., 1966, pp. 363-364.)

news agencies, and republications of statements from North Vietnam. All these statements were published after the first series of American air raids on North Vietnam in early February, and all concerned the role being played by Thailand in the Vietnam conflict. Included were a statement of the TIM declaring that the "Thai and Vietnamese peoples have a common fate" and a "common enemy" in their struggles against United States imperialism; citations from Western news sources that had (correctly) reported American use of Thai bases for bombing runs into Laos and North Vietnam; and a warning contained in the official Hanoi organ, *Nhan Dan*, that Thailand "certainly cannot escape having to bear the responsibility for the serious consequences of" permitting the United States use of its territory for "aggression" against the DRV.[55]

Thai Communist propaganda at this time, while continuing to give prominence to United States "neocolonialism" and its danger to Thailand in statements for both international and domestic (Thai) consumption,[56] also began to devote attention to issues relevant to Thai society. Evidently in an effort to generate popular support, the Communists broadened their appeal. Political repression, the Thai government's failure to institute genuine democracy, corruption, the economic plight of the northeasterners, unemployment, and police terrorism were among the subjects discussed.[57] If the one-sidedly anti-American flavor of the 1964 Thai Communist pronouncements reflected Chinese interests, the themes in 1965 may be said to have reflected Thai Communist concerns as well, some of which were quite legitimate.

Not until April 1965, after a curious hiatus of over two weeks during which the Chinese media said nothing about Thailand,[w] did a Chinese writer comment on Bangkok's policies. The anonymous but authoritative "Commentator," referring to the abovementioned statements of the North Vietnamese and the TPF, wrote:

Recently, U.S. imperialism has been intensifying its use of Thailand as a base for expanding its aggressive war in Vietnam, and moreover has exerted all efforts to drag Thailand into the Indochina war. The Thai authorities, following the aggressive policies of U.S. imperialism, have permitted U.S. military personnel and jet aircraft to enter Thailand continuously. U.S. aircraft have taken off from Thailand one after another to bomb the DRV and Laos. Under the urging of

---

[w]Between April 8 (Hanoi's abovementioned warning) and April 26, the Chinese press suspended attacks on Thai policy, apparently because of Thailand's participation in the tenth anniversary celebrations in Djakarta of the Bandung Conference (April 18-25). During the Djakarta conference, China's representatives (Premier Chou En-lai and Ch'en Yi) repeatedly assailed United States policy in Vietnam, but curiously refrained from condemning Thailand's "complicity." Thanat Khoman's recollection, four years after the event, was that "the very last [contact with Chinese Communist officials] was in Djakarta ... where I met Marshal Chen Yi, who incidentally drank many toasts to me." (Press Conference remarks, published by the Thai Permanent Mission, Press Release No. 16, April 2, 1968.) Thanat's statement, besides making Ch'en Yi's alleged prediction of a guerrilla war all the more questionable, also encourages speculation that at the Djakarta meeting Peking may have made a last attempt to sway Thailand's leaders away from their Indochina involvement before directly indicating support for the Thai Communists.

U.S. imperialism, the Thai authorities have also prepared to send military personnel to South Vietnam to participate in the aggressive war.

Having registered the reasons for China's hostility, Commentator went on to state that the Thai government was pinning its hopes on a lame horse and could end "only by accompanying U.S. imperialism to the grave and going to its death without reason. We want to warn the Thai authorities: beware of attracting the flames to burn yourselves."[58]

As the air war over North Vietnam moved into high gear, as additional American personnel arrived in Thailand, and as the United States prepared to increase its own forces in South Vietnam by about 75,000, Commentator, in July, issued a new kind of veiled threat. Charging, among other things, that the Thai government had increased its military support of the right-wing Laotian army and had permitted a step-up in United States bombing runs from Thai bases, Commentator for the first time linked these developments to the possibility of revolutionary violence. "All these things," he declared,

cannot but severely harm Thailand's sovereign independence and national interests, cannot but stimulate the fierce dissatisfaction and anger of the Thai masses. A popular war against the Thai authorities' selling out of the national interest and their serving as the accomplice of the United States is *arising* in Thai territory. *This is the inevitable result* of the Thai authorities' following a policy of toadying to the United States and selling out the country.[59]

It may be more than coincidental that the noticeable intensification of Communist-supported dissidence in northeast Thailand occurred soon after Commentator's remarks. In fact, once the first reported armed incident had taken place in Nong Khai (in August), the Chinese began to specify the northeast—and later the north—as the area where Communist forces were "arising" in response to Thailand's intransigence.[x]

Another three months passed without a significant Chinese warning on Thailand. Then, in October, Commentator again took to the editorial column. Pointing to the many new "crimes committed against the people of the Indochina countries" by the Thai government, Commentator said: "The Thai authorities must know that the ringleader [the United States] will be punished and that the accomplice [Thailand] cannot escape. Starting with the aim of harming others, one must end by harming oneself: This is the sad fate that the

[x]The Nong Khai incident was reported ibid., August 29, 1965, p. 3. It seems significant that neither in 1965 nor thereafter did Peking refer to the potential for a Thai Communist-led rebellion in the peninsular provinces of southern Thailand, which since 1948 have been a sanctuary for Chinese Malay guerrillas opposing the Malaysian government. In identifying the northeast rather than the south as the locale of potentially serious Communist revolution, Peking seemed to have selected the region not only where its support of the insurgents would be most credible, but also where Thailand's "collusion" with the United States was of greatest import for developments in Laos and Vietnam. If this assessment is correct, it further supports the proposition advanced earlier that China's decision to support the Thai Communist movement was primarily dictated by developments outside Thailand.

Thai authorities have set for themselves." Once more, Commentator made clear the connection between Thailand's efforts in the Americans' behalf and the strength of the insurgency:

It can be predicted that the more the Thai authorities let the wolf into their house, and the more the Thai territory changes into a new-type U.S. colony and military base, so will the patriotic struggle of the Thai people become even broader and more deeply developed.[60]

The concentration of United States air strikes against North Vietnam on targets north and west of Hanoi (including some less than 50 miles from the China border), and the increase of United States forces in Thailand,[61] may have been the chief reasons for Commentator's statement. There is no indication that Peking was concerned at this time about a threat to Chinese security stemming from the United States buildup in Thailand. Rather, Peking seemed determined to deter Thailand from expanding its role in the increasingly dangerous American escalation in Vietnam.

These apparent attempts to convince the Thai government that it was committing a grave Faustian error in selling Thai sovereignty for American dollars and military equipment still fell short of a definitive commitment to a Communist-run rebellion. For one thing, Chinese commentaries throughout 1965 referred to antigovernment developments in Thailand's northeast as the work of "the people's arms." Nothing had yet been said about a "people's war" or a Communist "people's army." For another, Commentator and other writers fell to silence about the Communist Party of Thailand; instead, the leading Communist groups were said to be the TPF, the TIM, and the "Federation of Patriotic Workers of Thailand."[62] In view of the importance attached by Mao and the Chinese leadership generally to a party-led revolution, this omission seems significant.

Of course, from the practical standpoint, the Chinese still had little of substance to identify with in Thailand's northeast. As indicated, the dissidence there had only become noticeable in mid-1965, barely worthy of being called a rebellion. Armed incidents were then still few and far between; and the estimated number of rebels was a mere 200 to 300, a figure that would jump roughly six times two years later.[63]

The Rebellion Viewed from Bangkok. If Peking was banking on the Thai government reading China's warning and reacting by changing course on Vietnam, it was making a low-confidence gamble. Not that the Thai leaders were unaware of China's threat; but they tended to believe that a certain risk had to be taken in support of the larger Thai interest in seeing aggression stopped in South Vietnam.

So far as the RTG was concerned, the appearance of the CPT merely reflected the culmination of longstanding Chinese efforts to foment an insurgency in Thailand. Whether or not Thailand assisted the American effort in South

Vietnam, China and North Vietnam were considered bound to have provided agents and weapons to indigenous Communists.[64] The suppression of insurrection in the northeast had, after all, begun well before Peking's broadcasts. Besides, RTG officials have gone on to contend, the steady increase in American Air Force personnel in Thailand was attributable to American needs in Vietnam and was never intended by either country to pave the way for American involvement in the Thai rebellion. Making Thai basing facilities available to the United States, though always stipulating clearly that the bases were Thai, was considered the best initial way that Thailand could contribute to the allied cause in Vietnam.[65]

Yet RTG spokesmen have also admitted that certain "sacrifices" had to be made when a large-scale American presence was permitted. As Foreign Minister Thanat said in two speeches during 1967, the Thai government's decision to allow the stationing of American forces and aircraft on its bases was taken "not because we enjoy seeing foreign troops on Thai soil, not because we enjoy seeing that destruction may enter by such a co-operation."[66] That decision, "though it affected our national sovereignty, is designed to give a meaning to the [Southeast Asia Treaty] Organization or otherwise it would be reduced to a useless carcass."[67] It was, in brief, reasonably clear to the RTG that the presence of Americans in large numbers in Thailand would be a useful propaganda target of the Communists in and outside the country.

Probably for this reason—to avoid making the Americans and their work more visible than necessary—the Thai government waited until March 1967 before publicly acknowledging that Thai bases were indeed being used by the United States for Vietnam bombing missions.[68] In doing so, Bangkok also announced that it was granting the United States "partial use" of the U Ta Pao base for purposes related to the Vietnam conflict, but on agreement that such use would continue "so long only as, in the opinion of the Thai government, the threat of Communist aggression against free nations in Southeast Asia still continues."[69] (Actually, U Ta Pao had been officially opened in August 1966.) The Thai government's reluctance to admit what everyone had known for years was indicative of its sensitivity to criticism, at home as well as abroad, of the growing American presence. As had been the case in the mid-1950s and again in 1962, when the question of a foreign military presence on Thai soil was raised, the Thai leaders were concerned that the size and length of stay of any foreign force might compromise national independence and might even provoke outside agitation.[70] They were therefore caught in 1964 and afterwards between their desire to demonstrate unity of purpose with the United States and their anxiety about the domestic impact of a large, geographically dispersed American presence of unknown duration. Their answer was not to refuse to accommodate the Americans—which would have contradicted their own criticism of United States policy in Laos between 1961 and 1962—but instead to seek to deflect or reduce the adverse consequences they foresaw.

The Thai Situation in the Context of a Global Chinese Reassessment. The failure of threatening Chinese statements to budge the Thai government from its course coincided with a number of developments abroad between late 1965 and early 1966 that were interpreted in Peking as symptomatic of an "adverse international current." The first of these developments was the outbreak of fighting in August 1965 between India and Pakistan along the cease-fire line in the Kashmir. Peking's ultimata to India to cease her "aggression," and the encouragement of Pakistan to continue in armed resistance, were deflated in two respects. On September 22, agreement was reached to a cease-fire that had been called for by the United Nations Security Council. India and Pakistan also accepted Soviet mediation of the dispute that led, in January 1966, to the Tashkent Declaration. Tashkent not only brought about the withdrawal of Indian and Pakistani forces to preconflict lines; it also boosted the Soviet image and influence throughout Asia.

In Indonesia, as a result of the abortive coup attempt by the Communist Party and dissident members of the Indonesian Army (the Gestapu incident of September 30–October 1, 1965), the party's ranks were decimated, a major Chinese political ally in Southeast Asia (Sukarno) was deposed, local Chinese were among the victims of a massive bloodletting, and Sino-Indonesian relations quickly reached the breaking point. In Algiers that November, Peking's hope that a broad anti-American united front of Afro-Asian nations could be constructed at the "second Bandung" conference was dashed when few governments proved receptive to China's uncompromising stance on Vietnam and other issues. The Algiers Conference never was held, thanks to Chinese pressure that twice forced its postponement.[y] Chinese efforts to extend their influence in Africa and Latin America also suffered setbacks. Relations were disrupted with Burundi, Kenya, Malawi, and Ghana, in the last instance when a coup ousted Kwame Nkrumah at a time when Nkrumah was touring China (February 1966). And China's major ally in Latin America, Castro's Cuba, also turned on Peking early in 1966, charging the Chinese with having reneged on trade agreements covering Cuban sugar and Chinese rice.

That the Chinese leadership was disturbed with these developments is clear enough from the statements and analyses that appeared in an effort to minimize the long-term significance of them. Ch'en Yi, for instance, acknowledged to a Japanese Communist interviewer that "setbacks in individual areas" not only had occurred, but might well occur again in the future. But the foreign minister considered these "only temporary phenomena," since "The course of advance of a people's revolutionary struggle is never straight, it is bound to be wavelike."[71] Actually, according to another argument, revolutionary class struggle could only take place in times of upheaval; without upheaval and even occasional reversals,

---

[y]The Second Afro-Asian Conference was originally scheduled to be held in June 1965. The Chinese, in pressing for both postponements, were also opposed on other key demands besides Vietnam: that the Soviet Union not be permitted to attend the conference; that no representative of the United Nations be allowed in; and that Indian "aggression" along the border with China be condemned. (*Jen-min jih-pao* editorial, October 23, 1965, p. 1.) In addition to these rebuffs, Peking also lost favor when it quickly recognized the new Algerian regime of Colonel Boumedienne, who had overthrown the respected Ben Bella government days before the conference was to have opened in November.

there would be no opportunities for revolution and for "reactionaries" to be overthrown.[72]

Revolutionaries were urged to ride out the storm since, eventually, their resistance would overcome "the forces of decay."[73] in the Chinese view, the international situation had entered a period "filled with contradictions and conflict," with great "splitting and agitation." There would always be "zigzags in the road forward," it was suggested, but these could be used to advantage, especially by making more people in the countries concerned aware of their government's reactionary policies and eager to join the revolutionary forces.[z]

The succession of events adverse to Chinese foreign policy interests perhaps made a major impact on policymakers in Peking because the reversals abroad occurred amidst dissension at home on two fronts.[74] In response to United States air actions in North Vietnam close to China's border, differences apparently developed in the Chinese leadership over the implications for the preparedness, force posture, and mission of the People's Liberation Army (PLA). Mao was pressed by Lo Jui-ch'ing, the chief of staff of the PLA (who probably was speaking for others as well), to augment China's air and possibly land defenses in south China. But Mao, concerned far more about a flagging ideological rectification campaign and dissension in the party's ranks toward his authority, rejected any suggestion that the PLA be diverted from its domestic political and security functions to meet a hypothetical American threat. Lo Jui-ch'ing, who also held a key post in the CCP Secretariat, was purged in December 1965—the first victim of an extensive cleanup of party and other dissidents. The PLA would play a pivotal role in these dramatic developments—what became known in 1966 as the Great Proletarian Cultural Revolution.

These volatile situations at home and abroad may have constrained Chinese foreign policy choices. The Chinese leadership, itself probably unsettled as the first purges were made, perhaps had only one general course of action available to it. Positive, even dramatic action to attempt to recoup perceived setbacks would have entailed too many risks. On the other extreme was retrenchment and withdrawal from foreign affairs, as by abandoning the united front approach on Vietnam, curtailing state-to-state diplomacy, and reducing verbal and material support of revolutionary movements to a bare minimum. But, to judge from the commentaries of 1965 and 1966, that alternative would have been counter-revolutionary, an intolerable capitulation before temporary adversity and Soviet-American pressures. Instead, it may be speculated, the basic decision was

---

[z]Ibid.; Hsiang Tung-hui, "The Big Agitation is a Good Thing," *Jen-min jih-pao*, March 1, 1966, p. 4; and *Ta-kung pao*, February 25, 1966, p. 4. Later, in August 1966, when the Eleventh Plenum of the Eighth CCP Central Committee met to confirm Mao's intention to institute a sweeping purge of the party apparatus, the international situation was again described (in the plenum's communiqué) in terms of a "great upheaval, great division and great reorganization." "Zigzags and reversals" were once more explained as being signs of imperialism's last gasp and as small steps backward on the road to victory. *Peking Review*, No. 34, August 19, 1966.

to retain a low-keyed diplomacy but to reduce, or not expand, commitments (of prestige, political support, and aid programs) to all revolutionary movements and friendly governments except those of immediate interest in the Indochina region.

The Thai Communist movement, while having no special claims on the Chinese, was sufficiently important to Peking because of the Indochina situation to warrant continuing encouragement. In response to the RTG's inflexible position, remarks in the Chinese news media on dissidence in Thailand changed in 1966 from indirect hints of impending trouble to direct reference to "people's war." This effort to upgrade the character of the Thai Communists' campaign was accompanied by an intensification of the rebellion during 1966 and, as 1967 began, by Peking's allusion for the first time to the leading role of the CPT in it.

On January 1, 1966, the first anniversary of the TPF, a letter to the Thai people was issued by the Front and published two weeks later in *Jen-min jih-pao*.[75] The Front spoke of the necessity to resort to armed struggle in the northeast. Now, the letter said, "the only road is: We people must take up arms and begin an eye-for-an-eye, tooth-for-tooth, tit-for-tat struggle with the enemy. Moreover, only by broadening the people's armed struggle into people's war can our country destroy the enemy's armed power and achieve final victory."

Shortly thereafter, Chinese comments gave official blessing to the new enterprise. On January 28, no less than six articles appeared in *Jen-min jih-pao* on developments in Thailand. The gist of these articles was that the Americans were continuing to entrench themselves in Thailand, that "Thailand has already completely lost its national independence," and hence that the Thai people's determination to carry out a people's war "is absolutely correct." In fact, one commentary added, the Americans were worried about the possibility of another Vietnam occurring in Thailand; but in their efforts to suppress the developing revolution, they would inevitably meet with the same results as in Vietnam.[76]

The oblique reference to "another Vietnam" soon became more direct, and may have been linked to the renewal of intensive air action over North Vietnam after a 37-day bombing "pause." Perhaps to deter United States consideration of risky air actions close to the China border, Peking asserted, beginning in April, that the Thai government's anti-Communist efforts would inevitably "make Thailand even more quickly become a 'second Vietnam'. . ."[77] When, in early May, the Thai government indicated its preparedness to reinforce a small naval and air contingent in South Vietnam, the Chinese press first reported a DRV protest[78] and then published a statement of the Chinese Ministry of Foreign Affairs that was the most threatening to date. Calling the latest Thai decision a "grave step" and noting that the American presence had increased once more to "over 18,000," the Foreign Ministry strongly intimated that the northeast rebellion was bound to intensify in direct proportion to Thailand's involvement in Vietnam. The statement said:

. . . the Thai authorities should know that Thailand is beside Indochina, and that if you openly participate in U.S. imperialism's aggressive war in Vietnam, you cannot escape the linking together of the Vietnam battlefield with Thailand itself and your becoming the enemy of the people of the Indochinese and Southeast Asian nations. We warn the Thai authorities: if you have no care about selling out the country's sovereignty and national interests and willingly serve U.S. imperialism, you will certainly be derisively cast aside by the people of the Indochinese countries, will raise strong opposition from the Thai people, and thus will further hasten your own downfall.[79]

What is significant about these statements is, first, that they now specified that Thailand had *already* lost its sovereignty and was a full-fledged American colony, thus rationalizing a people's war. Second, the statements made clear that stepped-up dissidence in the northeast would be the penalty the RTG would have to pay for not only permitting the United States use of Thai air bases and granting occupation privileges to American personnel, but also for taking on a direct combat role in South Vietnam. Finally, the implication of the Chinese statements was that the penalty would be meted out by the "Indochinese" people in cooperation with the Thai Communists, thus warning of increased North Vietnamese and Pathet Lao support of the Thai insurgents. Phayom Chulanond, in a statement of May 8, 1966, to NCNA, held that inasmuch as the Thai government was sending forces to other countries, it was perfectly appropriate for "the Vietnamese people . . . to rise up to oppose and moreover to pursue and destroy the enemy in Thai territory. . ."[80] This new "hot pursuit" thesis recalled an earlier statement of Chou En-lai on April 10 to the effect that if the Americans attacked China, China would be free to retaliate by land elsewhere than in Vietnam.[a]

Politics Takes Command in the Thai Communist Movement. One important component missing from these Chinese pronouncements on a people's war in Thailand was the ascription of the northeast revolution to the Communist Party of Thailand. Not until January 1967 did any overt Chinese communication state that the CPT was leading the Communists' fight to overthrow the Royal Thai Government.

As was the case with the shifts from characterizing dissidence in the northeast first as a popular uprising, then as "armed struggle," and finally as a people's war, China's moves to enhance the role of the CPT were equally deliberate. Until early 1967, the Thai Patriotic Front was still held in commentaries from Peking to be directing revolution in the northeast.[81] A subtle hint, however, that more would be said about the Communist party came in mid-1966 when references to "modern revisionism" attributed to Thai Communists in exile took on much

---

[a]With reference to United States escalation in Vietnam, Chou warned that the Americans were indulging in "wishful thinking" if they supposed that an air and naval attack on China would eliminate the need to fight a ground war. "Whereas the war may start in the air or sea," Chou said, "how the war continues to be pursued need not be determined by the United States. If you can come by air, why can't we go by land? . . . " Interview with the Pakistani newspaper, *Dawn*, reprinted ibid., May 10, 1966, p. 1.

stronger tones—for instance, by specifying Soviet revisionism.[82] Inasmuch as the Soviet Union had chosen virtually to ignore the Communist-led rebellion,[b] Thai Communist leaders in Peking may have decided, or been finally persuaded, to take a much stronger stance against Moscow.

The party's commitment to the Chinese camp was sealed when it sent a message of greetings to the ninth congress of the Albanian Workers Party that convened in Tirana during November 1966.[83] Not only had the CPT thus chosen to issue its first statements since October 1964 to China's major ideological ally; the party also replaced neutralism with Communism as its goal and adopted the Chinese position on "no third road" in the dispute over Marxism-Leninism. "In the struggle against all forms of opportunism," the message declared, "there is no third road. There is no middle road, and compromise is never allowed." This was precisely the formulation of Teng Hsiao-p'ing in May 1966 when, as CCP General Secretary, he indirectly slapped at North Vietnam's fence-straddling in the Sino-Soviet controversy.[84] The CPT had consequently become not simply anti-Soviet, but also antineutralist in the international Communist movement.

Shortly after the Tirana meeting, on December 1, 1966 (the party's twenty-fourth anniversary), another message was said to have been issued by the CPT central committee. In it, the party declared it had "become an important political organization leading the masses in the struggle against U.S. imperialism and the traitorous [Thai] government." The message called attention to the favorable revolutionary situation in Southeast Asia and especially to the fight being waged by the Viet Cong, which was "the nucleus of the revolutionary struggle of the world's people." China's "brilliant achievements" in the Cultural Revolution were cited and, by contrast, Soviet revisionism was. vigorously condemned. Party members were instructed to "prepare for long and arduous struggle" and "to form a nationwide patriotic and democratic front"; to do so, they would have to "study seriously Mao Tse-tung's thoughts, which are the very essence of Marxist-Leninist theory," and his guerrilla war tactics as well.[85]

Despite having taken steps to align with the Chinese position on international affairs, the CPT still referred to itself as only "an" organization in the Communist united front, a point underscored in the December 1 message's avowal of continued support of the TPF. Such, however, was not Peking's interpretation of the message. Radio Peking had once before spoken about the

---

[b]To the limited extent that Soviet writers commented on developments in Thailand, they studiously avoided referring to the CPT. Not only in 1964 but thereafter as well, the Soviets confined their remarks to the debilitating consequences of the American presence for Thailand's economy and on Thailand's too-close alignment with SEATO. But hope was held out that Soviet-Thai relations would improve and that the Thai leaders were in the process of rethinking their country's dependency on the United States. (See, for example, Iu. Lugovskoi, "When Will They Ring Off in Bangkok?" *Krasnaia zvezda* [*Red Star*], December 24, 1964.) Evidently, it was the Soviet conviction that cultivating relations with the RTG was a far more fruitful pursuit than hinging hopes on a Thai Communist Party whose leaders were in Peking.

Front's leadership of the rebellion in a Thai-language broadcast.[86] In the Chinese version of this latest CPT message, not only was the CPT said to be the nucleus of the anti-U.S., anti-RTG effort, but also the TPF was not mentioned at all.[87] One possible explanation of this clear-cut difference[c] is that Peking, in the throes of its Cultural Revolution, was eager to demonstrate that the familiar tripod of party, army, and united front had been completed in Thailand in accordance with Mao's prescription for successful people's war. As we shall see, this old formula also was revived following trouble between China and Burma in the summer of 1967. Another motivation may have been to create the appearance of a new addition to the Chinese international front against the Soviet Union; the Thai rebellion could now be said to be led by a pro-Chinese party. A third possible factor was that Peking, dissatisfied with the failure of the Thai Communist fronts to generate popular support, pressed for the CPT's assumption of the leadership. Finally, reference to the CPT's leading role may have related to Peking's step-by-step escalation of its characterization of the Thai insurgency. That is, having first brought the CPT and its fronts into the open, and having later called their struggle a people's war, Peking now chose to sanction the rebellion by pointing up the CPT's dominance. If this last consideration was operative, it may have related to further developments in Thailand's involvement with the American effort in Vietnam.

By January 1967, two circumstances in particular may have given Peking cause to identify the Thai Communists' struggle with the CPT. The first was the announcement of the Thai government that it would send additional ground forces to South Vietnam to bolster its 300-man naval and air transport units already there.[d] The second was discussion in the American press about the

---

[c]Subsequent CPT and Chinese Communist commentaries have sought to obscure the fact that the Thai party was for some time not accorded vanguard status in the Thai Communist movement. The CPT's ten-point program of December 1, 1968, for instance, declared: "Our party has been leading the people in organizing patriotic armed forces to heroically fight the enemy for more than three years." (VTP broadcast of December 6, 1968.) Similarly called into question is the CPT's claim that it led the first "uprising" in Nan province (northern Thailand) in February 1967. (VTP broadcast of January 31, 1968.)

[d]The RTG indicated that it would call for volunteers to form a new 2,100-man combat team, later named the Queen's Cobra Task Force. It was later revealed in testimony before a Senate subcommittee that Thai forces in South Vietnam had been paid for by the United States at an average cost of $50 million since 1966. This arrangement, formalized in an agreement of November 9, 1967, covered equipment, training, logistical support, and overseas allowances, and also included $30 million in additional military assistance and a battery of Hawk antiaircraft missiles for Thai armed forces in Thailand. The Thai government's insistence that it was only motivated to send troops to South Vietnam because of the anti-Communist struggle there consequently represented only part of the story. See *Senate Hearings on Thailand*, p. 657, and *New York Times*, June 8, 1970, pp. 1, 3.

basing of B-52 bombers in Thailand.[e] To the Chinese, this latter possibility, prematurely presented in the official press as an accomplished fact, meant that the United States was not only colluding with Thailand over Vietnam but was also bent on "directing the spearhead of its aggression against China." A statement of the CPR Ministry of Foreign Affairs rhetorically asked Thai leaders:

... aren't you afraid that the war flames lit by the United States may spread to yourselves? Since you are not concerned about selling out the national interest, and willingly serve the aggressive and war policies of the United States, the Vietnamese people and the peoples of the Indochinese nations will certainly firmly counterattack, and the Thai people will also certainly further unite and move even further against you.[88]

For the first time in a statement for international consumption,[89] Peking charged that the Thai bases had become part of the American base system that was being used to "encircle" China and give the United States added capability to "attack the 'underbelly' of China."[90]

At the same time as Peking began speaking of the Thai bases as China-directed rather than as Vietnam- and Laos-oriented, additional color was added to the Maoist picture of revolutionary activity in Thailand. A number of statements were issued purporting to show that the Thai Communists, under the party's leadership and guided by Maoist guerrilla doctrine, were proving that the large-scale presence of American military personnel could be turned to advantage. Mention was made for the first time that the Thai Communists had (in good Maoist fashion) established rural base areas from which armed forays could be launched and assets protected from hostile attack.[91] "The thoughts of Mao Tse-tung" were held aloft as the inspirational and directional bases of the Thai Communist movement.

But the most important new theme in Chinese accounts was that protracted struggle was the necessary precondition to successful revolution. This was

---

[e]News reports in late 1966 had cited comments by American officials to the effect only that no decision had yet been made to assign B-52s to Thai bases. See, e.g., *New York Times*, November 18, 1966, p. 5. In fact, the U.S. decision to begin enlarging U Ta Pao for possible use by B-52s was made early in 1966, and construction work began in August. (*Senate Hearings on Thailand*, p. 668.) On April 16, 1967, the *New York Times* reported that three B-52s had been moved from Guam to the massive air-naval complex at Sattahip. As Hanson Baldwin, the *Times's* military editor, further reported (ibid., April 8, 1967, p. 3), these three aircraft were to be the first of a 15-plane squadron to be sent to Thailand along with supporting tanker planes. The move, he said, was designed to cut the flying distance to targets in South Vietnam from 2,550 miles to 425 miles. But Baldwin pointed out that B-52s in Thailand could serve a larger purpose. They would "be symbolic of an expanded strategic interest in the Southeast Asian-Indian Ocean area." Sattahip would slightly cut the flying distance for U.S. aircraft to such potential strategic targets in China as Nanning (850 miles), the atomic test grounds at Lop Nor (2,000 miles), and Peking (2,100 miles).

Peking's way of telling the Thai Communists that they faced an uphill fight—a conclusion supported by the state of the rebellion in Thailand and increased Chinese attention to the dissident Meos in the north (see below). The fact that, from 1967 on, the Chinese apparently did not increase their role in the rebellion (for example, in the supply of trained cadres, arms, and ammunition), and may even have decreased it in certain respects (in money, for instance), was also in line with that conclusion. Peking may simply have decided, propaganda claims notwithstanding, that the rebels' circumstances and capabilities did not justify any further increases in material assistance. While continuing to support the Thai Communists' struggle, Peking seemed to be saying that the rebels were essentially on their own and could not expect substantial additional aid even though the guerrillas were known to be only partially armed and in need of money.

Commentator's article of October 1967 established China's dual line:

The CPT, guided by Marxism-Leninism and the thoughts of Mao Tse-tung, has dauntlessly led the Thai people in taking up arms and making a courageous fight against the U.S. aggressors and their running dogs. It is precisely in the northeast where U.S. imperialism's military bases are concentrated that the Thai people have lit the torch of armed struggle. It is precisely under circumstances where U.S. imperialism has directly participated in suppression that the ardent flames of armed struggle have burned ever higher. These facts fully prove that even in a country where U.S. imperialism's forces are garrisoned, where U.S. military bases are firmly established, and where extremely brutal fascist rule is being carried out, revolutionary people, so long as they have correct leadership, have a fearless spirit of daring to struggle and daring to win, and unite all forces that can be united, not only can launch armed struggle, but can also persist in it and ultimately be victorious.[92]

Commentator advised that the Thai peasantry must be the "main force" of the "national-democratic revolution." A people's army led by the Communist party should seek to mobilize the peasants. "In this way, they [the Thai Communists] can gradually establish and expand their bases for armed struggle, and, through protracted struggle, encircle the cities from the countryside, ultimately capture the cities, and gain victory over the entire country." In short, by "taking the road of Mao Tse-tung," the Thai Communists were bound to succeed against seemingly insurmountable odds *provided* they had the will, the leadership, and faith in Maoist political and military doctrine.

Chinese Communist comments on developments in Thailand after October 1967 kept to the position outlined by Commentator. The rebellion was said to be proceeding satisfactorily: the CPT, as the "core" of the revolution, was becoming stronger thanks to its adherence to Marxism-Leninism and Mao's thoughts; the so-called Thai People's Liberation Armed Forces was performing brilliantly in working among the masses of peasants; the united front had succeeded in mobilizing people from a broad social strata. By late 1968, it was averred, the Thai Communist rebels had rebuffed attacks by government troops, had consolidated their base areas, and had expanded operations to "over 100 districts in 31 provinces." Yet, Commentator's conclusion was only cautiously optimistic: "Although the people of Thailand may still be confronted with difficulties of all kinds on the road of struggle, so long as they persist in this correct line of Marxism-Leninism and Mao Tse-tung's thought, they will certainly win final victory."[93]

Imagery and Reality in the Thai Communist Movement

Despite the fact that Chinese commentaries had begun in January 1967 to describe the CPT as the leader in the northeast rebellion, Thai Communist spokesmen seemed to have trouble agreeing. Not until August 7, 1967, did the leader of the TPF, Phayom Chulanond, publicly acknowledge the party's leading role; and, it appears, not until December did the CPT do likewise.[94] It may be that factionalism had come to the fore within the Thai exile group in Peking, factionalism brought on by differences over the movement's organizational and personal leadership, and over the degree of closeness the movement should profess to Maoist doctrine.[95] Peking's support of the CPT's leading role may, in this light, have constituted an imposition of Maoist direction on the exiles. In contrast to those Thai Communists who may have wanted to keep the movement a loosely united alliance of separate groups having their own leadership and program, the Chinese Communists and certain Thai exiles loyal to them perhaps were insistent that the situation in Thailand required central party direction and absolute identification with Maoism.

Peking's possible adamancy on these points may have also stemmed from its embroilment in the Cultural Revolution. While externally Chinese statements of this period had emphasized anew the *sine qua non* of Maoist ideology and revolutionary strategy for Thai Communist insurgents, internally, toward the Thai exile groups, the stress seems to have been on making Soviet revisionism as much the target as United States "imperialism." A communiqué of the CPT central committee on December 1, 1967, responding to greetings from the CCP, agreed with the Maoist position that "if we resist imperialism, we must resist modern revisionism as well." The communiqué also held that "The achievement of the party depends mainly on the belief of all party members in Mao Tse-tung's thoughts."[96]

Thai Communist spokesmen and organizations continued to follow the Chinese line on international and mainland developments. Chinese views on Vietnam, Laos, Cambodia, and the Soviet intervention in Czechoslovakia were upheld to the letter by the Thai Communists. Similarly, the Maoist personality cult, the "brilliant achievements" of the Cultural Revolution, China's nuclear program, and the opening of the CCP's Ninth National Congress in April 1969 were quickly endorsed. From Peking's standpoint, the Thai Communists' encomiums added weight to worldwide revolutionary sentiment in favor of China's position vis-à-vis Moscow, a commodity of some importance to Peking at a time when the number of pro-Chinese parties had dwindled markedly.

The CPT's domestic line, meanwhile, sought to keep pace with political events in Thailand. On December 1, 1968, the party again used the occasion of its anniversary to issue an important statement, this time the first party program since 1942. Like the 1942 platform, the one announced in 1968 contained ten points and, except for manifestations of allegiance to Peking, did not substantially differ in its proposals regarding civil liberties and treatment of indigenous capitalists. Primarily, the program aimed at exploiting anti-American, anti-neocolonialist, and ethnic autonomist sentiment.*f* Its timing suggested an effort to preempt the Bangkok municipal elections held December 23—the first elections in a decade—and the national assembly (parliamentary) lower-house elections that were being planned for early 1969 (and were held in February).

Although the Thai Communist movement had taken on an unblemished Maoist character by 1967, Peking, as was suggested, had good reason to intimate publicly that it was aware of the rebels' deficiencies. The rebellion has developed spottily and the Communist political organization has been weak. On the military side, rebel groups were operating in the northern, central, and southern regions. But the geographical spread of their actions from 1967 on did not bring with it territorial control. Organizationally, the Communist party apparatus, at least on paper, became more extensive; but some of its leaders in the field had been arrested, and the question persisted whether the CPT had really been coordinating the actions of the armed bands that it claimed to be directing. Finally, in terms of adherents, the total number of CTs reportedly increased between 1967 and 1969 compared to previous years. Again, however, a qualification needs to be made, for not all those said to be CTs necessarily operated under the banner of the Communist movement.

These three areas—activities, organization, and strength—require some elaboration. In the north, dating roughly from the end of 1967, when the CPT acknowledged its leading role, more frequent reports were heard concerning Communist-provoked incidents. There, Communist agents evidently sought to exploit antigovernment sentiment among the minority Meo and Yao hill tribes. There are roughly 55,000 Meo and 10,000 Yao tribesmen living in the north. Bangkok officials pinned the blame on outside Communist *provocateurs* who infiltrated among these tribes to sow dissension through armed propaganda

---

*f*In brief, the ten-point program discussed: (1) waging a people's war to overthrow the RTG and establish a united-front government "composed of representatives of the proletarian classes, peasants, minor and nationalist-minded capitalists, including all patriotic and democracy-loving people, to carry out a genuinely independent and democratic policy"; (2) civil liberties and laws; (3) confiscation of lands and punishment or rectification of "counterrevolutionaries" and "reactionaries"; (4) abolition of "traitorous and unjust agreements and treaties" and cooperation with and support of other revolutionaries; (5) autonomy for ethnic minorities; (6) abolition of feudal conditions, reform of landholding and indebtedness conditions; (7) promotion of state-owned industry, but allowing for private industry; (8) job security for workers; (9) promotion of the rights of women and youth; (10) promotion of Thai culture and elimination of the "reactionary" culture, Thai and American. The complete statement was broadcast by VTP on December 6, 1968.

meetings.[g] According to Premier Thanom, the aim of the Communists is to promote the setting up of a separate Meo state embracing the whole of the northern region from Loei province in the east to Tak province in the west.[97] Yet, the methods used by Thai government officials to resettle the tribespeople in the lowlands and isolate the Communists in the hills may well have pushed some minorities to work for the Communists rather than be evicted from their traditional homeland and forced to abandon their opium trade. One official American estimate indicates that the mostly Meo CTs in the north numbered 1,300 to 1,600 in 1969, a sizable increase from only a few hundred in 1967.[98]

In the northeast, the tactic of armed propaganda meetings used during 1967 gave way to increased and heavier fighting by 1968—much of it due, however, to greater Thai government attention to, and military pressure on, the insurgents. In contrast to the north, the reported number of CTs had declined in the northeast—from roughly 2,000 armed guerrillas in 1967 to 1,700-2,000 in 1968 and to 1,200-1,500 in 1969.[99] No distinctions were apparently made, however, between externally infiltrated Thai-Lao, common bandits, and the assortment of other antigovernment types that together make the northeast a complicated picture. Nor has the Communist side, despite its apparently increasing numbers, made any claims concerning territorial holdings, popular support, or size of its forces.

The important but always difficult distinction between pro-Communist and local antigovernment sentiment among the rebels applied also to southern Thailand. Although there has been speculation concerning a connection between the northeast and southern dissidence,[100] neither the Chinese Communists nor the Thai Communists have claimed any such link-up. In their propaganda, both Communist parties assert their support of rebellion in the south by so-called "people's forces," but the Thai government has been more successful there than elsewhere in containing armed violence. Most of the incidents have occurred along the Thai-Malaysian border, where the two governments are cooperating to suppress several kinds of antigovernment forces: Thai terrorists; bandit gangs, which made headlines in Bangkok beginning in 1969 although they had long been active in the south; Thai-Muslim separatists, whose organization, the Moslem National Liberation Front, advocates union with Malaysia but does not have the Malaysian Government's support; and Chinese guerrillas belonging to the Communist Party of Malaya, which has been in rebellion under Chin Peng's leadership since 1948. Figures on antigovernment forces in the central and deep

---

[g]*Bangkok World*, December 31, 1967. The charge of external involvement has yet to be proven, but it is interesting that the Chinese Communists, at about the same time they began to reveal disenchantment with the northeast Communists, seemed to have shifted their propaganda attention to the northern tribes. Broadcasts in the Meo and other minority dialects began about late 1966 and were followed by steadily increasing attention in the Chinese media to north Thailand. Conceivably, the Chinese leadership decided to disengage from the northeast Thai Communists and to devote the limited resources given them to the northern minority groups, channeling some arms and supplies through the Pathet Lao.

south—ranging from 800 to $1,400$[101]—are, consequently, not very meaningful, since they refer to rebel groups with quite distinct objectives and ethnic and religious makeups.

Organizationally, the Thai Communists have expanded, but with little indication of having made significant headway in popular support. An impressive hierarchical chart could be prepared on the basis of present information concerning the numerous front organizations and armed forces branches said to be under the CPT's control. In the northeast, for instance, the Communists are reported to have established their own provincial administrative boundaries and within these to have formed front organizations on the basis of social group and age. Theoretically, each one of these fronts is responsible to the next highest echelon (e.g., the district farmers' front is responsible to the province farmers' front); at the national party level, all the fronts are under the direction of an internal relations section which, it is speculated, may be one of five sections that comprise the party organization.[h]

The party's leadership, however, may have suffered a major blow in 1967 when the RTG announced, on August 31, that 33 members of the CPT, including five central committee members, had been arrested. (Another police raid in July 1970 reportedly resulted in the capture of the senior central committee member.)[102] This reversal, it may be hazarded, was partly responsible for the subsequent Chinese emphasis on protracted struggle. Although these and other captives have told of the existence of party-run lines of command from the national organization down to the village, the actual capabilities of the CPT have probably been exaggerated. To date, the quasiinsurgent system still seems to comprise small, scattered, largely autonomous military bands that move about within perhaps several districts of a given region, neither responsible to nor even necessarily aware of a central directing agency.

Regional Developments and Thai Foreign Policy

The roles of China and North Vietnam in the Communist-supported portion of the rebellion, the vulnerability of Thailand to hostile penetration by dissident groups or *agents provocateurs* from neighboring countries, and Thailand's nearness to major conflicts in Laos and Vietnam combine to give regional dimensions to events in northern, northeastern, and southern Thailand. The Thai government has tried, through border-control arrangements with neighboring

[h]Thai officials believe the other four sections to be foreign relations, fund raising, intelligence, and the military. In connection with military operations, a new development in 1969 was the announcement on January 1 that a Supreme Command of the Thai People's Liberation Armed Forces would henceforth be the primary coordinating body for the Communist rebels. The Supreme Command would, of course, be responsible to the CPT. A ten-point disciplinary program was also announced to govern good relations between troops and the people—yet another borrowing from Mao. VTP broadcasts of December 31, 1968.

governments,[i] to reduce transnational traffic in Communist guerrillas (from Laos and Malaysia), in opium (by Chinese Nationalist remnant forces who travel between Laos and Burma), and in ethnic minorities (for whom the border is an artificial separation). With the exception of Thai-Malaysian cooperation, however, these control arrangements have not been dependable, and Thailand's borders have remained porous.

But the Thai government's major security problems cannot be managed through improved relations with neighboring governments. They are the product of the conflicting policy aims of the United States, China, North Vietnam, and, to a lesser extent, the Soviet Union in Southeast Asia. Especially since 1968, the Thai government, while consistently supporting United States policy objectives in Vietnam and elsewhere, has also been eager to emphasize its independence by espousing the theme of Thai self-reliance, by continuing in the role of regional mediator and advocate of regional nonmilitary cooperation, and by developing a more flexible approach to relations with the Communist world.

Ever since the Laos crisis of 1961-1962 when, in Bangkok's view, SEATO's response was belated and ineffective, the RTG has considered the organization of limited immediate value to Thailand's defense. By 1967, Thai spokesmen were alluding to a further retrogression of SEATO as some of its members became inactive or reduced their commitments in Asia.[103] This perception, together with developments in Vietnam, spurred the conviction of such politically different men as Foreign Minister Thanat and Defense Minister Praphat that Thai foreign policy also had to evolve. The immediate stimulus was President Johnson's March 31, 1968, speech in which he announced a major deescalation of the air war over North Vietnam and his decision not to stand for reelection. Some Thai leaders went farther than others in projecting the unfortunate consequences of the President's announcement for the future United States role in Asia. But all concluded that the ensuing months would be trying ones for Thailand, and that the post-Johnson period would require new Thai efforts at self-reliance.[104] As matters developed, self-reliance was to take several directions.

---

[i]Briefly, a joint Thai-Burmese committee has been operating since May 1963, when an economic and border agreement was signed, to eliminate misunderstandings concerning the border and to cut down the number of illegal crossings by Shan, Karen, and Kyaw peoples, some of whom are in rebellion against the Burmese government. Thus far, no joint efforts have been undertaken to police the border. The infiltration problem is most serious from Laos. Despite the exchange of intelligence and the establishment of special Mekong River crossing points, the magnitude of the task of patrolling the river boundary makes effective control very difficult. A mutual border security agreement was reported by General Praphat to be under discussion in February 1968, but as yet no agreement with the Royal Laotian Government has been announced. (*Bangkok Post*, February 29, 1968.) Thai-Malaysian cooperation, on the other hand, led to agreement in March 1965 to permit Malaysian forces to move up to 5 miles into Thailand in pursuit of Communist guerrillas. A new agreement in March 1970 permits cross-border operations for 72 hours (instead of 24) and sets up a combined military headquarters.

Within Thailand, sensitivities were beginning to show because of Communist propaganda and Western news reports that intimated it was only a question of time before American troops took a direct part in the government's counterinsurgency program. Some members of the Thai government, including General Praphat, were believed to have long been dismayed at the rising number of Americans on Thai soil.[105] By early 1967, the United States troop total stood at 35,300, of whom about 8,000 were said to be engaged in non-Vietnam related activities. The total jumped to 43,000 a year later, with an estimated 10,000 not contributing to the Vietnam effort.[106] Thai government leaders went to great pains, therefore, not only to reiterate that American personnel were in Thailand because of the Vietnam war, but also to affirm that the rebellion in Thailand was a Thai responsibility to be carried out entirely with Thai manpower.[107] Once the Vietnam war was over, it was made clear, and barring an external attack on Thailand, most United States forces would be asked to leave, since the Thai people were "not too happy about the presence of foreign troops on Thai soil."[108]

In Thailand's approach to Southeast Asia as a region, Thanat's longstanding commitment to the solution of common problems through primarily political and economic cooperation has been emphasized.[109] With over ten years of service as foreign minister behind him, Thanat has been outspoken on the theme that Southeast Asian nations must "take our destiny into our own hands instead of letting others from far away mold it for us at their whims and pleasures."[110] In particular, this has meant the retention of Thailand's traditional unwillingness to put all her eggs in one basket; instead, the Thai, with an eye to the period following an American withdrawal from Vietnam, have stressed the pivotal role Thailand can play in harmonizing disputes within Southeast Asia and in pulling together those nations willing to cooperate to bolster the stability of all. Regionalism has therefore come to mean three things for Thailand: a mediator's role; a leading part in regional associations; coordination of bilateral and multilateral cooperative enterprises toward the end of making independent Southeast Asian nations strong enough to resist subversion without the need of foreign (extraregional) assistance.

"Bangkok," Thanom Kittikachon said in May 1968, "has become the center for harmonizing actions and resolving intra-regional differences. The concept that Asian problems should be resolved by the Asians themselves has indeed been implemented."[111] In keeping with the Thai government's aspiration to be a regional leader, Bangkok had by then undertaken the peacemaker's role in several disputes. Conferences had been convened in the Thai capital to discuss differences among Indonesia, Malaysia, and the Philippines over the movement of Indonesian forces into Sabah and Sarawak (February-March 1964). Thai inspection teams were asked to verify the withdrawal of those forces (June 1964). Further Malaysia-Indonesia discussions were held in Bangkok between May and June 1966. The Thai government also sought to prevent the dismemberment of the Association of Southeast Asia (ASA) by providing a forum for exchanges of views between Filipino and Malaysian representatives regarding the Sabah question (summer, 1968).[112]

In similar fashion, the Thai government took special pride in providing home bases for a large number of international and regional organizations. The Mekong River Development Committee, several of the Specialized Agencies of the United Nations—including UNESCO, UNICEF, ILO, FAO, and WHO—and the Economic Committee for Asia and the Far East (ECAFE) all have their headquarters in Bangkok.

In hosting these organizations and in belonging to several others—the Asian Development Bank, ASA, the Association of Southeast Asian Nations (ASEAN), and the Asian and Pacific Council (ASPAC)—Thailand seeks not only to demonstrate her commitment to the notion of cooperative economic development and improved communications among the region's nations, but also to strengthen political unity as the cornerstone of security against hostile threats. On the one hand, the Thai government is perhaps more aware of, and certainly more vocal about, the limitations upon these organizations to perform security functions. Foreign Minister Thanat, for instance, has frequently and unequivocally stated that Thailand would not want to see ASEAN or ASPAC transformed into new security organizations that might supplant or supplement SEATO. Yet, Thanat has also said that whereas the Southeast Asian member states obviously lack military resources, their very unity constitutes a political commitment to "the preservation of peace and stability in the area."[j] The RTG seems now to believe that self-reliance, in the regionalist sense, should mean that multilateral economic and political associations can begin to fill the gap that will exist once the United States withdraws from Vietnam and, under President Nixon's Guam Doctrine, begins to play a less direct role in Southeast Asia's security. Regionalism, then, has the dual purpose of reducing Thailand's direct ties to U.S.-supported alliances and increasing her own importance within all-Asian organizations.[113]

China Policy. Viewed as a hedge against future developments in Asia, Thailand's involvement in regional organizations is further motivated by consideration of Communist China's power and the possibility, however remote now, of a rapprochement with Peking.

Asian regionalism emerges as Thailand's alternative to a neutralist or "accommodationist" policy, and to foreign neutralization schemes, in the period when American power has receded from the area. Regional cooperation, Thanat has said, insulates participating countries from manipulation by foreign powers, friendly and hostile. It answers the "need for a more effective effort to neutralize any eventual interference or intervention on the part of others into our affairs and our interests."[114]

---

[j]Interview with Frances L. Starner, "No 'Camouflage Surrender,' " *Far Eastern Economic Review*, October 17, 1968, p. 156. Since then, Thanat has distinguished between military and security cooperation. While ruling out Thailand's participation in a new NATO-type military alliance, Thanat suggested that *ad hoc* cooperation among Southeast Asian nations, including Australia and New Zealand, might be possible to deal with the common threat of guerrilla warfare. Interview with members of the British, Australian, and American press in Bangkok on February 13, 1969; Thai Permanent Mission, Press Release No. 13, March 12, 1969.

Expressing Thanat's position, Theh Chongkhadikij, a deputy editor of the *Bangkok Post*, has written that the foreign minister has been trying "to consolidate the Southeast Asian countries into the permanent balance to Peking's power. With such a balance, it may be possible that Peking would realize that it has to deal with these small countries on a basis of equality and mutual respect." Thanat was said to be anticipating the gradual evaporation of a permanent United States military presence in Southeast Asia, and to believe that collaboration among the independent nations of the area could somewhat offset that development.[115]

In another respect, though, Thailand's divorcement from too close an association with the United States—after, that is, an American withdrawal from Vietnam and a major reduction of the American presence in Thailand—may facilitate an eventual cooling off of China's hostility. Thai leaders have on one side condemned China's bellicosity and on the other left open the possibility that China will moderate her foreign policy. It is, however, up to China to change; once China "comes back to its senses, if it wants to deal with other nations on a sensible basis, Southeast Asia should not be caught unprepared to deal with it."[116] Should Peking "renounce the threat or use of force as a means of national policy," it will "be welcomed to work and cooperate with other Asian states for the peace and progress of the continent."[117] Foreign Minister Thanat has on more than one occasion said he would be willing to have "serious talks" with Chinese and other Asian Communist leaders on matters affecting the peace and security of the area. Beginning late in 1970, considerable discussion in the Thai government was reported about the desirability and feasibility of improving relations with the CPR.[118] According to these reports, some officials continued to oppose any dealings with Peking, but others were actively considering trying to "coax" China with prospects of trade and political relations. A special government task force was set up in the foreign ministry to weigh alternative policies toward China.[119]

This potential for increased flexibility toward the Communist world is further illustration of Thailand's pragmatic approach to shifting relations among the major powers in the Southeast Asia region. It is not a sign of neutralist sentiment or readiness to accommodate to China—phrases that have often been used by foreign observers who have tended to overlook the essentially nonideological, hardheaded Thai interpretation of events on the basis of Thailand's national interest. Yet past experience also indicates that the Thai government has sometimes held out the possibility of improved relations, especially with the Soviet Union, as a means of inviting a stronger American commitment to Thailand.[k] Thailand's partial opening of the door to China as announced by

---

[k]Thailand's displeasure with American policy in Laos in 1960 and with the augmentation of United States aid to Cambodia in the fall of 1962 had led to Thai feelers regarding formal trade and cultural relations with the USSR. See Nuechterlein, *Thailand and the Struggle for Southeast Asia*, pp. 178, 254-255. At the 1962 Geneva Conference on Laos, moreover, Thanat had authorized private discussions between Thai and Chinese Communist delegates. The subject was not disclosed and the attempt failed. *Bangkok Post*, February 21, 1969.

Thanat, and the negotiations that led, late in 1970, to the start of official trade relations with the Soviet Union,[1] can thus cut two ways: they may evidence Thailand's traditional sensitivity to the growing power and nearness of China at a time when the Laos situation remains uncertain, Soviet responsibilities continue to be important in North Vietnam and Laos, and the American presence in Asia may be reduced; they may also be intended to influence the United States against any significant reductions in either the American aid programs to Thailand or the American security commitment.

China and Thailand: A Concluding Assessment

The study of China's support of the Thai Communists' rebellion has developed the theme that the CPR was primarily motivated by concern over Thailand's and the United States' role in Laos and Vietnam rather than by the opportunity to implement long-term plans for an insurgency in the northeast. As it evolved from October 1964 to the end of 1966, China's support was intended to sustain a CPT-led uprising as a counter to the Thai government's active cooperation with United States policy. It was not a commitment to a Communist overthrow of the RTG. So far as can be discovered, China's part was (and has remained) more political than material; and it was staged in careful phases during 1965 and 1966, apparently to give Thailand time to reconsider *her* foreign commitments.

Although, in 1967, the full panoply of Maoist revolutionary devices—the leading party, the united front, the Thai "people's army," and Mao's "thoughts"—was said to have come into play in Thailand, China's role and responsibility for the rebellion did not increase. In part, this may have been based on diminished confidence in the rebellion, which Chinese commentaries seemed to recognize had made little concrete progress. Probably also influential was the fact that China's pressure tactics had failed; if the Thai government understood Peking's signals, it had chosen to ignore them. Putting these two considerations together, China's leaders seem to have decided that, rather than abandon the Thai Communists outright, it was practical to continue supporting them at a very modest level. Eventually, the Thai government might be persuaded that a long-term counterinsurgency effort would be more costly and

---

[1]Although the Soviet Union has been accused at various times of providing the Communist insurgents with arms—an accusation based on the capture of Soviet-made weapons—the strongly anti-Soviet stance of the CPT and the Soviet unwillingness to support the Thai Communists improved prospects for more formalized Thai-Soviet ties. Praphat reported in mid-1968 on a favorable RTG response to persistent Soviet overtures on concluding a bilateral trade agreement to replace the longstanding conduct of trade between individual firms only. (*Bangkok World*, June 27, 1968.) A thirty-man Thai trade mission visited the Soviet Union and six other East European countries in May and June 1969. The mission returned with a number of contracts. During the first half of 1970, trade agreements were concluded with Bulgaria and Rumania, followed by more intensive discussions with Soviet officials that led to the trade agreement on December 25, 1970. Thai-Soviet agreement was also reached on May 6, 1971 to permit Aeroflot, the Soviet national airline, to have stopover privileges in Bangkok.

of less predictable benefit than would an alteration of Thai foreign policies in ways favorable to China.

The conditional but critical extent of China's involvement in the Thai Communist rebellion has major implications for future Sino-Thai relations. Although Peking cannot be said to have exclusive control over the fate of the rebellion, it does unquestionably exert predominant influence over the Thai Communist leadership, its political appeals, and its strategy. This circumstance does not make the Communist movement a "creature" of Peking, but it does mean that, without Chinese political backing, the movement's key spokesmen would be isolated in China, deprived of an outlet for their programs and propaganda (perhaps including Thai-language broadcasts of the VTP, which may be located in south China) and of opportunities for public appearances. Moreover, a major cutback in Chinese support of the CPT would put great pressure on North Vietnam to stop infiltrating guerrillas and military supplies.*m* The Thai Communist movement would then probably revert to what it was before 1964: a politically ineffective, militarily weak, and fragmented organization with an exile leadership and no means of outside assistance.

How far Peking, and Hanoi, would go toward ceasing to support the Thai Communists seems to depend on how much the Thai government would be prepared to adjust its foreign policy, principally its interaction with United States policy in Indochina. In large part, the course the Thai government chooses to travel will in turn depend on American policy. The size and purposes of the American presence on Thai bases during and after American withdrawal from Vietnam, and the nature of United States involvement in Laos and Cambodia (since the March 18, 1970, overthrow of Prince Sihanouk), will be critical factors in any foreign policy reassessment by the Thai government. So may the circumstances in which the United States leaves Vietnam—in particular, as Thanat Khoman has said, whether the Saigon government is given responsibility for a political settlement or the United States imposes an unacceptable solution on South Vietnamese leaders.[120] If the United States is willing to continue paying a price (in aid and security promises) for Thailand's friendship and for access rights to the bases, and if the American commitment to non-Communist regimes in Indochina is considered steadfast, Thai interest in self-reliance and foreign policy change may be retarded.

Thailand's commitment to the West is thus very much context-dependent rather than philosophically derived.[121] Should the United States prove unwilling to assure the survival of non-Communist regimes even while sustaining support of Thailand's security, modifications in Thai foreign policy can be

---

*m*This is not to suggest, however, that North Vietnam's actions with respect to the Thai Communists are wholly dependent on Chinese decisions. A variety of situations can be imagined in Laos that might sustain North Vietnam's interest in northeast Thailand even if Sino-Thai relations improved. But at present, since China's and North Vietnam's interests in the northeast are congruent, the Hanoi regime would probably find it very difficult to counteract a Chinese move to abandon the Thai Communists, especially but not exclusively because of North Vietnam's dependence on Chinese aid and policy support.

expected. While accommodation, neutralism, nonalignment, and neutralization have long been criticized as viable alternatives for Thailand,[122] a policy of greater independence of the United States already is taking shape. This has occurred, as noted before, primarily because of American policy pronouncements and policy changes in Vietnam; but it has also been in response to unflattering American congressional and newspaper discussion of present and potential Thai dependency on the United States. A more independent foreign policy would mean continuing to accept foreign (i.e., American) advice and support, particularly in order to maintain the counterinsurgency program, but modifying foreign policy statements and actions to fit with the new Asian situation that Thai leaders foresee "after Vietnam."

Several possible steps can be mentioned that the Thai government might take in the future with an eye to improving relations with China.[n] The RTG might close down several air bases now being used for the Vietnam conflict, might reduce the American presence to a strictly limited number of advisers, and might maintain only formal ties to SEATO. A sharp reduction in the American presence in Thailand,[o] less vocal Thai support of American policies, and a softening of criticism of China by government sources might spur Peking's interest in an amelioration of relations with Bangkok. Chinese interests would not appear to require that Thailand first extend Peking diplomatic recognition or sever ties to Taiwan, although these would surely be issues if Thailand wished to pursue such questions as the nationality of the overseas Chinese and trade and cultural relations. From China's standpoint, the major roadblocks to a

---

[n]For further discussion, see the author's *Southeast Asia Tomorrow: Problems and Prospects for U.S. Policy*, Johns Hopkins Press, Baltimore, 1970, pp. 69-74. It may be, however, that Thailand will become more interested in trying to lessen tensions with Hanoi than with Peking, since it is the North Vietnamese, through the Pathet Lao, who are most immediately concerned with the training and supplying of insurgents in Thailand's north and northeast. The previously mentioned meetings with North Vietnamese officials to discuss repatriation during 1970 may be the first step in the direction of improved DRV-RTG relations. As Thanat Khoman reportedly said, the fact that Hanoi chose to send a delegation to Bangkok was "a sign for a more favorable trend in the future." (*Bangkok Post*, December 29, 1970). North Vietnam's decision may have been made in response to two decisions of the RTG: the first was not to send troops into Cambodia after the overthrow of Prince Sihanouk in March 1970; the second was to withdraw all Thai troops from South Vietnam by January 1972. By the same token, implementation by North Vietnam of agreements reached on the repatriation of northeastern Vietnamese may depend on whether or not the RTG sticks to those two decisions and reduces its involvement in Indochina.

[o]A reduced American presence, but Thailand's maintenance of the major air bases for future contingencies that might bring U.S. forces back, would be one way whereby the RTG could test China's interest in a rapprochement without throwing away the opportunity for continued close defense cooperation with the United States. By July 1970, approximately 6,000 U.S. servicemen had been withdrawn from Thailand under an agreement reached on September 30, 1969. Several thousand more were scheduled to follow by mid-1971. What effect these reductions will have on Chinese and North Vietnamese evaluations of Thai policy remains to be seen, however, inasmuch as American use of Thai air bases for missions over Laos and North Vietnam continued unabated into 1971.

satisfactory relationship with Thailand probably are the American presence and Thailand's direct participation in the fighting in Indochina.[p] Until these policies are abandoned by Bangkok, Peking probably sees very little risk or cost in sustaining the pressure on the Thai government through support, both actual and potential, of the CPT and other insurgent forces.[q]

A substantially diminished support role in behalf of the Thai Communists would probably be a price Peking would willingly pay for a looser Thai-American alliance. A less clearly aligned Thailand, which would not be without precedent, would probably encourage Peking to attempt to perpetuate a Thai-American divorcement through diplomacy. Peking, after all, has found in the past—as shall be discussed in the Burma case—that its interests can sometimes better be served by wooing a non-Communist government than by throwing support to an unpredictable Communist movement disadvantaged by internal weaknesses and historical circumstances.

---

[p] As has become public knowledge, personnel of the Thai armed forces have for some years served as advisors, as pilots of T-28 bombers, and in artillery support units to assist the Laotian government under Prince Souvanna Phouma. See, e.g., New York Times, May 27, 1967, p. 2, and Los Angeles Times, March 22, 1970, p. 7. Following the overthrow of Sihanouk, the RTG agreed to train ethnic Khmers living on both sides of the Thai-Cambodia border, to provide them with uniforms and equipment, and to carry out air raids against Communist troops in northwestern Cambodia. Just prior to the entry of South Vietnamese battalions into the Ho Chi Minh Trail area of southern Laos in February 1971, Thai ground involvement in Laos was said to have stepped up. Senator Walter F. Mondale of Minnesota charged—without challenge from Administration officials—that about 1,000 Thai troops had been airlifted into southern Laos. New York Times, January 22, 1971, p. 5.

[q] A recent illustration of Peking's ability to heighten Bangkok's concern over the Communist rebellion is the Chinese roadbuilding activity in northwestern Laos, which began on a small scale with Laotian government approval in 1962. Thailand's concern became conspicuous toward the end of 1969 when the construction of motorable and smaller feeder roads by Chinese engineering battalions began extending southeast from Muong Sai to Muong Houn in the Nam Beng Valley, less than 60 miles from Thailand's frontier. Although the principal purposes of the roads may be to improve the Chinese position and the logistical system of Communist forces in northern Laos, Peking leaves Thai officials with food for thought about an increased Chinese potential to assist insurgents in North Thailand. On the Chinese roads, see Senate Hearings on Thailand, p. 652, and U.S. Senate, Committee on Foreign Relations, Subcommittee on United States Security Agreements and Commitments Abroad, Hearings: Kingdom of Laos, 91st Cong., 1st Sess., part 2, October 20-22, 28, 1969, Government Printing Office, Washington, D.C., 1970, p. 372.

3

Cambodia and China: The Politics of Accommodation

Cambodian Foreign Policy under Sihanouk: Some Critical Values

The key elements in Cambodia's foreign policy are as much the result of circumstance as of history.[a] The country's geographical position—sharing a 549-mile border with South Vietnam, a 240-mile border with Laos, and a 380-mile border with Thailand—has made Cambodian governments ever-conscious of security threats from all sides and has entangled them in the civil strife that has dominated the post-World War II history of Indochina. Like Thailand, Cambodia has been caught in the vortex of major-power conflict over mainland Southeast Asia; unlike Thailand, Cambodia eventually chose to reconcile her external policies to those of Communist China. Accommodation to China did not, however, mean a foreign policy of submission but rather one of adjustment to what Cambodia regarded as the political realities of Asia.

Under the guiding hand of Prince Norodom Sihanouk,[b] Cambodia's foreign policy had four main themes: territorial integrity, independence, a Cambodian world role, and "positive" neutralism.[1]

Territorial Integrity

Cambodia's overriding concern for the security of her borders stems from historical conflict with Thai and Vietnamese forces. The bitterness and suspicion that characterize Cambodia's attitude toward present-day Thai and Vietnamese governments and political movements exist against a background of centuries of hostility.[2] These feelings have been kept prominent by the strong personalities who have headed the governments of these countries. In Sihanouk's view, the

---

[a]This chapter, and parts of chapters 5 and 6, were written prior to the overthrow of Sihanouk in March 1970. Rather than qualify every statement about Sihanouk's policies by mentioning that event, I have decided to retain the original version and to add a postscript (in Chapter 6) that brings the Cambodia story up to date.

[b]Sihanouk became Cambodia's monarch in April 194i. He abdicated the throne in March 1955 to become Head of State, Cambodia having become a constitutional monarchy in 1947. When King Norodom Suramarit, Sihanouk's father died in April 1960, the prince did not name a successor. Instead, in June 1960, Sihanouk held a nationwide referendum on his leadership that resulted in nearly 100 percent popular approval.

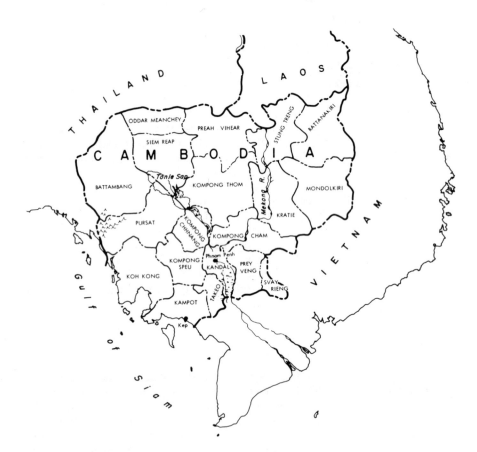

Figure 3-1. Cambodia.

basic threats to Cambodia originate in the traditional annexationist ambitions of Hanoi, Saigon, and Bangkok.[3]

The specific issues in Cambodian-Thai and Cambodian-Vietnamese relations concerned the border regions but also involved broader political differences. A major issue with Thailand was the dispute over the temple of Preah Vihear (Pra Viharn) which, the International Court of Justice determined in 1962, belongs to Cambodia. Prior to the Court's decision, numerous attempts were made to negotiate an agreement. These efforts broke down, recriminations were exchanged, diplomatic relations were suspended (in November 1958, after Sihanouk's second trip to Peking), briefly restored (February 1959), and broken anew (October 1961). Armed incidents were reported in the temple area and elsewhere along the border; these have occurred sporadically since 1962 despite Thailand's acceptance of the Court's verdict.[4]

As to the border itself, the Sihanouk government was not convinced that Thailand had dropped all interest in recovering Cambodian territory (principally, the provinces of Siem Reap and Battambang) that had been granted the Thai by the French in 1941 under the auspices of Japanese occupation authorities. Although the two provinces were restored to Cambodia in 1946, and although Bangkok insists that the validity of the frontier is not questioned, Sihanouk's suspicions—which apply equally to the Thai Communists—led him to demand as the prerequisite to a restoration of RTG-Cambodia relations that Thailand, along with all other nations, declare her respect and recognition of the existing border.[c]

Finally, Cambodia maintained that the Thai government, with American backing, had long harbored the former Khmer nationalist leader, Son Ngoc Thanh, and his band of rebel Khmer Serai (Free Khmer). Although the Thai wartime government under Pridi may have actively supported Son Ngoc Thanh's forces, then known as Khmer Issarak,[5] the extent of its involvement with the movement has probably varied. (Thai authorities have denied any connection with the movement, though they have not denied sympathy for its aim of overthrowing Sihanouk.)[6] Sihanouk was certain, however, that many armed incidents in Battambang province over the years were attributable to the Khmer Serai who, he claimed, continued to receive equipment from and shelter in Thailand.

---

[c]In September 1966 and again in May 1967, for instance, Sihanouk reported that his representatives, meeting in Peking with members of the Thai Patriotic Front, had been rebuffed in efforts to gain agreement on mutual respect of the existing borders. The prince concluded that the Thai Communists were as expansionist as their brethren in Bangkok. Press conference of September 20, 1966, broadcast by Phnom Penh Radio to Southeast Asia, same date; speech of May 9, 1967, broadcast by Phnom Penh domestic service, same date. (Although reference is made here to statements by Sihanouk contained in broadcasts, his remarks were considered "official" only when reported in the daily dispatches of the Agence Khmère de Presse news agency or were reprinted in the government's periodic compilation of the prince's speeches.)

Differences with Vietnam ranged over questions of Communist subversion, alleged Vietnamese territorial interests in Cambodia, treatment of the minority Khmer people who live in Vietnam, and Saigon's economic pressure tactics. Since the early 1950s, the Cambodian government has been concerned about the subversive activities of so-called Khmer Viet Minh (or Khmer Reds) who, in the name of the Khmer People's Liberation Army, had fought against Sihanouk and French authorities and were part of the Viet Minh movement. After the 1954 Geneva Conference, these primarily Vietnamese Communist forces did not entirely dismantle their cells or turn over their arms.[d] These remnant Communist forces were said by Sihanouk to have resurfaced early in 1967. Sihanouk claimed they were supported by Hanoi and the Viet Cong, despite the fact that Cambodia was cooperating in several ways with the Communists' effort in South Vietnam. To Sihanouk, the militant behavior of the Communists and their evasiveness during several negotiating sessions concerning the status of the border only demonstrated the perfidy of the "Annamese," be they Communist or non-Communist.

The Cambodian-Vietnamese border is considered delimited by Cambodia but still open to dispute by the Saigon government. The government of Vietnam (GVN) has consistently refused to issue a statement recognizing the legality of the present border. Saigon, unlike the DRV and the National Liberation Front of South Vietnam, has also refused to relinquish its claim to several small islands in the Gulf of Siam, near the Cambodian seaside resort of Kep. Saigon's attitude on the Khmer minority in Vietnam and Cambodian access to Mekong River traffic further aggravates relations. The minority Kampuchea Krom, numbering perhaps 500,000, live primarily in Cochinchina, a region that used to be part of the Khmer Empire. At various times, Phnom Penh has accused the Saigon government of harassing these people. Periodic closures of the Mekong River to ships destined for Cambodia represent a different kind of harassment. The construction and deepening of the port of Sihanoukville over the last decade is Cambodia's alternative to dependence on Saigon's whim for an outlet to the

---

[d]Officially, all Viet Minh soldiers were evacuated from Cambodia to North Vietnam in October 1954. The Cambodian government charged then and thereafter that in fact some Viet Minh had remained behind, hidden their arms, and either continued to roam the countryside or merged with the Vietnamese minority. But the International Control Commission in Cambodia could not confirm these charges. See Great Britain, *First Progress Report of the International Commission for Supervision and Control in Cambodia for the Period Ending December 31, 1954*, Cambodia No. 1 (1955), Cmd. 9458, H.M.S.O., London, May 1955; and *Second Progress Report . . . for the Period January 1 to March 31, 1955*, Cambodia No. 2 (1955), Cmd. 9534, H.M.S.O., London, July 1955. Background information on Viet Minh activities in Cambodia between 1949 and 1954 may be found in Smith, pp. 32-51, and David J. Steinberg, et al., *Cambodia: Its People, Its Society, Its Culture*, rev. ed., H.R.A.F. Press, New Haven, Conn., 1959, pp. 106-112. Sihanouk, writing in April 1966, charged that the Khmer Viet Minh were "created" by the Vietnamese Communists between 1946 and 1947. Quoted in *Le Monde*, April 5, 1967.

sea.[e] All these issues became particularly pronounced with the intensification of the conflict in South Vietnam and charges of Cambodian complicity in the supplying of Viet Cong and North Vietnamese forces.

Although history has not left the same legacy of bitterness with Laos as with Thailand and Vietnam, the Sihanouk government disclosed a certain anxiety about Laotian intentions toward Cambodia. A sizable Laotian population resides in the Cambodian province of Stung Treng, which was once a part of Laos. According to Phnom Penh, the Royal Laotian Government's Ministry of Foreign Affairs informed Cambodia in a note of October 2, 1964, that "there has never been a question of the Laotian kingdom reclaiming any portion of Khmer territory."[7] But this disclaimer said nothing about the legal status of the border; and, in 1967, when Sihanouk called upon all nations to affirm or reaffirm their recognition and respect of Cambodia's existing frontiers, the RLG did not respond. (The Pathet Lao, whom Sihanouk accused of being involved in Communist-provoked agitation in Stung Treng in 1967, eventually issued a statement of recognition and respect late in 1968.) So far as Sihanouk was concerned, the Laotians had become like the Thai and the Vietnamese in aspiring to regain lost territory in Cambodia.

Centuries of conflict and unresolved disputes that intermix frontiers and politics may not, however, fully explain Cambodia's much-publicized concern about her security. Domestic political considerations may also be involved. Thai-Cambodian hostility, for instance, may at times serve the separate purposes of the two governments. The existence of an external threat can be exploited as a rallying point for nationalism. The Thai government could claim that Cambodia's closeness to Communist China raised the danger of subversion of Cambodia's neighbors under the cloak of neutralism, while Cambodia could claim that Thailand's alignment with the United States accentuated the danger of infiltration by the Khmer Serai. By virtue of these claims, moreover, the Thai and Cambodian governments could seek to strengthen their argument for obtaining military assistance and defense commitments from their respective allies. In this respect, Cambodia and Thailand are no different from other developing countries that have used foreign policy for domestic purposes.[8]

The fears expressed by the Cambodian government about the intentions of Thailand and Vietnam, together with Sihanouk's uncertainty about the readiness of any major power to come to his assistance if Cambodian security were directly threatened, were behind the prince's constant efforts to gain big-power commitments to Cambodia's territorial integrity. Beginning at the Geneva Conference on Laos, Sihanouk sought out big-power agreement to extend to

---

[e]A related matter of contention, though not one that Sihanouk gave much attention to publicly in recent years, is Cambodia's share of customs receipts collected at Saigon when that port served as the trade center for the French-established Indochina customs union. The money is tied up in Paris and the amount due Cambodia is in dispute. See Bernard K. Gordon, "Cambodia: Where Foreign Policy Counts," *Asian Survey*, Vol. V, No. 9, September 1965, p. 446.

Cambodia the same guarantees of her neutralism that had been granted Laos. The prince wanted much more than obliging letters from heads of state assuring Cambodia of respect for her territorial integrity; he also wanted an international conference that would result in fairly explicit guarantees of that respect.[9] The position of Thailand and South Vietnam at that time, and since, was that there were no boundary problems to be resolved, and hence that Sihanouk was mainly interested in using a conference to publicize his groundless suspicions of Thai and Vietnamese expansionism.[10] Sihanouk did not forget that at the same time as his neighbors and the United States demurred on his appeal, Communist China gave it total support.[11]

The persistence of border difficulties amid failure to gain the consent of all the major powers to an international conference was partly responsible for Sihanouk's call upon all nations in May 1967 to clarify their position on Cambodia's existing borders.[f] On July 10, Sihanouk went further, announcing that his government would freeze diplomatic relations with nations that refused to declare their recognition and respect of the border.[12] By mid-1967, Cambodia's security was far more seriously in jeopardy than at the time of the Geneva Conference on Laos. The alleged threats from South Vietnam and Thailand had taken a back seat to a small-scale rebellion in Battambang province that was said to be supported by Vietnamese as well as Cambodian Communists. Yet, in mid-1967 as in 1961 and 1962, Sihanouk's motivation was apparently to publicize his border problems and in that way pressure the major Western and Communist powers to declare their acceptance of Cambodia's territorial integrity. His assumption, which was to be seriously challenged by subsequent events, was that the major powers would be willing and able to restrain their respective allies in Thailand, Vietnam, and Laos from interfering in Cambodia's affairs.

Independence

Prince Sihanouk often stated that his ultimate concern was not whether Cambodia fell to Communism or whether he remained as head of state, but whether Cambodia could survive as an independent entity, as the repository of the Khmer culture. His admiration for Ho Chi Minh and Marshal Tito stemmed from their ability to have maneuvered so as to avoid compromising their countries' independence for the sake of other nations' interests.[13]

Sihanouk warned that Cambodia could not afford to be the servant of any great power or foreign ideology. Alliances are always transitory, and today's friend can quickly become tomorrow's enemy. The prince—pointing, for

---

[f]At that time, only France (at the time of De Gaulle's visit of August 31-September 2, 1966), East Germany, and Singapore had issued unequivocal statements on Cambodia's borders. Sihanouk's particular interest in forcing China's hand on the border question is discussed below.

instance, to the hesitancy of Cambodia's professed friends to respond unequivocally to his call for statements of recognition and respect of Cambodia's borders—observed many times that certain nations praise and aid Cambodia not because they value her independence but because they have need of Cambodia's antiimperialist foreign policy.[14] But in looking at Saigon's and Bangkok's relations with the United States, Sihanouk's government saw a lesson for itself: once having inextricably aligned with a great power, smaller nations begin by sacrificing their independence and may end by collapsing once the great power decides that the alliance is no longer in its interest.[g]

This principle found expression in Sihanouk's persistent attempts to steer clear of an irrevocable commitment to any one great power and to leave open the alternative of leaning "left" or "right" as circumstances dictated. The competition for influence in Southeast Asia between China and the United States was therefore critical to Cambodia's survival as an independent nation. Even if Cambodia appeared to side with Peking, it was Sihanouk's view that the maintenance of American power and influence in the region (but not in Cambodia) sufficiently balanced off that relationship to preserve Cambodia's freedom of maneuver. As he put it in an address before the Asia Society in New York on September 26, 1961:

The day we find ourselves facing only one all-powerful bloc, the days of our independence—perhaps even of our very existence—will be counted. This is why we are absolutely sincere when we say that we want the United States and our other Western friends to preserve and maintain their influence, their position in our area.[15]

For all the criticism Sihanouk leveled at Thailand's openness to American "domination," furthermore, he admitted that were Thailand neutral or Communist-dominated, the Communist nations would lose interest in Cambodia's independence and leave her vulnerable (as in 1941) to renewed Thai incursions.[16] A victory for the Communists in South Vietnam was deemed equally disastrous for Cambodia.[17] The American role in both those countries was perceived as a kind of lightning rod that protected Cambodia by assuring, first, that Sino-American hostility was played out beyond Cambodia's borders, and, second, that the Thai and South Vietnamese governments would be prevented from attempting to reoccupy lost territories. One writer has proposed

---

[g]Referring to the American impact on the South Vietnamese government, an editorial in the weekly newspaper, *Neak Cheat Niyum (Le Nationaliste)*, official organ of Sihanouk's political movement, said: "The unprecedented humiliation inflicted upon the Saigon authorities and their probable abandonment by the United States are in the nature of things and are part of the customs and habits of the great powers in their relations with small countries. . . . It is appropriate to recall the excellent advice which former King Norodom frequently gave: 'Never associate with someone who is stronger and richer than you; otherwise, you will always lose.' " Issue of November 4-10, 1968.

that Sihanouk "needed" a certain amount of tension nearby to make Cambodia's survival an interest of larger nations:[18] Cambodia's independence stands the best chance of enduring in an environment of low-level tensions and divergent foreign policies in adjacent countries.

The preservation of an independent foreign policy required that Sihanouk be sensitive not only to relations among the major powers in Asia, but also to the factionalism and dissension that have characterized Cambodian politics. Neutralism, by appealing to Cambodian self-reliance, was consistent with the diversity of political persuasions of the Cambodian governmental elite and the intellectual community. Smith suggests that a neutral foreign policy may have been decided upon in part to unify a disintegrating party system.[19] The political movement which Sihanouk headed—the Sangkum Reastr Niyum or People's Socialist Community, which was launched in March 1955—symbolized the prince's determination to bring diverse personalities and policy preferences into a single organization; it also was in keeping with the personalist nature of his rule.[20] Yet, Sihanouk's unquestionable popularity and the remarkable degree of loyalty he commanded in and outside his government did not always assure the removal of foreign policy from the arena of political conflict. At the same time as neutralism and independence may have been sensible priorities for both Cambodia's external and internal stability, they at times also led to Sihanouk's being challenged for every supposed deviation toward the "red" or "blue" camp.

Cambodia's World Role

If Cambodia under Sihanouk seemed to gain more prominence in the news and in foreign offices than her size and power appeared to justify, this feat can be attributed to the prince's perseverance. His concern for Cambodia's tenuous security situation led him to do everything possible to publicize his country's weakness and turn it into an asset. His constant reiteration of the theme that Cambodia constitutes a particular model of independent national development worthy of emulation by other small countries anxious to preserve their sovereignty and culture was Sihanouk's way of attempting to maximize Cambodia's drawing power with governments of every political persuasion.

Sihanouk's view was that while Cambodia's exposure to hostile interference needed to be stressed to the outer world, Cambodia also had to evoke an image of positive contributor to regional and world peace. By gaining prominence as a force for stability, Cambodia would further enhance her claim to worldwide support against her external enemies. Sihanouk took special pride in mediating big-power disputes—for instance, in having helped convene the Geneva Conference on Laos[21]—because such efforts seemed to him to bolster Cambodia's as well as his own reputation. And his well-known sensitivity to criticism of Cambodia—a sensitivity, however, that he shared with other leaders of developing nations—came into the open whenever Cambodia was denied an opportunity to play an important role in settling major conflicts—as, for instance, when Phnom Penh was rejected by the United States as a suitable location for opening negotiations with North Vietnam in 1968.

Neutralism, Cambodian Style

Although foreign policies tend to defy strict definition, Cambodia's foreign policy under Sihanouk may be labeled positive neutralism rather than nonalignment or neutrality.[22] It was not a policy of nonalignment inasmuch as the Cambodian government, while rejecting permanent affiliation with any single major power, did take stands on specific cold-war issues. It was not a policy of neutrality since, despite Cambodia's adoption of a Neutrality Act in September 1957,[23] Cambodia's status was not juridically established as neutral by the international community (unlike Switzerland, for example); and Sihanouk himself many times distinguished Cambodia's foreign policy from that of a strictly neutral nation.

Sihanouk seemed to have concluded that neither nonalignment nor neutrality could ever serve Cambodia's interests. He apparently came to regard nonalignment as too negative a response to the demands of the cold war on small nations. From Cambodia's standpoint, being noncommittal (and hence silent) on major international issues—such as the Test Ban Agreement of 1963 and the Vietnam conflict—could create far more trouble than issuing an uncompromising statement of position. Moreover, for all the lip service paid by the nonaligned nations to anticolonialist, antiimperialist themes, Cambodia could not expect to receive practical assistance from them against her enemies to the east and west.[24] As he told the delegates of the nonaligned nations represented at Belgrade in 1961, Cambodia's interests were best preserved by maintaining "a balance in our friendship with the two blocs," not by joining a third bloc of the nonaligned.[25]

As for neutrality, Sihanouk commented that few governments can completely avoid having to make certain kinds of "compensation" for aid received from major powers.[26] Nonalignment would require that Cambodia refrain from deferring to Peking or Hanoi on critical international issues, but neutrality would cost Cambodia the significant assistance of Moscow and Peking that could be expected in return for such deference. Thus, although the prince's neutralism meant identification with the antibloc philosophy of the nonaligned nations and a refusal to join military alliances, it also meant a commitment to certain outstanding international issues along lines consonant with Cambodia's relations with the Communist world.

Neutralism in Practice

Sihanouk's style of neutralism depended upon his degree of confidence in other nations' willingness and ability to protect Cambodia from her traditional enemies, his fear of Communist intentions and hopes of China's readiness to intervene in Cambodia's behalf, and the overall security situation in the Indochina region at any given time. Cambodia's closeness to the United States after the 1954 Geneva Conference, in particular Phnom Penh's interest in American protection under the SEATO umbrella, was based on the conviction that China and North Vietnam were the main threats to Cambodian security and that only the United States could be relied on for protection. But an exchange of visits with Nehru (November 1954 in Phnom Penh, March 1955 in New Delhi), and Chou En-lai's soft-pedaling of peaceful coexistence at Bandung, apparently kindled Sihanouk's interest in avoiding a possibly compromising association with the United States. By early 1956, when Sihanouk paid a visit to Manila, he was saying that involvement in an anti-China alliance such as SEATO at a time when China was extending a friendly hand might invite the very antagonism Cambodia wished to avoid.[27]

When the prince traveled to Peking for the first time in February 1956, as he later recollected,[28] Mao advised him that Communism was perhaps a good thing for Cambodia. The prince replied that Communism was ill-suited to Cambodian nationalism and Buddhism, and that Cambodia would resist the attempts of any nation to impose its ideology on Cambodia. Mao is said to have replied: "This is very good; it is necessary always to defend the interests of one's country and to face the dangers which menace it." Evidently from this and previous conversations in Bandung, Sihanouk drew the conclusion that he could count on China to respect and support Cambodian territorial integrity so long as Cambodia did not adopt policies hostile to China. He specifically disavowed SEATO's protection in February; Cambodia signed her first trade and payments agreements with China (to receive industrial and communications equipment in return for minerals and other products) in April; and, in June, the Chinese made their first aid grant to a non-Communist country—$22.4 million—toward the construction of plywood, textile, paper, and cement factories. These steps toward normalizing relations with China were greeted with decisions in Saigon and Bangkok to close their borders with Cambodia, moves that Sihanouk charged were instigated by American displeasure over the results of his trip to Peking. But the pressure subsided, friendly relations with the United States were reaffirmed, and Sihanouk had made stick his determination that Cambodia would henceforth balance her aid program and political dealings between Communist and Western sources.[29]

Neutralism and Cambodia's China Policy

Beginning in 1956, Prince Sihanouk was wary of offending Peking and damaging the carefully cultivated relationship that began with his visit there in February. Although well aware that Cambodia had no special place in Chinese foreign policy interests, Sihanouk long considered China to have the highest value for Cambodian security and hence to be worth a certain political price.

In July 1958, Cambodia and China agreed to establish diplomatic relations and to exchange ambassadors. Two months later, Sihanouk attended the Thirteenth UN General Assembly meeting to propose the admission of Communist China to the Organization. Several visits by officials of the two countries were exchanged thereafter, and additional economic trade and agreements were signed. Liu Shao-ch'i's visit of December 1960 was particularly influential: it led to the signing of a Treaty of Friendship and Mutual Nonaggression. A China-Cambodia Friendship Association was formed in Peking that same month (although the Phnom Penh branch was not set up until September 1964). In December 1963, the month after Sihanouk announced the termination of the American aid program, the first Sino-Cambodian military aid agreement was signed.

These developments were motivated by a number of basic policy conclusions Sihanouk had arrived at over some time: that the Americans were bent on using their aid program to keep Sihanouk tied to them, holding over him the threat of fomenting a rebellion against him; that the Chinese not only respected Cambodian territorial integrity, but would also use their influence in Hanoi to keep the Vietnamese Communists out of Cambodia; that the Americans were not firmly committed to stopping the Communist threat in Laos, were unwilling to interpose themselves in Cambodia's behalf by guaranteeing the country's neutrality, and were supporting a weak reed in Ngo Dinh Diem—whom they later had to cut down—against a powerful national-Communist movement in South Vietnam. Uncertainty over and mistrust of American intentions on the Southeast Asia mainland thus combined with the hope that friendly relations with China would safeguard Cambodia against undesirable future contingencies in Sihanouk's policy of moving farther away from the United States and closer to Peking.

By the mid-1960s, Sihanouk was apparently convinced he was pursuing the proper course. The American effort in Vietnam did not then appear to him to have stymied the Viet Cong, and it still looked as though it would only be a matter of time before the Communists ruled in Saigon. The United States would then be compelled to withdraw from Vietnam and from an active, influential role in Southeast Asia generally. In 1965 no less than in 1963, after Diem's overthrow,[30] Sihanouk concluded that America had no future in Asia and hence that Chinese hegemony in the region was inevitable. Publicly, he said he had no illusions about the fate that awaited Cambodia once China dominated Asia;[31] but by his actions, it became apparent that his aim was to preserve Cambodian sovereignty through political accommodation. And, as Sihanouk would write in 1966, friendship with China had resulted in some important benefits, in particular that China respected and rewarded Cambodian neutralism where the United States had not:

Certainly we are the friends of the People's Republic of China. But this is not by any propensity to follow Marxist ideology in the "hardest" line. It is in all simplicity because we have never, throughout our history, quarreled with this great nation, and because the regime in power in Peking has never ceased to display to us its comprehension and sympathy in supporting our resistance to American imperialist aggression and to the annexationist attempts of our neighbors, according us, incidentally, military and economic aid without condition. Peking makes no subversive propaganda in our house and well accommodates to our neutrality. . . . For we who apply the principle of reciprocity in our foreign relations, how can we not respond with friendship to the amicable treatment which the Chinese reserve for us? We are friends of China, but not her "satellite."[32]

In linking friendship with China to Cambodia's survival,[33] Sihanouk was not only placing his chips with the player he considered potentially the strongest, but may also have been hoping to influence Peking to continue in the role Cambodia wanted it to play. Yet, his assumptions regarding Communist China's preparedness and capacity both to deter the pro-American regimes in South Vietnam and Thailand and to restrain North Vietnam had little in fact to support them.

Peking then (and thereafter) was hardly willing to give the prince a firm commitment to intervene, directly or indirectly, in response to threats from Saigon or Bangkok. China's leverage in Hanoi had only slightly more evidence to justify Sihanouk's hope. At the 1954 Geneva Conference, Peking's delegates, led by Chou En-lai, had prevailed upon the Viet Minh to drop most of their extravagant and baseless demands concerning their Communist Khmer clients. Aside from that event, which occurred before North Vietnam became an independent state, the only other—and rather circumstantial—indication of possible Chinese influence over Hanoi was North Vietnam's dropping of claims to the off-shore islands just before Liu Shao-ch'i arrived in Phnom Penh from Hanoi in May 1963.[34] Not until four years later, however, would Sihanouk be given reason to consider that he had overestimated the extent of North Vietnam's attentiveness to Chinese advice.

Cambodia's gratitude for China's unconditional assistance,[h] political support, and noninterference in Cambodian affairs was expressed in numerous ways between 1958 and mid-1964, when the Vietnam war introduced new elements into Sino-Cambodian relations. Peking's leadership and China's economic

[h]In addition to two aid grants in 1956 and 1960, the CPR sent over 400 engineers and technical workers to Cambodia between 1956 and 1962. China also accepted about 200 Cambodian trainees for courses of instruction on the operation of the four factories donated to Cambodia. See the comments of the Chinese ambassador to Cambodia, Ch'en Shu-liang, in *Réalités cambodgiennes*, July 13, 1962, as quoted in Michael Field, *The Prevailing Wind: Witness in Indo-China*, Methuen and Co., London, 1965, p. 198. Subsequent charges from diverse sources, including the Soviet Union, have held that these Chinese factories actually produced poor quality goods, were not properly constructed, and were of little assistance to Cambodia's economic development. See Michael Leifer, "Cambodia: The Politics of Accommodation," *Asian Survey*, Vol. IV, No. 1, January 1964, p. 676, and a Phnom Penh radio broadcast of July 22, 1965, responding to Soviet charges, in *The China Quarterly*, No. 24, October-December 1965, p. 211.

progress were periodically extolled. Cambodia broke off diplomatic relations with Thailand in October 1961 and with South Vietnam in August 1963. (Relations with the United States were finally severed in May 1965.) The Albanian government was recognized by Phnom Penh in September 1962; and in October 1963, the two countries cosponsored a resolution to seat mainland China in the General Assembly. Of more immediate interest to Peking was Cambodia's attitude on the Sino-Indian border war in the fall of 1962. Whatever Sihanouk's private thoughts on the matter may have been, he recognized the delicacy of the situation and evidently decided that Cambodia should not be thrust into the position of arbitrating the dispute. At the December 1962 Colombo Conference called by Nehru to help resolve the issue, Cambodia joined with Burma in urging only that negotiations between New Delhi and Peking be resumed, and in rejecting Egypt's suggestion that a demilitarized zone be established in Ladakh (a measure China would never have accepted). In the end, Nehru accepted the conference's proposals regarding a cease-fire line, thus enabling both Sihanouk and Ne Win to emerge with their positions unscathed.[35]

China's opposition to the formation of a third-world bloc of nonaligned nations, especially one headed by Nehru, Nasser, and Tito, received more direct support from Cambodia. Having made clear his distaste for third-world politics at the Belgrade Conference in 1961, Sihanouk acted accordingly in March 1964 when, at Colombo, Sino-Soviet differences split the delegations between those in favor of a second nonaligned "bloc" conference at Belgrade and those in favor of a second Bandung conference composed of Asian and African nations. Cambodia sided with the Bandung group which, supported by Communist China, proposed to meet at that site (later switched to Algiers) to give support to Sukarno's new theme of the New Emerging Forces, to ignore the Yugoslav-Indian pleas that a conference of the developing nations emphasize peaceful coexistence, and to play up anticolonialism and antiimperialism.[36] The differences between the pro-Belgrade and pro-Bandung groups carried over into 1965 and finally led to the dissolution of the Algiers Conference.

When the Nuclear Test Ban Agreement was signed in 1963, Cambodia adopted China's position that the treaty was a poor substitute for general disarmament. Sihanouk reportedly referred to it as a "bargain of dupes and a demagogic act."[37] Whether or not he actually thought so may have been beside the point, for as he wrote in explaining his government's position: "All things considered, we prefer after all to be isolated *with* China rather than against China, which is the only country ready to fight at our side for our survival if this were directly threatened."[38]

These gestures by Sihanouk in China's direction were made at the same time as the prince took steps that demonstrated Cambodia's independence of Peking in politics and foreign affairs. Domestically, friendly relations with China did not prevent Sihanouk from curtailing the political activities of certain leftist Chinese. Although Chou En-lai, when he visited Phnom Penh in December 1956, admonished the overseas Chinese to stay out of politics and obey Cambodian law,[i] the CPR economic mission, once established in Cambodia in 1958, reportedly began financing a number of leftist newspapers and seeking to influence leftist control of the Chinese schools and regionally based Chinese clubs (*congrégations*).[39] To deal with these problems, the Cambodian government restricted foreigners from engaging in eighteen professions (several of which affected the Chinese in particular), abolished the *congrégations*, and placed controls over the Chinese schools.[40] Sihanouk was careful then, as he would be in 1967, to differentiate Chinese government policy from the local activities of the CPR mission.[j]

Two years later, in 1960, "several hundred" Chinese were reportedly arrested by the government for various illegal activities, including subversion. Between sixty and seventy were deported to China, apparently after Chou agreed to the arrangement during a visit to Cambodia in May 1960.[41] Then, in December 1963, Sihanouk instituted a nationalization program that affected the largely Chinese-run import-export trade. The Chinese community generally acquiesced in the program, however, since its hold on Cambodia's trade, real estate, and industry would not be substantially altered by the changeover to state administration.[k]

Close supervision of the Chinese community was paralleled during the 1958-1964 period by concerted internal security measures to defeat the subversive activities of the Cambodian left-wing. These radicals, belonging to the Pracheachon (People's Party), had on occasion participated in elections in the country;[42] but their strength and appeal had always been minimal. Sihanouk's concern was that Pathet Lao successes across the border beginning in 1960 might embolden the Pracheachon to press its own cause.[43] Early in 1962, 15 members of this crypto-Communist organization were arrested on charges of having received North Vietnamese instructions to carry out subversion. The unfolding of this plot, as it indeed appears to have been,[44] probably further strengthened Sihanouk's conviction that the North Vietnamese threat from Laos and South Vietnam demanded Cambodia's political identification with China on inter-

---

[i]William E. Willmott, *The Chinese in Cambodia*, University of British Columbia Press, Vancouver, 1967, p. 79. This book is the most comprehensive treatment available of the overseas Chinese there. Willmott (Table 1, p. 12) puts the Chinese population of Cambodia at about 400,000 (as of 1964), with 150,000 in Phnom Penh.

[j]In a March 1958 article in *Réalités cambodgiennes*, for instance, Sihanouk contrasted Chou's "official warning" with the CPR mission's belief in "the necessity of communizing the Chinese and the Khmers." Quoted in Smith, *Cambodia's Foreign Policy, loc. cit.*

[k]Willmott, pp. 100-101. Willmott makes a strong case for the high degree of assimilation of the Chinese into Cambodian society despite their dominant position in transportation, trade, and rice-milling industries. Control of commerce by the Chinese and the emergence of a Sino-Cambodian elite, economic and political, have not, he argues, created a conflictual situation inasmuch as direct competition between Khmers and Chinese has not occurred. Racial antagonism is directed far more at the Vietnamese (numbering perhaps 300,000) than at the Chinese—as became apparent with the violence against Vietnamese in Cambodia following the deposition of Sihanouk.

national issues of significance to Peking. Thereafter, however, the Pracheachon became virtually a defunct political force, and although its existence was permitted, it was more "to let the party stand as a target of popular abuse" than to show the government's tolerance toward pro-Communist organizations.[l]

In the international arena, the Cambodian government adopted positions different from those Peking took or might have wished Phnom Penh to take. Contrary to Peking, Cambodia praised the Yugoslavs for their independent position in the international Communist movement. Although Sihanouk did not agree with Tito's third-world bloc proposals, he frequently paid tribute to the Yugoslav leader's tenacity in avoiding compromising alliances.[45] Relations between Cambodia and the Soviet Union remained friendly and profitable despite the Sino-Soviet rift. Soviet economic assistance to Cambodia between 1955 and 1960 totaled $28.8 million; in April 1963, eight months *before* the Sino-Cambodian military aid agreement was concluded, Moscow and Phnom Penh signed Cambodia's first military aid pact with a member of the socialist camp. Soviet economic and military aid between 1960 and 1964 came to $20.5 million, compared with $25.7 million in the same period for Chinese assistance.[46] In terms of total bilateral assistance from the Communist countries (including Yugoslavia) compared with the non-Communist countries between 1960 and 1964, the balance favored the latter, $169 million to $65.5 million.[m] Although the American contribution ($130.5 million for these years) ended in 1963, China's aid never rose above 20 percent of total assistance given Cambodia. Finally, the Cambodian trade pattern also favored the West. Imports and exports were primarily kept (as is still the case) within the so-called French franc zone, whereas the China trade has consistently been small (between 15-20 percent of Cambodia's imports and 5-10 percent of her exports).[47]

From Peking's viewpoint, these aspects of Cambodian policy were probably minor irritants at most, considering the other kinds of political support China was receiving from Sihanouk. Nevertheless, they did show that Cambodian neutralism, though oriented toward Peking, was not dominated by considerations of Chinese interests and retained considerable flexibility.

---

[l]Leifer, "Cambodia and China," p. 337. The U.S. State Department's sourcebook, *World Strength of the Communist Party Organizations*, states that the Pracheachon may have "less than 1,000 members and several thousand sympathizers." It is listed as the front organization of the People's Revolutionary Party, estimated to have under 100 Khmer members. The PRP received rare public mention in March 1968 when *Neues Deutschland*, organ of the East German Communist Party, mentioned it as a Marxist-Leninist party that should be invited to the preparatory meeting of world Communist parties.

[m]Aside from the United States, other Western contributors for 1960-1964 were France ($34.4 million) and Japan ($4.1 million). On the Communist side, Czechoslovakia ($8 million), Poland ($0.3 million), and Yugoslavia ($6 million) gave economic aid in addition to that of the USSR and the CPR. Figures are drawn from ibid.

China's Cambodia Policy

Cambodia's departures from a strict alignment with Communist China on political and foreign policies did not diminish the value of Cambodia to China's external interests. As Cambodia drifted away from the United States, that value tended to increase. Simultaneously, however, Peking was confronted with the possibility that Sihanouk's friendship, by increasing Cambodia's susceptibility to pressures from the American camp, might impose unwanted obligations on Peking regarding Cambodia's defense. After Tonkin, with Cambodia caught up in the tension of the U.S.-DRV conflict, Sihanouk's stock in Peking rose, but the Chinese leaders gave no indication that they would be any more generous than previously regarding commitments to Cambodian security.

Cambodia's Value to China

Sihanouk's pursuit of a neutral, independent foreign policy served an exemplary purpose for Chinese foreign policy by demonstrating China's toleration of governments that do not align with the American security system. The prince's friendly relations with the Soviet Union and with members of the Western bloc were not nearly as important as was his rejection of American aid, bases, and forces.

Cambodia also symbolized, for China, the feasibility of a relationship based on the five principles of peaceful coexistence: nonaggression; noninterference by one nation in the other's internal affairs; mutual respect for each other's sovereignty and territorial integrity; equality and mutual benefit; peaceful coexistence. These principles, and Cambodia's agreement not to join a military alliance directed against China, were incorporated in the 1960 friendship and mutual nonaggression pact. The treaty in effect underscored the assurance implied in Cambodia's Neutrality Act that Cambodia would not become a member of SEATO or any other "anti-China" alliance. When the 1960 treaty was concluded during Sihanouk's trip to Peking in December, Chinese commentaries intimated that a relationship based on the five principles carried certain rewards for the smaller nation. As put in an editorial of *Jen-min jih-pao* of December 22, China would not interfere in the other nation's internal affairs, and would give "energetic assistance and support to those countries in the development and consolidation of their national economies. . . ."[48]

Cambodia's value also included her support of Chinese positions, particularly those that reflected opposition to imperialism. In the early 1960s, when Yugoslavia, Egypt, and India were leading a drive to unite the nonaligned nations, Peking had sought to head it off by appealing for the formation of a "broad united front" against imperialism. At the same time, Peking was also contesting the Soviet Union's "softness" on revolutionary war; but Chinese policy in action chose to overlook the character of individual governments and instead to emphasize their antiimperialist convictions.[n] Sihanouk's Cambodia was therefore an important addition to Peking's united front. This was all the more so after Tonkin, when outspoken criticism of United States policy in Vietnam was a scarcity among the Afro-Asian nations.

The nature and limitations of China's "compensation" for Cambodian friendship and support may be gauged by looking at Peking's reaction to the events surrounding the severance of the American aid program to Cambodia. Reporting new and serious armed incidents along the Vietnamese and Thai borders late in 1963, Prince Sihanouk had warned he would replace American with Chinese aid unless Washington put a stop to them. In particular, Sihanouk demanded the cessation of broadcasts that he charged were being beamed with American radio transmitters on behalf of the Khmer Serai. The intrusion of other events, including Diem's overthrow, precipitated Sihanouk's demand in November that the United States aid mission leave the country; and, in December, the first Cambodia-CPR aid agreement was drawn up.

Peking was, needless to say, heartened by Sihanouk's dismissal of American aid. But a Chinese government statement of November 21 was careful not to go too far in pledging "resolute support" of Cambodia against alleged American-engineered provocations and violations of the Geneva accords.

The Chinese Government solemnly declares: If the Kingdom of Cambodia, which firmly supports policies of peace and neutrality, should actually come under armed incursions planned by the United States and its lackeys, the Chinese Government and the Chinese people will steadfastly stand on the side of Cambodia and moreover will give her full support. U.S. imperialism must accept all the consequences of this. . . .[49]

As would be typical of Chinese statements thereafter, the CPR voiced confidence that Cambodia under Sihanouk would be able to deal with the United States on her own. China's thinking, and no doubt Sihanouk's too, was probably that Cambodia should have available a CPR pronouncement that could be used to deter American, Thai, or South Vietnamese moves into Cambodia. Rather than committing China to any particular course of action, Peking seems then to have been interested in convening another Geneva Conference that would, through big-power agreement, neutralize Cambodia and make it politically more costly for the United States or Cambodia's neighbors to violate her frontiers.[o]

---

[n]Peking claimed that the antiimperialist forces in the third world included "not only workers, peasants, intellectuals, and petty bourgeoisie; [they] also include the patriotic national bourgeoisie and even a segment of the patriotic kings, princes, and aristocrats." See *Kuan-yü kuo-chi kung-ch'an chu-yi yün-tung tsung lu-hsien ti chien-yi (A Proposal Concerning the General Line of the International Communist Movement)*, Jen-min ch'u-pan she, Peking, 1963, p. 14.

[o]In a statement of the CPR Ministry of Foreign Affairs on December 5, China reiterated her support of Sihanouk's proposal for an international conference to neutralize Cambodia. The ministry proposed that the conference be held in Djakarta, Bandung, or Rangoon, and pledged full support in manpower, materials, and authority to the International Control Commission to assure Cambodia's neutralism. Ibid., December 19, 1963, p. 1.

Although the Chinese government statement was also careful not to promise that China would take up the slack created by the elimination of the United States aid program, new military assistance was sent to Cambodia soon after the December 1963 CPR-Cambodia aid agreement. During early 1964 mortars, rocket launchers, trucks, and automatic and other weapons with ammunition were delivered by Peking. These items were in addition to Soviet, Czech, and Yugoslav weapons and aircraft that began to be delivered in the same period.[50] Sihanouk doubtless had these gifts in mind when he boasted in a speech of May 5 that Cambodia, having eliminated United States aid, was in a position to compel the Communist nations to support him.

The convergence of Chinese and Cambodian views on the desirability of bringing Cambodia's security problems before an international meeting became more apparent beginning in the spring of 1964, when conflict in Laos again heated up. China's view, which Sihanouk shared, was that fourteen-nation Geneva conferences should be held on both Laos and Cambodia, a view apparently based on the perception that the United States was expanding its Vietnam effort to include military and diplomatic pressure on Laos and Cambodia.[51] An article by Commentator in July favorably reported Sihanouk's position that the conference method was the "only way" to restore peace throughout Indochina.[52] At the same time, Sihanouk was praised for coming out, as Peking already had, against any suggestion that the United Nations play a peacekeeping role, such as by establishing an international force to patrol the Vietnam-Cambodia border.[53] China and Cambodia, in short, had evidently concluded that at a time of growing danger in Vietnam and Laos, an international conference would be the best (and, for China, the least costly) way of freezing the border situation.

Sino-Cambodian Relations after Tonkin

The increase of tension in Indochina after the Tonkin incidents occurred amidst continuing disagreement between Cambodia and the United States over the Vietnam-Cambodia border and charges that the Viet Cong were using Cambodian territory to evade pursuit.[54] As a general negotiated settlement became increasingly remote, Sihanouk's conviction strengthened that Cambodia would have to move still closer to China if there were to be any hopes of coming to terms with the North Vietnamese. The prince's calculation in the spring of 1964 had been that Cambodia would either try to obtain a written internationally sanctioned guarantee concerning the border from the South Vietnamese government, or would negotiate with the National Liberation Front (NLF) on the same problem. Sihanouk seems to have expected that if Saigon would agree at an international conference to recognize and respect the existing border, even the Viet Cong, were they to win, would have to do likewise inasmuch as both Moscow and Peking would also have put their signatures to the conference's instruments of guarantee.[55] By mid-year, with no possibility in sight for Cambodia-GVN talks on the border and other issues, Sihanouk evidently concluded that his only remaining option was to seek out North Vietnamese and NLF agreement.

Sihanouk's hopes were carried to Peking late in September 1964 when he met with Chinese, Vietnamese, and Laotian Communist representatives. During his visit, Sihanouk heard Liu Shao-ch'i speak of China as Cambodia's "most trustworthy friend" and promise that in the event of an "armed invasion" Cambodia could expect the "full support" of "the Chinese people."[56] Sihanouk responded with appropriate remarks on China's friendship, the Taiwan issue, and the Tonkin Gulf incidents. Vietnam figured prominently, too, in the final communiqué of October 5, in which American policies were condemned, the withdrawal of United States forces and bases from South Vietnam was demanded, and settlement of the war by the Vietnamese (though, curiously, without mention of the NLF's key phrase, "in accordance with the NLF program") was asserted. China's "all-out support and assistance" in case of "foreign armed aggression" was once more pledged to Cambodia by Liu Shao-ch'i.[57]

Talks with the Vietnamese and Laotians went less cordially, and the substance of them was not reported in the Chinese media. Sihanouk wanted Hanoi's promise to respect and recognize the existing border, but Premier Pham Van Dong cleverly referred the prince to the NLF, no doubt in order to force a trade of Cambodian recognition of the Front in return for NLF promises. Sihanouk, although having broken relations with South Vietnam, was not yet prepared to make that kind of deal. The outcome was that the Communists would only state their recognition and respect orally, not in writing.[p]

Returning to Phnom Penh, Prince Sihanouk revealed that Cambodia had not obtained the kind of specific Chinese backing she would have liked, but sought to balance this disappointment by exaggerating the extent of the Chinese commitment. In a speech on October 8, the prince said Cambodia had tried and failed to have China agree to a mutual defense treaty, or at least to a statement making an attack on Cambodia equivalent to an attack on China. The Chinese refused both suggestions, he reported, saying with respect to the second that Cambodia, unlike North Vietnam, was not a member of the socialist bloc. But Sihanouk also alleged in a speech broadcast October 8 that China had promised to meet an attack on Cambodia by the United States and its allies through assistance in the same manner as in Korea, implying that Peking would dispatch volunteer contingents of the People's Liberation Army. Bolstering this report, Sihanouk gave details over the radio the following day of Chinese military aid,

---

[p]Leifer, *Cambodia*, p. 158. High-ranking Cambodian officials also held talks with Hanoi's leaders in late November. These did not enlarge upon Hanoi's verbal promise but led to the scheduling of further talks in Peking. A third round of discussions was reported from Peking in January 1965, with Ch'en Yi and other Chinese foreign ministry officials in attendance alongside Cambodian, NLF, and North Vietnamese spokesmen. See *Jen-min jih-pao*, November 30, 1964, p. 5, and January 16, 1965, p. 3.

said China had promised to provide MIG-19 jets, and stated that Chou had told him China would not object to Cambodia's acquiring aircraft from France and the Soviet Union.

By contrast, China's reporting of Sihanouk's speeches made clear anew her intention that the commitment to Cambodia's defense remain ambiguous and limited. On the critical point in Sihanouk's October 8 speech concerning a direct Chinese military response to U.S.-backed attacks, Sihanouk was quoted as having said that "once the peace-loving Royal Kingdom of Cambodia comes under foreign armed attack, the 650 million Chinese people will give all-out support."[58] No mention was made of new Chinese military aid to Cambodia. Peking, perhaps wary of Sihanouk's radical alterations of mood, was not about to let him misconstrue its commitment and take undue risks.[q] From Sihanouk's standpoint, the magnification of China's commitment—implying that the PLA would be available to take up Cambodia's ground defense—was probably deliberate. Although almost certainly aware that China's promises were offered for their deterrent value, he used them to try to convince potential aggressors that they amounted to an unequivocal commitment to Cambodia's defense in case of attack.

Diplomacy under Pressure in 1965

Sihanouk's inability to reduce the military pressure he felt on Cambodia's borders by interesting the United States and its allies in a negotiated settlement on his terms[59] sustained his efforts to attract the support of his Communist neighbors for similar talks and guarantees. Although rebuffed by Hanoi in his attempt to gain a written promise regarding the Vietnam-Cambodian border, Sihanouk indicated by word and deed that he was willing to maintain a pro-Communist image if that would purchase Communist support of his neutralization scheme. But between February and April 1965, Sihanouk discovered not only that neutralization had become of secondary interest to the Vietnamese Communists and the Chinese, but also that Peking was not about to intervene in his behalf so long as the Vietnam war had not been settled on terms favorable to the Communists.

---

[q]The differences in emphasis and conditionality of Chinese and Cambodian statements became quite apparent when Ch'en Yi visited Phnom Penh in November 1964. General Lon Nol said, with reference to Sihanouk's October visit to Peking: "China and the Chinese people recently assured us again that if the imperialists have the gall to carry out large-scale actions against our territory, they will give us unconditional support." Ch'en replied by reiterating the theme of "all-out support" contained in the Sihanouk-Liu Shao-ch'i communiqué, and added that China backed "the Cambodian government and people in their just struggle to defend national sovereignty and territorial integrity." (Ibid., November 10, 1964, p. 3.) Ch'en's statement was hardly equivalent to "unconditional support." And, in his farewell speech of November 13, he made the distinction even more explicit by expressing China's belief that Cambodia, with her valiant leader, nationalistic spirit, and unity, could overcome all adversities on her own. Ibid., November 14, 1964, p. 3.

Hoping to maintain China's interest in a big-power conference on Cambodia, as well as to repay China's "all-out support" of Cambodia against the perceived threats to the west and east, Sihanouk praised China's explosion of her first atomic device in October 1964.[60] Of greater importance, Sihanouk initiated the convening in Phnom Penh of an Indochinese People's Conference (IPC), which was actually a propaganda forum for a diverse gathering of Vietnamese, Laotian, and Cambodian left-wing and Communist organizations. The preparatory session of the IPC was held during February; its agenda condemned the U.S.-GVN alliance, called for a new Geneva conference on Cambodia, demanded respect for the 1962 agreements on Laos, and raised the possibility of creating a permanent secretariat of the Indochinese states to symbolize and promote the area's solidarity.[61]

The ensuing discussions, however, produced divergent positions so far as Cambodian interests were concerned. China (not in attendance) and North Vietnam wanted the conference to demonstrate, particularly to the Afro-Asian nations, the unity of viewpoint of the politically powerful antiimperialist forces in Indochina. Sihanouk, while agreeable to that objective, wanted in return acceptance of his program for a conference that would be convened fairly soon to extend Cambodia guaranteed neutrality. At the same time, he probably also hoped to impress upon the United States his preparedness to move closer toward Hanoi and the Viet Cong if that would enhance Cambodia's security. China's priorities were made clear when Chou En-lai sent a message to the conference, prior to its first plenary session of February 25 (which was then postponed to March 1). In the message, Chou specified that any international agreement (such as Sihanouk's proposal entailed) to settle Indochina's problems, together or separately, would have to await the complete withdrawal of American forces and bases from South Vietnam.[62] Sihanouk was forced to cancel his address scheduled for February 25; but it was published and circulated at the meeting. In it he was to propose several points at odds with the Chinese position: "solid guarantees" to the United States regarding the neutrality of Laos, Cambodia, and South Vietnam after an American withdrawal; the implementation of a mutual East-West "disengagement" from all three countries (though he would have assured his Vietnamese Communist listeners that he did not believe they had intervened anywhere in Indochina); an augmentation of the capabilities of the International Control Commissions in the three countries; finally, by implication, the implementation of his neutralization plan *before*, and in fact as a condition of, a total U.S. withdrawal.[63]

The subordination of Sihanouk's neutralization plan to Chinese and Vietnamese Communist interests became plain with announcement of the IPC's final documents.[64] The conference resolutions of March 9 focused on Laos and South Vietnam, following Hanoi's position very closely, and avoided mention of the innovative aspects of Sihanouk's suggestions. Sihanouk's proposal that a Geneva conference on Cambodia be quickly summoned was resolved upon; but in the ensuing weeks, controversy among the major powers, sparked by rumors that a conference on Cambodia would merely provide a convenient setting for negotiations concerning Vietnam, led Peking to demand the NLF's right of representation. By raising the representation issue, Peking assured the quick demise of plans for a conference on Cambodia.[r]

It was hardly surprising when, amidst these developments, Cambodia broke diplomatic relations with the United States on May 3, 1965. Both Washington and Peking had, in fact, been interested in using Cambodia for their own purposes in Vietnam; but Washington had proven itself totally uninterested in giving Sihanouk the guarantees he wanted, whereas Peking's influence might still be useful to Sihanouk in his ongoing struggle to obtain Vietnamese Communist agreement on the border. Responding to the Cambodia-United States break, Chou En-lai hailed Cambodia's courage, advised Sihanouk that his best recourse to (possible) "invasion and occupation" was "people's guerrilla war" following the Viet Cong example, and said that China would "certainly [not] sit by and watch without paying attention" should Cambodia fall victim to the Vietnam conflict.[65]

Once again, the Chinese government had refused to elaborate on its commitment to Cambodia. Yet, with the disruption of American relations with Cambodia, Sihanouk was an even more valuable commodity than before. As an editorial in *Jen-min jih-pao* remarked, the fact that Phnom Penh had been forced to sever all ties to the United States proved that the United States was indeed the "deadly enemy" of Cambodians and all other peoples in the developing countries; it also proved the ineffectuality and arrogance of the Americans, who had to resort to subversion of peaceful Cambodia when all else failed.[66]

Sihanouk between Peking and Moscow

The continued need of Sihanouk and the Chinese Communists for one another was accentuated when the prince traveled to Peking for the sixth time in October 1965 to be feted as China's principal guest at the National Day

---

[r]Peking had initially replied favorably to the IPC resolution, on March 17, stating that "the interested countries" should be invited. The United States and France also agreed to attend. Once the rumors of a Vietnam conference began to circulate, however, the Cambodian government, on May 1, declared that the only acceptable conference would be one that excluded the Saigon government and agreed not to discuss problems related to Vietnam and Laos. The following day, Peking, going beyond Cambodia's position, said that the "test of American sincerity on guaranteeing Cambodian neutrality was Washington's willingness to acknowledge the National Liberation Front's right of representation." Peking's statement assured not only that the United States and its allies would end their support of a conference, but also that Moscow, which had from the outset been willing to exclude the NLF, would also back down. Sihanouk applied the *coup de grâce* on May 15 when he informed British Prime Minister Macmillan that the major powers would have to agree on the question of South Vietnam's representation before any progress on a Cambodia conference could be made. For documentation of this account, see Great Britain, *Recent Diplomatic Exchanges Concerning the Proposal for an International Conference on the Neutrality and Territorial Integrity of Cambodia*, Cambodia No. 1 (1965), Cmd. 2678, H.M.S.O., London, 1965.

celebrations. In view especially of the importance China attached to the formation of a "broad, anti-imperialist united front" on Vietnam that would exclude the Soviet Union, Sihanouk's stamp of approval to China's Asian policies must have been highly desired.

Sihanouk was greeted with tumultuous receptions wherever he traveled, according to the Chinese press. He responded by adopting China's stance on several key issues: the four- and five-point programs of the NLF and Hanoi for a Vietnam settlement; the Soviet-American nuclear monopoly; American manipulation of the UN; and the Algiers Conference which, he agreed, should either adopt a firm stand against United States policy in Vietnam and the Congo or "lose its significance."[67] Thereafter, Cambodia would also back China's demand that the Algiers Conference be postponed rather than face deadlocks over Vietnam and Soviet participation.[68]

Although Sihanouk had refrained from identifying Cambodia with any direct Chinese criticism of the Soviet Union, his support for Peking's inflexible line on Vietnam and his agreement that Soviet delegates should be barred from the Algiers Conference may have been too much for Moscow. The Soviets showed their annoyance by snubbing him when he arrived in Pyongyang from China, and then by abruptly cancelling his scheduled trip to Moscow in November. In an "authorized" statement, Tass said the reason for the cancellation was "events which could not be foreseen and require the participation of the Soviet leaders."[69] Needless to say, the Chinese press made a good deal of the Pyongyang incident.[70] When Sihanouk returned to Phnom Penh in late October, he said he could "afford" to quarrel with Moscow but not with Peking, since a Russian invasion or subversion did not have to be feared. But he also said he wanted to retain good relations with Moscow, whose aid he needed, and reported that China's leaders had not been opposed when he told them he wanted to be neutral in the Sino-Soviet dispute.[71]

The Chinese nevertheless used the brief rupture in Cambodian-Soviet relations to step up their military aid program, perhaps in an effort to become Cambodia's primary, or even sole, source of arms and technicians. An agreement had already been signed June 23 to bring Chinese military technicians into Cambodia.[72] In October, Chou urged Sihanouk to send a military aid team direct to him; Chou would see to the details personally. According to Sihanouk, Chou also said that China would provide all the military aid Cambodia needed to defend against both large- and small-scaled attacks.[73] Sihanouk dispatched General Lon Nol, then commander of the armed forces, who reported to Sihanouk in November that China had promised enough arms to outfit 20,000 men; these, together with previous Chinese deliveries, would provide weapons for 49,000 men, or 19,000 more than the total manpower of the Cambodian army at that time. In addition, the first Chinese jets were promised—three MIG-17's, compared with five the Soviet Union had already shipped—as well as four transport planes and four trainer aircraft.[74]

These substantial new aid promises were compatible, too, with the global reassessment that, it was earlier suggested, China's leadership was making at this time, and with China's consistent message to Sihanouk that Cambodia should be self-reliant in defense. On the one hand, Cambodia was sufficiently important to Chinese interests that additional aid was warranted. On the other, no additional *commitments* to Cambodia should be made. In fact, the nature of China's latest aid package was such as to have further *reduced* the likelihood that China would become more directly involved in Cambodia's security problems. The military equipment promised would cover a variety of war contingencies and could be (but were not) used by Sihanouk to build up his army, thus presumably facilitating resistance of border incursions. These mutually reinforcing self-limitations on China's responsibility became clearer during the first months of 1966, when Cambodian and Chinese sources reported increased American and Thai military pressures. As before, Peking qualified its support while Sihanouk plainly exaggerated it.[s] Concerned mainly about internal political order and escalation in North Vietnam, and probably confident that an invasion of Cambodia was highly unlikely anyway, China's leaders were hardly about to authorize an increased stake in Cambodia.

Leftists and Communists in Cambodia: Seeds of Cambodia's China Crisis

During 1966 and 1967, coincident with Sihanouk's ongoing effort to deflect pressures on his frontiers by magnifying the Chinese commitment, threats of an entirely different kind began to preoccupy him. The prince's charges concerning American-backed incursions were answered with countercharges that the Viet Cong were making extensive use of Cambodian territory with Sihanouk's knowledge and consent. While these allegations could no more be proven than could Sihanouk's insistence that the Americans were somehow behind the hostile acts of Bangkok and Saigon, they soon were overshadowed by a domestic political crisis in Phnom Penh that Sihanouk declared was being pushed by the Khmer Viet Minh and radical leftists in the capital. Taken together, these developments further complicated Cambodia's security problems and may have prompted serious doubts in Sihanouk's mind about China's usefulness in deflecting the Vietnamese Communists, much less the Americans and their allies. In the midst of all this, the CPR Embassy's links to the overseas Chinese were revealed as indicating Chinese Communist interference in Cambodia's affairs.

---

[s]Compare, for instance, the statement of the CPR Ministry of Foreign Affairs on January 3 and an editorial of January 4 (both in *Jen-min jih-pao*, January 4, 1966, pp. 1, 3) with Sihanouk's statement on January 4 that China had promised to aid Cambodia with volunteers, as in Korea, and that the North Koreans were only waiting to be asked to send troops. (Broadcast the same day by Phnom Penh domestic service radio.) Thereafter, the Chinese press reported the *success* of Cambodian forces in repelling Thai and South Vietnamese encroachments, strongly implied that only a massive *American* invasion might prompt a change in China's policy, and reserved threatening words for Thailand to Thailand's role *in Vietnam*. (See *Jen-min jih-pao*, January 30, 1966, p. 3; February 2, p. 3; February 3, p. 4; February 5, p. 4; February 11, p. 4; and March 13, p. 3.)

Viet Cong in Cambodia?

Once Sihanouk had exhausted all diplomatic channels to the South Vietnamese in 1964, his belief probably hardened that accommodation to China's international position, especially when the Viet Cong seemed well on the way toward victory, was the most practical course still open to him. A Communist victory in South Vietnam would give Cambodia the advantage of having sided with the winner and enable her to draw on China for political compensation—that is, China's influence against any Vietnamese Communist ambitions in Cambodia. Perhaps as an added inducement to Hanoi, Sihanouk agreed to having a North Vietnamese embassy opened in August 1966 in Phnom Penh, though Cambodia still had not recognized the Democratic Republic (DRV). His planning, as he explained in September 1966, was still to get Viet Cong recognition of the frontier:

Even if they [the Viet Cong] come to mistreat us in the future, our position will be strengthened by this signed agreement. . . . We must make the decision before the Viet Cong and Viet Minh defeat the Americans, for they will surely be victorious in the future. When they achieve victory, they will become arrogant and will refuse to sign an agreement with us to respect our frontiers. They have agreed to sign this agreement now because they are grateful to us, for we have agreed to recognize them at a time when they have suffered so much. . . . When they sign with us, our position will be made stable by their signature on the paper. . . .[75]

Sihanouk had anticipated too much, for the negotiations then in progress with the Viet Cong proved no more fruitful than previous talks.[t] But his conviction seemed to have remained that there was little alternative to supporting the Viet Cong cause: if the Viet Cong were defeated, Cambodia could easily revise her relations with the United States and the GVN; if the Viet Cong prevailed after Cambodia had adopted a pro-American policy, the penalties might be high.

How much beyond publicizing the Viet Cong's programs and aims and condemning American policy in Vietnam Sihanouk went in 1966 and 1967 may never be fully known. It is by no means clear, for instance, how significant the North Vietnamese-controlled trail network at the intersection of Laos, Cambodia, and South Vietnam was to the Viet Cong effort. Nor is there very reliable evidence concerning the alleged role of Sihanoukville as a port for the transfer of war goods to the Viet Cong. The extent to which Viet Cong and North Vietnamese units used remote Cambodian territory for recuperation and

---

[t]Although the Viet Cong were reported by Sihanouk to have rejected claims to the offshore islands, they refused to go farther. Sihanouk admitted that his negotiators had adopted a tough stance, demanding agreement on mutual noninterference in one another country's affairs and a guarantee of religious and cultural freedom for the Khmer Krom living in the former region of Cochinchina. Phnom Penh broadcast to Southeast Asia reporting Sihanouk's press conference on September 20, 1966; also, Sihanouk's speech of November 20, 1966, broadcast domestically November 21.

resupply, as well as for sanctuary from pursuit, seems to have depended a good deal on local circumstances, such as the attitude of individual Cambodian military commanders, the location of the encampment, and the ethnic makeup of the villagers asked to provide food and shelter.[u] Moreover, unlike Laos, the Cambodian government's announced policy on Vietnam precluded active efforts to secure evidence concerning Communist forces; by the time an ICC team was dispatched, those forces had almost always managed to slip away without leaving a trace of their identity. And, of course, the small Cambodian army was in any event not equipped, much less prepared, to patrol the border or oust Vietnamese Communist intruders.

Finally, Sihanouk's own thinking on the Viet Cong presence must be taken into account. Conceivably, he knew that some Communist units were encamped in remote corners of Cambodia for short periods of time—he would admit to this late in 1968—but reasoned that these units did not disturb his villagers, establish a permanent presence, or create a legitimate pretext for United States retaliatory raids. The prince may simply have considered that the Communists' limited use of Cambodia was a relatively small price to pay for assuring their noninterference in Cambodia after the war; so long as it remained limited, it would not bring disrepute upon Cambodian neutralism. In this respect, he may have miscalculated, in that the pressure of the war would, by 1968, make the Communists' presence too large to be denied, much less eliminated by force. Sihanouk may also have been misinformed, in that what started as a limited presence may have grown quickly in scope and organization beyond what he had been led to believe by those who were reporting to him.

The Chinese Interest

So far as Peking was concerned, it mattered little how much Sihanouk was aware of the Viet Cong's activities in Cambodia so long as he continued to cooperate by adopting a hands-off policy. Although this attitude was never made crystal clear, it was implied in statements such as the one by Vice-Premier Li Hsien-nien when he said that China considered aid to be a two-way street involving mutual assistance.[76]

The kinds of Cambodian assistance Li had in mind must have included Vietnam policy. Aside from assailing American policy there and upholding the Viet Cong's position, Sihanouk had earned China's thanks for rejecting a mediator's role in Vietnam unless asked by the NLF and the DRV.[77] He joined with China in demanding that termination of the war only required an American withdrawal, and in denouncing the prospect raised at Manila of an all-Asian

---

[u]This conclusion is based on the author's survey of RAND Corporation interrogation reports of captured or surrendered Viet Cong soldiers who, during 1966 and 1967, traveled or operated in Cambodia. The entire interview series is on file in The RAND Corporation, Santa Monica, California.

peace conference on Vietnam.[78] Although he stopped short of saying he hoped to see a Communist Vietnam, he expressed compassion for the Communists' struggle and asserted that all non-Vietnamese forces should be withdrawn in order that the contending factions might fight it out among themselves.[79]

In return, the CPR military and economic aid program was stepped up in 1966. A new pact was signed concerning Chinese military technicians, though details were not provided.[80] Chinese aid was also reported to have been received for laboratory construction and equipment in a national university, for a 200-bed hospital, for a tea-processing plant, and for a glassworks, among other projects.[81] (Through 1968, completed major Chinese aid projects in Cambodia included a cement plant, two textile plants, a paper mill, and the glassworks.) Sihanouk said that were it not for Chinese assistance, "Cambodia would not be able to fulfill the duty and mission entrusted to us by all our dear friends."[82]

As in previous years, however, Sihanouk refused to follow the Chinese line completely or to place exclusive reliance on China's assistance. At a time when the Chinese were trying to substantiate the legitimacy of the Thai Communists, Sihanouk said China was the "father and master" of the TPF.[83] The prince also continued to speak favorably of Yugoslavia, and indirectly taunted China in one speech for refusing to consider Yugoslavia a socialist country when he did.[84] Furthermore, Sihanouk was silent on the Cultural Revolution. In the spring of 1967, in fact, he would criticize it in speeches to Cambodian audiences. Finally, despite any Chinese hopes to ease out the Soviet Union as an arms supplier of the Cambodians, a $2.3 million military aid protocol was signed with Moscow on March 18, 1966. Sihanouk, in announcing the deal on March 23, said it was an unconditional grant that would provide Cambodia with five additional MIG-17's, two transport planes, and antiaircraft artillery.[85] This aid, together with substantial new ruble loans, gifts, and technical staff on a variety of enterprises,[86] more than matched Chinese aid and restored Moscow to Sihanouk's good graces. When P. Demichev, leading a delegation of the Supreme Soviet, departed December 10 from the Cambodian capital, he renewed Moscow's "firm support" of Cambodian foreign policy and expressed satisfaction at the increased pace of Soviet-Cambodian cooperation.[87]

The Beginnings of Domestic Upheaval

The interplay of Cambodia's persistent border problems and unstable political alignments became significant late in 1966 when radical leftist politicians precipitated a government crisis over the selection of a right-of-center cabinet with General Lon Nol as premier. Dissatisfied with Sihanouk's offer that they participate in an opposition (shadow) cabinet, the radicals provoked student demonstrations against the new government which Sihanouk charged were the work of the Khmer Reds and the Pracheachon backed by the Vietnamese Communists.[88] The prince refused to take over the premiership, vowed that the Lon Nol cabinet would not fall before November 1967 (one year away), and defiantly left the country for medical treatment in France. By the time he returned, on March 9, 1967, dissension had spread from the capital to Pailin district of Battambang province, and had forced Lon Nol to dispatch army units to the scene. Organized elements of the Khmer Reds had taken advantage of local grievances, a history of dissidence, and the district's physical isolation to promote antigovernment violence.[v] By March, Sihanouk faced new demonstrations and violence in parts of Pursat, Kompong Speu, and Kompong Thom provinces; and on April 2, a village chief was killed, causing Sihanouk to wonder aloud why, despite all the aid he had given the Viet Cong and despite China's support of him, the Khmer Reds had been allowed to strike. He made his charge against the Khmer Reds' external ties explicit: "The masters of the Khmer Viet Minh are the Viet Minh and the Viet Cong."[89]

As the situation in the provinces worsened during March and April, Sihanouk took firmer security measures, but eventually found it necessary to capitulate. Arrests, accusations, and conciliatory measures had failed to pacify Battambang.[w] On April 30, besides ordering reforms of the province's conditions and administration, he accepted Lon Nol's resignation and announced that he would form an interim government.[90] (The stated reason for Lon Nol's resignation was declining health following an automobile accident.) The radicals had forced him to abandon the Lon Nol regime six months ahead of his deadline; but they had also turned his attention to some of the underlying political and economic problems that may have made the dissidence possible.

---

[v]The violence consisted of an attack on a youth camp and a province guard post in February. The special features of the district and the province are their history of banditry and rebellion, their isolation from the center of the country, peasant grievances over the favorable terms on which Khmer Krom refugees were sold land, and the relative inferiority of farming conditions (including a high incidence of absentee landlordism and tenant farming, and the lesser availability of government credit). Added to these were the corruption of officials and maltreatment of citizens by civil and military authorities in the province, to which the government admitted. For the background to and explanations of the events in 1967, see Royaume du Cambodge, *Battambang et son passé*, Ministry of Information, Phnom Penh, 1968; "Une crise politique denouée en cinq mois," *Études cambodgiennes*, No. 10, April-June 1967, p. 3; Jacques Decornoy's article in *Le Monde*, April 7, 1967; and Leifer, "Rebellion or Subversion in Cambodia?" *Current History*, Vol. LVI, No. 330, February 1969, p. 113.

[w]Early in April, 48 members of the Khmer Viet Minh were reportedly arrested in Battambang, paratroopers were sent in to assist village guards, and alleged partisans of the Khmer Serai were arrested or executed. (Ibid., pp. 111 ff.; Phnom Penh broadcasts of April 7 and 11, 1967.) Soon afterwards, Sihanouk publicly identified the chieftains of the Reds in Phnom Penh as the three leading radicals in the National Assembly: Hou Youn, Hu Nim, and Khieu Samphan. (*Paroles, 1967*, pp. 159-160; on April 30, Sihanouk said Hou Youn and Khieu Samphan had disappeared; they may have been executed.) But the prince also sought to conciliate the radicals by removing three cabinet ministers unacceptable to them.

Involvement of the Overseas Chinese
and the Chinese Embassy

In the midst of these outbreaks of antigovernment violence in the provinces, Sihanouk's administration also had to confront an upsurge of proleftist activity among some overseas Chinese. Influenced by the Cultural Revolution on the mainland, the Chinese Embassy in Phnom Penh became a center for the distribution of Maoist propaganda and for the encouragement of local Chinese to emulate the Red Guards. Before this episode ended in early September 1967, Sino-Cambodian relations reached the breaking point and Sihanouk sharply questioned the sincerity of China's professions of friendship.

When he announced Lon Nol's resignation on April 30, Sihanouk, apparently for the first time publicly, disclosed that some overseas Chinese were engaged in illegal foreign exchange dealings and in smuggling with Vietnamese. These activities, he went on, were seriously hurting the national economy. In succeeding days, the prince made more serious accusations. He said that Sino-Khmer "who, however, have remained very Chinese at heart" were busily circulating Communist publications in the schools, propagandizing Communism in newspapers, movies, and the arts, and putting up wall posters Red Guard-style that were insulting to the Sangkum. He specifically indicted the Khmer-China Friendship Association (KCFA), which had "organized an exposition, and certain guides whom it recruited for visitors unjustly criticized our regime." Persons in his cabinet like Penn Nouth, the prince's personal adviser and not a member of the so-called Lon Nol group, were complaining about the KCFA's activities; and there was evidence that the Chinese had been assisted in their subversive actions by the leftists Hou Youn and Hu Nim. The Association's pro-Chinese orientation had become so serious that its chairman, Leng Ngeth, had submitted his resignation in protest. The prince concluded that "Such agitations dangerously compromise the traditional friendship between Cambodia and China"; but later on he was more cautious, observing (as he had during trouble with the Chinese Embassy in the late 1950s) that "in all these cases of subversion, there isn't proof that official China is responsible."[91]

In dealing with the leftist Chinese, Sihanouk authorized a number of countermeasures. His government cracked down on the Chinese school system, imposing controls over their curricula, teaching practices, and Chinese language training in an effort to stop the spread of Maoist doctrine. Black-marketing was dealt with more severely than before, and the prince related that two Chinese had been deported to the mainland for their involvement in it.[92] Thereafter, government authorities kept a close watch on suspected Chinese leftist sympathizers. But Sihanouk, doubtless concerned that restrictions on the Chinese might, as in Indonesia, create trouble with Peking, reportedly spoke out in mid-May against commentaries in the Cambodian press hostile to China.

Sihanouk's hope to keep alive the distinction between Peking's policies and locally generated subversion could not contain some public figures from venting their annoyance with China. Prominent among them was Tep Chhieu Kheng, a member of the shadow cabinet and editor of the journal *Khmer Ekreach*, who published an article critical of the Cultural Revolution. The Chinese Embassy expressed its regrets over the article and its hopes for a more favorable press coverage in a letter published May 22 in *La Nouvelle Dépêche*, the newspaper of Chau Seng, a leftist spokesman. Unwilling to let the matter rest, *Khmer Ekreach* defended itself, repeated its adverse comments on the Cultural Revolution, and added that the Embassy was guilty of subversion in Cambodia. This time, the Embassy not only lashed out at the newspaper but also sought to justify the involvement of local Chinese in activities that venerated Chairman Mao and demonstrated patriotic devotion to the motherland. In a second open letter, the Embassy disputed charges of subversion and insisted it was perfectly proper that news of "important political events in one's country" be brought to the attention of foreigners. If the overseas Chinese were displaying their ardor for Mao by reading books and hanging portraits, "This is the right of every Chinese," for "only those patriotic Chinese nationals who listen to Chairman Mao's recommendations can constantly apply the friendly policy of the Chinese Government toward Cambodia."[x] The Embassy's statement came about as close as possible to declaring outright that, contrary to Chou En-lai's position of 1956 during his trip to Cambodia, the overseas Chinese might praise the prince but should look for guidance and inspiration to the chairman. And since, as shall be seen, the chairman was occupied with more important matters, his "recommendations" were in fact those activities the Embassy chose to carry out as a show of support for the Cultural Revolution.

The Chinese Embassy's attempts to justify exuberant displays of pro-Mao sentiment in the Chinese community were particularly rankling to Cambodian government and other politically influential spokesmen not only because these activities seemed designed to exploit Sihanouk's problems with the radical left, but also because, as the prince said, they ran so contrary to his continued policy statements in support of China and the Vietnamese Communists. Yet, certain statements and actions by the prince may have been interpreted by the Embassy and later by an harassed leadership in Peking as unfriendly to China. Under the extraordinary pressure of developments on the mainland, CPR officials on the scene may now have reported to Peking that Sihanouk was shifting to a hostile policy toward China that required a warning. And the recall of China's ambassador to Phnom Penh, Ch'en Shu-liang, on June 8 may have freed the CPR Embassy to display its agitation.[y]

---

[x]The open letter, dated May 28, was broadcast by Phnom Penh domestic service, May 30, 1967. It closed by stating that "the real enemy and the real subverters" in Cambodia were "a handful of Chiang Kai-shek partisans" working in behalf of United States imperialism.

[y]The Embassy was left in the hands of the chargé d'affaires, Cheng Szu-hsiung. Ch'en's recall was in line with the worldwide return to Peking of CPR ambassadors, though it came later than most.

Apart from Sihanouk's accusations concerning the Embassy-financed KCFA, the restrictions placed on Chinese schools, and the hostile caricatures of the Cultural Revolution in the Cambodian press, the prince himself had on occasion sniped at the folly of events in China. In speeches broadcast within Cambodia but no doubt known to the Chinese Embassy, he refused to indulge Mao's "genius" in directing the Cultural Revolution as had certain pro-Chinese Communist parties (e.g., the CPT). During one particularly caustic speech on March 12, 1967, Sihanouk labeled the Cultural Revolution "an erroneous policy" that, with its Red Guards, "has won contempt and not admiration" for the CPR. China, he went on, was formerly "highly honored; at present it has lost much." But he said that since Cambodia had to rely on Chinese aid, Cambodia was required to follow "the policy of 'belly gratitude' because we must praise anybody who has kept us and we must not criticize him."[93] Of course, he had been anything but laudatory; the prince and other officials rarely had a kind word for the Cultural Revolution, although the Chinese media often reported that Cambodians had spoken well of it.

A second major issue that may have produced the first fissures in Sino-Cambodian relations concerned Cambodia's borders and China's failure or inability to assist Cambodia in dealing with the worsening "Viet Minh" threat. Perhaps to draw out a definitive Chinese statement of respect and recognition of Cambodia's existing borders that would compel Hanoi and the NLF to do likewise, Phnom Penh officially announced on May 19 that all countries were being asked to make clear their attitude on the frontiers. Actually, the government's appeal had been unofficially sounded nearly two weeks before, when it was pointed out that only France, East Germany, and Singapore had stated their respect and recognition. In essence, Sihanouk was telling the Chinese that previous expressions of support were not good enough, and that he needed a more explicit documentation of their view if he was to be assured of their friendship and if he was to force Hanoi's and the NLF's hands.[z] As he frankly put his attitude toward China: "China herself dares not intervene very flatly in the question of the Cambodia-Vietnam frontiers, and this despite her being our number one friend. It doesn't matter who may declare that he respects our territorial integrity, because it is a question of a vague expression which does not commit its author to anything major."[94]

Sihanouk's challenge to the Chinese was not answered, however, until after the Soviets had responded favorably, a circumstance that surely must have upset

---

[z]The royal government's stated reasons for insisting that other nations clarify their stand on the borders were to "freeze" the frontiers and put a "definite and reciprocal end to territorial claims by either Cambodia or its neighboring countries." (*Études cambodgiennes*, No. 11, July-September 1967, p. 10.) In part, no doubt, Sihanouk wanted to spotlight anew the failure of the United States and its allies to renounce their former positions on the borders. But their refusals were well known and, in the context of Sihanouk's difficulties with the Khmer Viet Minh, it seems probable that he particularly had in mind using China's and the Soviet Union's declarations as levers against the Vietnamese Communists, North and South.

Peking. While in Moscow, Prince Norodom Phurissara, the foreign minister, gained Soviet agreement on June 1, and Sihanouk announced on June 6 that the USSR had become the first Communist state to issue a formal statement on the borders. Forced now to emulate Moscow or fail Sihanouk's test of friendship, Peking, on June 13, made its declaration;[95] but perhaps to show China's displeasure, the declaration merely indicated respect for the borders, not recognition of them—and recognition would not be bestowed until July 31. Sandwiched between the Soviet and Chinese actions were those by the NLF and Hanoi; both announced their positions on June 8.[96]

Sihanouk responded by informing Pham Van Dong on June 15 that Cambodia now recognized the DRV *de jure* and hoped to raise diplomatic relations to the ambassadorial level.[97] The NLF, meanwhile, was granted the right to establish a permanent representation in Phnom Penh. Insofar as Sino-Cambodian relations were concerned, however, the damage had been done: Sihanouk had been forced to rely on the Soviets to obtain Chinese and Vietnamese Communist written promises on the borders, and said so. He was aware that Peking would have preferred not to commit itself on the border question at that time.[a] But, after eight unsuccessful negotiating rounds with the North Vietnamese and the Viet Cong, he could draw satisfaction that, at least *pro forma*, Cambodia had finally cornered the Communists into accepting the legality of the border.

In seeking to explain the near rupture in Sino-Cambodian relations later in 1967, and in underscoring the suggestion that the initial conflict of viewpoint was between Phnom Penh and the CPR Embassy rather than between Phnom Penh and Peking, these developments need to be balanced against others in the same period that betokened continued cordial relations. Foremost among these latter was the continuation of China's aid program. A new textile mill built with Chinese aid was inaugurated in Battambang on May 3. Sihanouk, speaking a few days later, gave a rundown of this and other Chinese aid projects and managed to include a few perfunctory words of praise for the Cultural Revolution.[98] Later in the month, Radio Phnom Penh reported the arrival of three teams of Chinese experts in aviation, naval administration, and health.[99]

Secondly, Sihanouk had after all given in to the demand of the radicals that he take over the government, and had placed two of them—Chau Seng and So Nem—in the new cabinet. If Peking (or the Embassy) was concerned that Sihanouk was going to use the Battambang incidents to eliminate leftist influence in his administration, the makeup of the May 1 government showed otherwise. In fact, Chou En-lai's congratulatory telegram of May 6 lent China's

---

[a]Speech of June 7, 1967, broadcast by Phnom Penh domestic service, June 8. The author's interviews with high-ranking Cambodian government officials in Phnom Penh in August 1968 brought out the view that had it not been for the Soviet statement, the Chinese and Vietnamese parties would not have acted. One official commented that the Chinese preferred to deal with the Vietnam border problem after the war, and then on a bilateral basis.

endorsement to the prince's action.[100] Thereafter, the prince several times sought to deflate rumors that he was preparing to move toward the Americans. Had he not refused to welcome Ambassador Averill Harriman in August 1966,[b] had he not sustained his political and material support of the Viet Cong, and had he not accepted the resignation of the allegedly pro-American Lon Nol?

If Peking took a jaundiced view of some developments in Cambodia, it did not indicate dissatisfaction the way the CPR Embassy had in its second open letter of May 28. Resistance to the Chinese Embassy's efforts to propagandize the Cultural Revolution, and the Cambodian government's suppression of proleft dissidence, were given prominent attention in issues of the *Ts'an-k'ao hsiao-hsi (Reference News)*, the special newsletter circulated among Chinese party and other officials on the mainland. Also spotlighted there was Sihanouk's laudatory message of thanks to Soviet Foreign Minister Gromyko for the Soviet decision to recognize and respect Cambodia's borders.[101] Yet through July 1967, Sihanouk received only one "signal"—by his own account—that might have indicated Peking's disenchantment with him: China's failure to respond to his congratulatory telegram to Chou following China's first explosion of a hydrogen device on June 18.[102] Not until August, when Prince Phurissara traveled to Peking for a first-hand assessment of China's official attitude, did the Chinese leaders, by then caught up in the final surge of ultraleftist officials and Red Guards, indicate their support of the Embassy's behavior and press the Cambodian government to accept Cultural Revolutionary activity in Phnom Penh.

The narrative will pick up with Phurissara's trip to Peking in Chapter 5, where the impact of the Cultural Revolution on China's relations with Cambodia and Burma will be discussed together. Before relating those events, the evolution of China's policy toward Burma, and the place of China in Burmese-style neutralism, shall be assessed.

---

[b]Ambassador Harriman's visit was cancelled when, just prior to his arrival, American aircraft bombed Thlok Trach village in Kompong Cham province, with loss of Cambodian lives and property. Washington apologized for the incident but insisted Thlok Trach was in Vietnamese territory, a claim that Sihanouk vehemently disputed and that led him to declare Harriman no longer welcome. Press conferences of August 8 and 13, 1966; broadcast on those days by Radio Phnom Penh to Southeast Asia.

4

Burma and China: The Politics of Discreet Neutralism

The interplay of great-power politics and rebellion has been no less prominent in Burma than in Thailand or Cambodia, and seems to have had a more pronounced effect in shaping Burma's foreign policy. Historically, Burmese governments have had to be attuned to the political and military power of their Chinese neighbor, and hence to the possibility of external interference. Taken together, these concerns, which have preoccupied civilian and military Rangoon administrations alike since independence from Great Britain (January 4, 1948), have led to the adoption of external policies that would desensitize the northern frontier with China and seek to avoid incurring China's displeasure. But the evolution of an accommodating approach to Peking, based on the perceived realities of geography and international politics, has not prevented the Government of the Union of Burma (GUB) from charting its own domestic political and economic course, including vigorous suppression of the revolutionary left.

Burmese Foreign Policy

In introducing some of the essential features of Burmese-style neutralism, and particularly in differentiating between foreign and domestic policy choices that have been made by Burmese leaders, some introductory comments on Communism in Burma shall be offered. The nature and precepts of Burma's foreign policy are discussed next. Against this background, the distinction in Burma's policymaking between a nonhostile policy toward Communist China and persistent efforts to eliminate internal threats to national unity can be better understood.

The Burmese "Ideology"

As a number of authorities on Burmese political thought have suggested,[a] the belated impact of Marxism in the 1930s on Burmese nationalists (in contrast, say, to Vietnamese) did not lessen its influence, but it did affect the ways in which it was adopted. Arriving in Burma at a time when British colonialism had

---

[a]See, in particular, John S. Thomson, "Marxism in Burma," in Trager, ed., pp. 14-27. Throughout, I shall use "Burmese" as the general term of reference to citizens of the Union of Burma, and "Burman" to denote the dominant ethnic and linguistic national group of Burma.

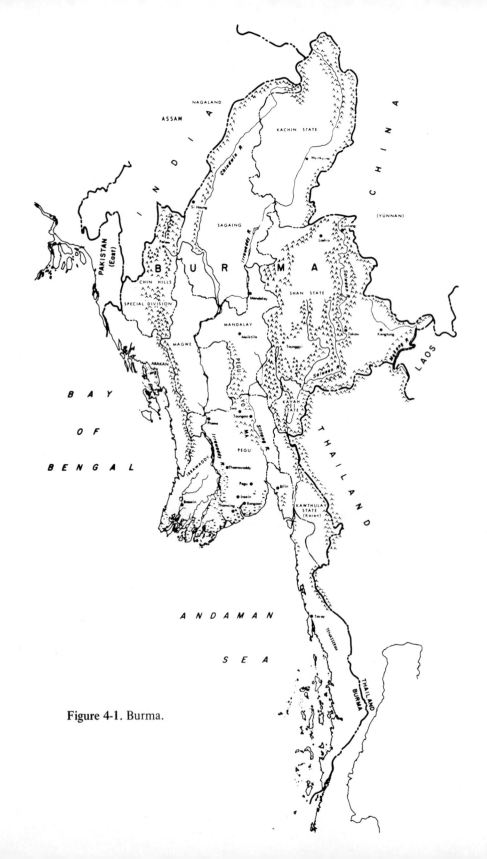

Figure 4-1. Burma.

already begun to stimulate a strong sense of Burmese identity and antiforeign sentiment, Marxism became useful to the nationalist cause mainly because of its anticolonialist, anticapitalist spirit rather than because of its broad philosophical appeal.[1] With the Japanese invasion, the independence movement of the young Thakins, as the nationalists referred to themselves, was further motivated to achieve the permanent displacement of British authority. Where "international Marxism"—that is, policies governing the worldwide movement as determined in Moscow—dictated resistance to the Japanese, and was in fact so read by the few genuine Burmese Communists of that time, the Thakins, however much attracted by Marxian economics, mostly favored collaboration to advance the ultimate anti-British struggle. When, toward the end of World War II (in 1944), the Thakins' resistance organization led by Aung San—the Anti-Fascist People's Freedom League (AFPFL)—decided upon cooperation with the Allies, it and not the Communists was in the vanguard of the independence struggle. Thus, in contrast to the situation in Vietnam (but like that in Cambodia), the non-Communist nationalists of Burma emerged as the standard-bearers of the independence movement, whereas the Communist Party of Burma (CPB), though a part of that movement, did not dominate it.[2]

While many Western observers of the Burma scene in the late 1940s and early 1950s were prone to regard the leaders of independent Burma as Communists, those more familiar with the profusion of philosophies represented in the AFPFL government cautioned against prejudgment. John S. Furnivall, for instance, who served for twenty years as a colonial administrator in Burma and stayed on as a government adviser, noted in 1949 that "what passes for Communism in Burma now is in fact little more than an extreme and impatient nationalism."[3] The fact that socialists of various persuasions remained in or were affiliated with the AFPFL after the expulsion of the Communists from that organization in October 1946 was apparently enough to convince some outsiders that Communism was not a misleading label. Yet pure ideological preferences neither then nor since seemed to be critical to interpreting Burmese politics, internal or external.[b] The multitudinous shades of leftist (socialist) doctrine manifested in the Thakins and non-Communist organizations that were formed subsequently were above all tools to be used in providing Burmese solutions, albeit noncapitalist ones, to pressing social and economic problems of the postindependence period.

As the AFPFL went through a succession of internal crises in the late 1950s, marked by a split in 1958 that brought General Ne Win to power at the head of

---

[b]The personal rather than the ideological element has perhaps been primary in Burmese politics, whether among non-Communists or Communists. Lucian W. Pye (in *Politics, Personality, and Nation Building: Burma's Search for Identity*, Yale University Press, New Haven, Conn., 1962, p. 162) proposes that what causes conflict among Burmese politicians is their failure to institutionalize conflicting interests, thus making every political issue the basis for personal hostility. This hypothesis helps account for the formation of cliques and factions based on loyalty to personalities rather than on identification with ideologies, programs, or particular issues. But personalist politics is not peculiar to Burma.

a caretaker administration, the distinctiveness of Burmese socialism from Marxist Communism was made plain. U Nu, the dominant figure in the AFPFL after the assassination of Aung San (July 1947), had long been enamored of Marxism's implications for welfare state programs. But, as he stated explicitly in a speech of January 29, 1958, Marxism was incompatible with the nonmaterialist, humanist traditions of Buddhism. The building of a socialist state was rightly Burma's economic goal, he indicated, but, for him as for other political leaders, Buddhism not only took primacy over any ideologies, but in addition "symbolized and embodied the culture and traditions of a renascent Burmese nation."[4] U Nu rejected Marxism as a binding state doctrine; but he, like other leaders of newly independent nations, still hoped to reconcile socialist economics with indigenous religious and cultural traditions.

Conflicting views of the role of religion in state life, which found U Nu advocating that Buddhism become the official state religion, helped precipitate the army coup of March 2, 1962, and the accession of Ne Win's Revolutionary Council. In Ne Win's view, national unity required that Burma be a secular state, built around radically socialist economic programs and the cultural Burmanization of the minority peoples.[5] Politically, Ne Win rejected Buddhism as a source for the legitimation of his government. Buddhism would continue to be valued for its ethical content and used to undercut the appeal of the Communist Party. This distinction was incorporated in the Revolutionary Council's program ("The Burmese Way to Socialism") and the principles of the government's Burma Socialist Program Party (BSPP).[c] Buddhism was to be supplanted by a radical non-Communist credo that would provide a rational, modernizing framework for and give ideological expression to the new government's policies. These differences in approach between a civilian and military leader should not, however, obscure the point that both were groping for some way to synthesize Burma's traditional (Buddhist) and modern (socialist-Marxist) heritages within a nationalistic framework.

In making the synthesis, Communism was never accepted as synonymous with Marxism or socialism. This was not a matter of ideological fine points; Communism, or more accurately the Communists, stood for political adherence to foreign powers, violence, civil war, and denigration of individualism and the Buddhist ethic.[6] The Revolutionary Council shared with U Nu a conviction that the Communist parties were a threat to national unity as well as to its own

---

[c]"The Burmese Way" appeared on April 30, 1962. Besides being a straight socialist economic tract, it also sought to justify the army's intervention following the asserted failure of parliamentary democracy. The BSPP's formation was announced on July 4, 1962; it was originally cast as an amalgam of all the major political parties but, when a single united party proved difficult to attain, it became the Revolutionary Council's own national party. In January 1963, the BSPP produced a "Party Philosophy" that elaborated on its socialist program and indicated ambitions to create a social democracy. All political parties except the BSPP were banned in March 1964. See Trager, *Burma—From Kingdom to Republic: A Historical and Political Analysis*, Praeger, New York, 1966, pp. 200-201.

power—much to the consternation of Soviet writers, who were heartened by Ne Win's socialist inclinations.[d] While several attempts were made after the Communist rebellion began in 1948 to bring about a reconciliation, the government's proposals never included terms that would sacrifice the political dominance of the non-Communist ruling circle, reduce the Burmese Army's military advantage, or weaken Rangoon's control of the Burmese Union's semi-autonomous ethnic states.

The Communists' place in Burmese politics has consequently been ambiguous. As John H. Badgley has suggested,[7] Burmese Communists are of two kinds, "national" and "international." The latter, being Party members, have been susceptible to the widespread Burmese suspicion of foreign political credos that incorporate appeals to non-Burmese loyalties. "Domesticated" Marxists have long been individually accepted in Burmese politics, since their social views have been in keeping with the socialist preferences of modern Burmese leaders. But the eclecticism that has marked political thought in Burma since the days of the Thakins has not accommodated the deterministic, anti-Buddhist qualities of Communism—and this circumstance, as shall be seen, goes far toward explaining the Burmese Government's suppression, with public approval, of the Communist movement and its allies.

The Molding of Burmese Neutralism

Although the colonial experience influenced Burmese leaders to experiment with socialism, their foreign policy orientation was not, at the time of independence, either neutralist or pro-Communist. As with Cambodia, neutralism was the successor to an initially pro-Western stance, though in Burma's case several factors, primary among which was the start of the Communist civil war in March 1948, made the first U Nu government reluctant to commit Burma to the Western security system for assistance against internal or external enemies. Still, until U Nu announced his "Program for Leftist Unity" in May 1948, Burmese representatives had twice indicated by agreement with British officials (in August and October 1947) that after independence Burma would rely for defense on a military alliance with the United Kingdom and the broad protective capabilities of the United Nations.[8]

---

[d]For all their satisfaction at the adoption of state socialism by the Revolutionary Council, Soviet writers have long been hard put to fit its rejection of Marxist materialism with its acceptance of Marxian economics. A typical explanation is that the BSPP "not only does not reject Marxism-Leninism, but in fact borrows many of its assumptions and positions." If, as was the case, the BSPP was critical of the Burmese Communists' philosophy, this "can be explained by . . . insufficient knowledge of the theory and practice of the world Communist movement." See Yu. N. Gavrilov, "Program Documents of the Revolutionary Council of the Burmese Union," in E.M. Zhukov, ed., *Sovremennye teorii sotsializma "natsional'nogo tipa" (Modern Theories of "National-type" Socialism)*, "Mysl'," Moscow, 1967.

The "Program for Leftist Unity," which was mainly designed to conciliate the rebellious Communist factions, made the first explicit references to Burma's hope for friendly relations with all nations, particularly including the Soviet bloc. At the same time, it announced that Burma would reject any foreign aid that might compromise her military, political, or economic independence. Subsequently, in a speech of June 14, 1948, U Nu spoke of Burma's need to "enter into mutually beneficial treaties or arrangements, defense and economic, with countries of common interest."[9]

This was hardly a neutralist formulation; quite the contrary, it signalled the GUB's intention to pursue diplomatic relations with Communist East Europe but also to seek membership in a United States-backed collective defense arrangement for Asia.[10] The lukewarm American response to this last approach, combined with Burma's failure to get British or American support against the rebels and with the Communist takeover of mainland China, decisively influenced the Burmese government's shift to a neutral foreign policy.[11]

For Burma as for Cambodia, neutralism was therefore a second-choice policy rather than a philosophical predisposition ready for implementation upon independence. Since late 1949, when U Nu spoke of adopting an "independent course" in foreign affairs, the characterization of neutralism has undergone several changes. It was referred to as "nonpartisanship" by U Nu in September 1950 and as "strict neutrality free from any entanglements" in October 1958.[12] When the Revolutionary Council was set up, it issued a statement on March 2, 1962, affirming a "policy of positive neutralism."

In a speech of August 4, 1952, entitled "Towards a Welfare State," Premier Nu gave the following as "the cardinal prerequisites for pursuance of a policy of neutrality":

(1) We must use our own consideration to either support or object to any matter on its own merits.
(2) We must establish the friendliest relations with all nations whenever possible.
(3) We must accept from any country any assistance for the creation of a Welfare State, provided such assistance is given freely and does not violate our sovereignty.
(4) We must render our utmost assistance to any country which needs it.[13]

U Nu likened Burmese neutralism to a meal in which the meat is eaten and the bones discarded, i.e., in which policy is determined by Burmese interests with respect to individual issues, and in which the decision reached reflects an independent viewpoint even as it may also support one or the other great-power bloc. Burmese neutralism thus has been heavily influenced by the Buddhist precepts of "right action" in particular cases and mutual benefit in foreign relations.[14]

Further elaborating on neutralism during a visit to the United States in mid-1955, U Nu sought to mollify critics by observing that alignment with a major-power bloc, far from helping preserve Burma's independence and reducing the danger of subversion, would probably have the opposite effects. Coming to conclusions similar to those drawn by Prince Sihanouk after the Bandung Conference, U Nu argued that a neutral foreign policy was the only one that could enable Burma to avoid domination by a foreign power, that had popular support, and that held out the possibility of promoting regional and worldwide peace. It was not a negative policy either, he said: "It is a positive policy of seeking peace and friendship with all countries. It is a policy of actively seeking to discover through negotiation and compromise and accommodation some acceptable basis on which the peace of the world can be secured."[15]

Neutralism as formulated by U Nu and as carried forward by Ne Win, though with important differences in emphasis and style, did not mean either noninvolvement or impartiality when dealing with international issues of relevance to Burma. Neutralism has rather been "positive" in the sense that it has not constrained the GUB, for example at the time of the Suez and Hungarian episodes in 1956, from taking stands.[e] Yet, on other occasions, particularly when Chinese Communist interests have been involved—as in Tibet, Korea, and Vietnam (discussed later)—official positions have not been taken, even though attitudes have unofficially been made known. It is this characteristic that distinguishes Burmese neutralism: interpreted in the light of Burma's interests, foremost among which is that of not antagonizing China, it sometimes requires prudently refraining from commenting on matters of importance to Peking. Whether or not that kind of neutralism has compromised Burma's independence by making Burma dependent on Chinese policies remains to be investigated.

Sino-Burmese Relations, 1950-1963

Burma's historic concern for the removal of tension in relations with China, especially in view of the vulnerability of the over 1,350-mile long border, made the question of diplomatic recognition of the CPR a priority matter after the Communist takeover in late 1949. The GUB, until then, had been on friendly terms with the Nationalist (Nanking) regime, which had been a sponsor of Burma's entry into the United Nations in April 1948. But Rangoon had also to take account of American and British disinterest in formal defense ties with Burma, and the serious threat to national unity posed by the rebel Communist forces, which in 1949 were at the height of their military advances. A further consideration was the presence in northern Burma of about 1,500 Kuomintang troops who had fled the mainland; the possibility existed that Chinese Communist forces might enter Burmese territory on the pretext of eliminating the KMT threat to Yünnan. As much, if not more, out of apprehension over Chinese Communist intentions—either to attack the KMT remnants or to assist

[e]In the Suez case, Burma condemned the Israeli and Anglo-French involvements in Egypt, backed the use of a UN Emergency Force there, and offered a troop contribution to it. In Hungary, although Burma's UN representative abstained from the critical votes on Soviet intervention, U Nu said later that Burma should have voted against the USSR. See Johnstone, p. 110, and Thomson, pp. 56-57.

the Burmese Communists—as out of faithfulness to the newly announced principle of friendly relations, the GUB became the first Asian government to recognize the CPR, on December 18, 1949.

The Korean conflict soon challenged the Burma government's neutralist aspirations and China policy. Burma supported the UN Security Council action on June 27, 1950, and later sent nearly $50,000 in rice to the Republic of Korea.[16] When the Chinese entered the war, however, the GUB no longer regarded the issue as one of clear-cut aggression and refused to join in the General Assembly resolution (February 1, 1951) condemning China's intervention. Nor did Burma favor the General Assembly resolution of May 18, 1951, that placed an embargo on strategic materials to China.[17] As with the recognition decision, Burma's abstentions on Chinese action in Korea no doubt were also taken with an eye on the internal rebellion.

Other developments during and after the Korean War further testified to Burma's dual interest in maintaining China's friendship and in separating the question of state-to-state relations from the Communist rebellion. The first Chinese cultural delegation arrived in Burma in December 1951, a visit reciprocated by a Burmese delegation the following April. Goodwill visits to China took place during 1952 and 1953. Below the diplomatic level, the problem of the KMT forces, by 1953 grown to about 12,000, persisted. Having failed to evict them through inquiries and protests to Washington and Bangkok, the GUB brought the issue before the UN in April 1953.[18] The ensuing resolution deploring the presence of "foreign" forces in Burma and urging their removal was not entirely satisfactory to Burma. But, beginning in August, more than half were evacuated to Taiwan with American and Thai assistance, thus easing the danger of a Chinese Communist unilateral military move.[f] A byproduct of these events was the termination of the 1950 United States-Burma economic aid agreement in March 1953. Primarily, Rangoon was expressing its extreme disappointment over American hesitancy to pressure Taiwan on the KMT presence, though the improvement of Burma's relations with China may also have been involved in the decision to terminate.[g]

---

[f]Other evacuations of Nationalist troops to Taiwan took place early in 1954 and in the spring of 1961, but without completely removing them. KMT soldiers still roam about the Burma-Laos-Thailand border area, conducting their opium trade and occasionally collaborating with Karen and Mon rebels. According to a former Chinese general who was in Burma in the early 1950s, and whom the author has interviewed, two Nationalist armies, based in northern Thailand, operate in Burma today. One, under General Tuan Wei-wen, may have about 1,500 men; the other, under General Li Wen-huan, at most has about 2,500 men. A useful survey of KMT activities from the north Thailand base has been written by Peter Braestrup, *New York Times*, September 8-9-10, 1966.

[g]The one remaining major agreement with a Western power—the Anglo-Burma Defense Agreement of 1947—was terminated by the Burmese side in 1954. But beginning early in 1956, United States economic aid to Burma was resumed, chiefly in agricultural surplus (P.L. 480) deliveries, but also in dollar loans. By 1968, however, an American development credit of $25 million granted in 1957 had run out, and only about $7 million of a $31 million 1959 aid grant was being retained by the GUB. (For complete statistics, see Senator Allen J. Ellender's *Review of United States Government Operations in South Asia*, 90th Cong., 2d Sess., Doc. No. 77, Government Printing Office, Washington, D.C., 1968, pp. 322, 330-331.) Figures on United States military aid to Burma have not been made public, but this program, which also ended in 1953, was resumed in 1958 on a very modest scale.

The end of the war in Korea and the onset of the so-called "Bandung" period upgraded the level and quality of Sino-Burmese contacts. A three-year trade agreement was negotiated in April 1954 and, when Chou visited Rangoon, the five principles were incorporated in the statement with U Nu of June 29. When U Nu returned Chou's visit in December, further agreements were reached: air, road, and postal communications would be instituted; barter trade between 1955 and 1957 would give Burma industrial facilities in return for rice; and each government would encourage its nationals residing in the other's country to abide by local laws and customs.[19] This last point, mainly relating to the over 300,000 Chinese then in Burma, about 1.6 percent of the population,[20] was to be reemphasized when Chou next traveled to Rangoon in December 1956.[h]

The one area where China's agreement could not be obtained concerned the border.[i] The Chou-U Nu communiqué of December 12, 1954, merely stated that the border question should be settled "in a friendly spirit at an appropriate time through normal diplomatic channels." Between that date and U Nu's next trip to Peking, in November 1956, at least one armed clash was officially acknowledged by both sides to have occurred (in November 1955) at the border,[j] and the Burmese public was aroused by belated press reports that Chinese troops had moved into the northeast (in Kachin State). U Nu's trip resulted in a mutual withdrawal arrangement from the Wa and Kachin States;[21] but the Chinese were in no hurry to yield on every one of the three disputed areas—perhaps for strategic, but more likely for political reasons—while the Burmese position, as it evolved from an all-or-nothing proposal toward the hint of concessions, gave Chou opportunities to maximize China's part of any subsequent bargain.[22] Further discussions in Rangoon and Peking between 1956 and 1958 produced new formulae for breaking the deadlock, but no agreement; and it remained until Ne Win's trip to Peking in January 1960 for a boundary treaty to be concluded.

---

[h]The details of Chou's remarks in Rangoon are important in light of events in the summer of 1967. In a speech of December 18, 1956, to overseas Chinese, Chou applauded the idea of cultural interchange and intermarriage with Burmese, and urged that the Chinese strictly abide by local customs, traditions, and laws. He insisted that overseas Chinese, whether of Burmese or Chinese nationality, should avoid all "political parties, elections, and every political organization in Burma.... At the same time, we also do not develop Communist parties or other democratic party branches among the overseas Chinese, ... [for] this can lead to misunderstanding on the part of the resident country." *Ch'iao-wu cheng-ts'e wen-chi* [*Collected Documents on Overseas Chinese Affairs Policy*], Jen-min ch'u-pan she, Peking, 1957, pp. 1-10.

[i]The three principal areas in question (see Trager, *Burma*, pp. 239-240) were a sixty-square mile triangle in which were located three Kachin villages; a tract of land in the Shan State, called the Namwan Tract, that had been assigned to Burma in 1897 by the British; and territory in the northern Wa State delineated by a 1941 survey and confirmed by the KMT and British governments, but subsequently disputed by both the Nationalist and the Communist Chinese.

[j]In Chou En-lai's report on the boundary dispute to the fourth session of the First National People's Congress on July 9, 1957, he described the clash as the result of an unfortunate "misunderstanding between the outpost units of the two countries in the border region." *A Victory for the Five Principles*, p. 17.

Despite the boundary question, Burmese leaders remained sanguine about China's adherence to the five principles. While in Peking in 1954, U Nu said he had given Chinese officials three assurances: that Burma would not be any power's lackey; that Burma would never "betray the people's trust," and that Burma would "exert her utmost towards the achievement of world peace."[23] Nearly three years later, in a speech before the Burmese parliament on September 27, 1957, he observed that China had lived up to her end of the five principles, despite having early given the Burmese Communists "moral support":

... as the years passed, and the Chinese saw from our actions that we were stooges of nobody and that we were embarked on an independent policy in internal affairs, they changed their attitude. Premier Chou En-lai's visit to India and Burma in 1954 proved to be the turning point in Sino-Burmese relations, and since then both of us have been guided by the five principles. . . .[24]

Before indicating how and why the border finally was defined by the two countries, it is important to relate the other side of China's relations with Burma—her attitude toward the internal rebellion.

China and the Rebels

In the KMT and the CPB, Communist China had two grounds for directly or indirectly intervening in Burma's affairs. Yet, between 1950 and 1963, China's contacts with Burma's Communists were more symbolic than subversive. At the most, they indicated that Peking had only a residual interest in the Burmese Communists' cause, an interest that could be activated, however, if Burma's foreign policy turned hostile toward Peking.

By the time of the establishment of Sino-Burmese diplomatic relations in late 1950, the Burmese Communist movement, though riven by personal and policy differences that had already split it in 1945 into Red Flag and White Flag factions,[k] nevertheless posed a substantial threat to the survival of the U Nu

---

[k]The CPB was founded on August 15, 1939, with its chief members being Thein Pe, Aung San, Goshal (a Burmese Indian also called Thakin Ba Tin), and Thakin Soe. Thakin Soe's more militant followers left to form the Red Flag faction, while Thakin Than Tun, who joined the party in 1944 and became its chairman the next year, headed the rival White Flags. Whereas the Red Flags have been an illegal organization since 1947, the White Flags, though in revolt since 1948, were not declared illegal until 1953. Throughout the early history of the party, questions of strategy in dealing with Rangoon were always grounds for divided opinions; but perhaps above all, the split of 1945, not to mention subsequent serious rifts that have plagued the Communist movement in Burma, can be traced to the party's lack of discipline, organizational unity, and cohesive leadership. Factionalism, based on personal rather than policy loyalties, has been the hallmark of Burmese politics in general and Communist party politics in particular. See Badgley, "The Communist Parties of Burma," pp. 292, 300-301.

On the pre-1950 history of the CPB, see ibid. and Badgley, "Burma's Radical Left," *Problems of Communism*, Vol. X, No. 2, March-April 1961, pp. 47-55; McLane, pp. 328-329, 371-378; and Ruth T. McVey, "The Southeast Asian Revolts," in Black and Thornton, eds., p. 146.

administration. Operating with a force variously estimated at from 15,000 to 25,000, the White Flags under Thakin Than Tun had captured a number of small towns in central Burma in the spring and summer of 1948, had taken Bassein (about 100 miles west of Rangoon) in January 1949, and were perhaps 50 miles southwest of Mandalay later in the year.[25] With the Chinese Communist victory across the border, the White Flags, conceivably anticipating logistical assistance, concentrated their efforts in northern Burma late in 1950.[26]

By then, it appears that the White Flags, in tactics, organization, and political strategy, were being considerably influenced by the Chinese Communists' example, but they were receiving little in the way of substantive help. In their adoption of antiimperialist slogans, of land and tax reform programs, and of a "People's Army" employing guerrilla tactics, the White Flags were certainly following in Mao's path. Their attempts to form alliances with other rebellious groups, and to set up a People's Democratic Front government (in March 1950), also bespoke some attention to Chinese united-front tactics.[27] So far as can be discovered, however, Peking responded halfheartedly. At best, a few senior White Flag leaders traveled to Peking sometime between late 1949 and 1950, probably followed in succeeding years by small groups of other party cadres to undergo political training.[28] If, as U Nu reported on returning from China in 1954, Peking's leaders had denied any connection to the Burmese Communists,[29] they were not being entirely truthful. But it does seem that in the early 1950s and even later on, when the unsettled border raised Burmese anxieties, Peking did not go beyond *sub rosa* encouragement of a handful of party faithfuls. A number of writers have linked this limited Chinese interest to preoccupation with the Korean and Indochina conflicts; but clearly, had Peking been determined to encourage the White Flags, it would have required only a minimal amount of verbal and material support.

Actually, there were already signs between 1951 and 1954 that the factionalism that has plagued the Burmese Communist movement virtually from its inception was eating away at its effectiveness and strength, thus making it a rather unattractive ally for Peking. The White Flags' attempts to sustain an antigovernment alliance were being steadily undercut by personal rivalries and differences over the appropriateness of negotiating with Rangoon to end the civil war.[30] These internal disputes coincided with increased government success on the battlefield and in its amnesty offer to the insurgents. One authority[31] has concluded that by 1954 over 23,000 rebels, Communist and minorities, had surrendered, of whom about 4,500 were White Flags. From that point into the early 1960s, the White Flags may have been able to count on no more than 1,000 full- and part-time supporters.

In the late 1950s, White Flag strategy, apparently influenced by Soviet interest in *détente* with the West[32] as well as by military weakness, switched from revolution to a peace settlement and a coalition government. The Burma Workers and Peasants Party (BWPP), which had been formed in January 1951, was reinvigorated to compete with the AFPFL in the 1956 and 1960 elections. The Communists had thus chosen temporarily to take the "parliamentary road," holding over the GUB the threat of renewed violence in the countryside.

In this period of superficially peaceful competition, fighting continued at a very low level and the White Flags focused on constructing a united front with other disaffected organizations. Extremist factions of the Karen, Mon, and Chin minorities were the main targets.[1] These groups were, in fact, brought into a National Democratic United Front (NDUF) in 1959; but it proved no more successful than previous such fronts, and its omission of dissident Shan and Kachin independence movements[m] revealed the difficulties of forming a cohesive alliance on the sole basis of opposition to the Rangoon government.

Peking and Rangoon: Solidification of Ties

While the fact of the White Flags' military setbacks, depletion in personnel, and political difficulties may have had some effect on Peking's attitude toward the GUB, China's preeminent concern was the trend in state-to-state relations. In that respect, developments between 1959 and 1963 gave the Chinese grounds for confidence in the friendship and loyalty of Burma. Peking had no reason to go beyond the low-level support it had been providing the White Flags before.

One such development was Burma's officially uncritical attitude toward Chinese suppressive action in Tibet during 1959. When the UN General

---

[1]Here, we can only very briefly mention the nature of these minority antigovernment groups. Among the largest minority, the Karens, was the Karen National Defense Organization (KNDO), then the military arm of the Karen National United Party (KNUP). The KNDO began armed insurrection late in 1948 and, during the 1950s, was allied to Thakin Soe's Red Flags. Basically, the KNDO was dissatisfied with the boundaries of the Karen State, which only took in about one-fourth of the Karen population, and espoused hopes for expanding it into a new state, autonomous from Burma, to be called *Kawthulay*. The neighboring Mon people also had aspirations for separate statehood; rebellious elements among them formed the New Mon State Party. The Chins, occupying the Chin Special Division bordering Indian Assam, revolted later than the other tribes, apparently in response to the State Religion Act of 1961 that for a time made Buddhism the official religion (many Chins professing Christianity). The rebellious Chin organization was known as the Chin National Organization.

For insightful essays concerning the minorities—the differences among them and within each, their linguistic and cultural affiliations, and rough estimates of their populations—see Peter Kunstadter, ed., *Southeast Asian Tribes, Minorities, and Nations*, Princeton University Press, Princeton, N.J., 1967, vol. I.

[m]Conflict between the Shan peoples and the central government goes back to the mid-1950s, when the Burmese Army reacted against expressions of a Shan cultural revival. Open rebellion has existed since 1959, and the presence of Shan peoples in northern Thailand—the Shan and the Thai being ethnically related—has long made Thailand a sanctuary for Shan rebels. Insurrection among the Kachins predates Burma's independence; since 1948, there have been reports of cooperation between some more radical Kachins and the Communist Chinese in Yünnan. It has long been assumed that Naw Seng, leader of the so-called Kachin Independence Army (KIA), fled to China in 1949 or 1950, after his forces were defeated, and became a full colonel in the PLA. Militantly nationalistic, the Kachins have been as difficult for the Communists to ally with as for the Rangoon government to placate.

Assembly's resolution of October 21 to condemn Chinese intervention came to a vote, Burma abstained. Guarded criticism of China's actions did occur in the Burmese press; but official silence was clearly the most discreet move, especially as Burma's own border problems with China had yet to be resolved.

The tragedy in Tibet, and Burma's reluctance to come out against it, may have contributed to the border settlement that finally was reached on January 28, 1960, between Chou and Ne Win. Although Ne Win, as head of the caretaker administration, had merely renewed U Nu's proposals, he found the Chinese favorably disposed toward them. The document agreed to in Peking set up a joint commission to study the particulars of competing claims in the three-village area and in the Wa State. Rather quickly, the difficult survey work was completed and the boundary treaty was signed in Peking on October 1. By its terms, China received the three-village area comprising 59 square miles, as well as 73 square miles in the Wa State area. Burma received 85 square miles in the Namwan Tract, and, by a redrawing of the so-called "1941 line," also gained control of four of six villages that had been situated on the line.[33] Only in the far western frontier, at the trination juncture with India, was no settlement produced.

The boundary settlement was not the only important outcome of Ne Win's visit. A friendship and mutual nonaggression treaty was also worked out on January 28, the most significant portion of which was the agreement by both nations "not to carry out acts of aggression against the other and not to take part in any military alliance directed against the other Contracting Party."[34] Conceivably, this provision may have been demanded of Burma as the *quid pro quo* for a border settlement. For China, the intent of augmenting the mutual nonaggression principle was probably to assure that in return for China's friendship, Burma would in the future—the treaty lasting ten years from the date of ratification, which was January 4, 1961—not join an anti-China alliance. Although it has since been contended that the GUB in effect agreed to limit its right of self-defense and its own policy options,[35] the Burma government probably—and rightly—looked upon the no-alliance clause as a means of further confirming China's friendly intentions without either forfeiting its sovereign right of self-defense or restricting the choices available to it under a neutralist foreign policy.

While the CPR probably regarded an affirmation of Burma's future foreign policy course as desirable in itself, the basis for China's decision to accept previously rejected terms can probably be found more in events in southern Asia than in Sino-Burmese relations. Tension, conflict, and diplomacy involving China and India, Tibet, and Nepal beginning in 1959 seem to have been particularly influential on China's changed attitude toward the Burma border. Chinese armed intervention in Tibet in the spring of 1959, the flight of the Dalai Lama to India, and armed incidents in the Ladakh region of Kashmir had created serious tension between India and China by late 1959, and may have had two effects on Sino-Burmese relations. First, these events stirred an almost universally adverse reaction to CPR policy that, at a time also of Chinese difficulties with the

Indonesian government over the overseas Chinese, may have led Peking's leaders to settle with Burma and recoup on the Tibetan events. Second, a treaty with Burma may have been viewed from Peking as a way of weakening India's claims of Chinese aggression by demonstrating China's flexibility and nonmilitancy in dealing with other less powerful neighbors on conflicting territorial claims. By April 1960, when talks between Chou and Nehru began, Peking had signed the boundary agreement with Burma, a boundary and economic aid agreement with Nepal (March 21), and a friendship treaty with Nepal (April 28). These actions not only enhanced China's negotiating position with India; the agreement with Burma, by incorporating mutual territorial concessions, also provided a precedent for a settlement along similar lines with India, in accordance with China's position that disputed territory in strategic Ladakh be given to China in exchange for Indian acquisition of disputed land in the North-East Frontier Agency.[36]

China's exploitation of ongoing negotiations with her neighbors for the purpose of eroding India's bargaining position did not end in early 1960. On August 26, during a visit by Ch'en Yi, a Sino-Afghan friendship and nonaggression treaty was signed. In 1961, aside from ratification of the Sino-Burmese border treaty in January, a visit to Peking by King Mahendra of Nepal resulted in a boundary treaty (October 5), along with agreement to construct a road from Tibet to Kathmandu with Chinese aid in men, money, and equipment.[37] When, in late 1961, clashes continued along the Sino-Indian frontier, Peking alluded to the settlements with Nepal and Burma as exemplary of how difficult problems might be resolved in accordance with the five principles.[38]

In summary, when Peking finally decided, several years after the boundary discussions had begun, that a settlement with Burma would further Chinese interests, it fit the negotiation of a treaty into an apparently patterned series of discussions with India's other neighbors.[n] Where previously Peking had dallied on the border question, perhaps using the uncertainty thereby generated to ensure Burma's friendly foreign policy (as on the Tibet intervention), in 1960, developments in China's external affairs created a new situation. Through the border and friendship agreements, China could appear to be magnanimous toward her neighbors—resolving potentially dangerous historical legacies peacefully and on reasonable terms, despite obvious differences in the size and power of the parties. Each such agreement became a model for the next, a demonstration of China's sincere interest in coexistence, in apposition to Indian "intransigence."

As with the other countries, Peking followed up successful negotiations with Burma by tendering economic "rewards." In January 1961, Peking promised a credit of £30 million (about $84 million) for trade promotion and technical

---

[n]By 1962, Pakistan was brought into the picture with the announcement in May of temporary agreement on the border pending the conclusion of a Kashmir settlement between India and Pakistan. A boundary agreement between Rawalpindi and Peking was eventually reached on March 2, 1963.

assistance, with no interest to accrue for ten years.[o] That October, the agreement was made more specific: thirteen projects were selected, and the first contingent of Chinese technicians—who would eventually number about 300, not including over 100 supporting personnel[p]—was scheduled to arrive during 1962.[q] (Chinese-financed aid projects in Burma are listed in Table 4-1.) Strictly speaking, Peking did not have to buy the friendship of its neighbors; but aid packages such as that of 1961 were probably meant to convey the message that certain practical benefits, as much as noninterference and nonaggression, would accrue to small nations that conducted their foreign policy in ways satisfactory to the CPR. And, as was revealed when Burma joined with Cambodia at Colombo in December 1962 to resist arbitrating the Sino-Indian war, this combination of benefits had important payoffs for Peking.

The 1963 Peace Negotiations. The parallel decline in political and military power of the White Flags during the early 1960s and the relatively smooth passage of Burmese diplomacy through potentially troublesome waters created by the Sino-Indian conflict combined to sustain cordiality in China's relations with Burma. The existence of an increasingly pro-Chinese Communist party in Burma did not intrude into those relations; in fact, Peking seems to have been highly influential in the CPB's decision late in 1963 to attempt again to resolve differences with the Burmese government through negotiations.

Communist China's intention to maintain only the most superficial support for the White Flags was reinforced after Ne Win's coup on March 2, 1962. The general's reaffirmation of a foreign policy of "positive neutrality," his radical socialist program, and his political plans for an essentially single-party

---

[o]The $84 million was China's second credit to Burma. In 1957, Burma had received a $4.2 million credit at 2.5 percent interest to be used in expanding a textile factory. (Trager, *Burma*, p. 334.) By contrast, loans made by the USSR in 1958, 1962, and 1965 for irrigation projects all carried interest charges (about 2.5 percent) for periods of from 12 to 30 years.

[p]The problem of classifying personnel belonging to Chinese aid teams is a difficult one. Members of aid teams are generally referred to as technical personnel, but this category includes everyone from cooks to expert engineers. Of the roughly 300 "technicians" who seem to have been in Burma at any given time between 1962 and late 1967 (when all personnel were withdrawn), conceivably no more than half qualified as experts, with the rest being skilled laborers.

[q]*Far Eastern Economic Review Yearbook*, 1963, p. 54. In seeking to dismiss the significance of the 1961 Sino-Burmese agreement, one Soviet writer, Byliniak, has commented that of the 13 enterprises, most had not yet been started and much of the loan was still unused by the end of 1967, when the projects were supposed to be finished. See S.A. Byliniak, *Gosudarstvennye finansy nezavisimoi Birmy (The National Finances of Independent Burma)*, "Nauka," Moscow, 1968, p. 179. His conclusions are partially confirmed in Senator Ellender's report (Table 2, p. 9), which states that only $21.4 million of the $84 million was expended through 1966. (By contrast, $12.9 million of $13.7 million in Soviet loans were spent by the GUB in the same period.) But any delays may also have been due to Burmese slowness in getting the projects underway.

Table 4-1

CPR Aid Projects in Burma, as Agreed Upon in April 1963*

Project	Location	Status
1. Suspension bridge	Kunlong	Completed, February 1966.
2. Suspension bridge	Takaw	Mainly completed, June 1967; remaining work taken over by Burmese and completed, July 1968.
3. Hydroelectric plant	Kengtung	Construction not begun when suspended in mid-1967.
4. Hydroelectric plant	Kunlong	Construction not begun when suspended in mid-1967.
5. Plywood factory	Swa	Construction in progress when work suspended, mid-1967; taken over by Burmese.
6. Paper mill	Sittang	Construction completed for trial production at time of suspension in mid-1967.
7. Sugar mill	Bilin	Completed, March 1966.
8. Textile mill	Meiktila	Nearly completed by mid-1967.
9. Tire factory	Insein	Survey work only.
10. Textile mill (expansion)	Thamaing	Completed, late 1964.

*Although selection of these (and three other) projects had been made in October 1961, the implementation stage was not reached until Liu Shao-ch'i's visit to Rangoon in April 1963. Only ten projects are listed; the remaining three evidently had still not gotten off the ground as of mid-1967.

state—which ensured the continued impotence of the legal Communist front party, now called the United Workers' Party of Burma[r]—all fit with Chinese interests and political preferences. As the Moscow meeting of 81 Communist parties in December 1960 had determined, furthermore, "national democracy" was an acceptable stage in the transition to the Communist state—and the

---

[r]The UWPB, actually not announced until December 1962, was an outgrowth of a series of mergers of leftist parties that began with the previously mentioned Burma Workers and Peasants Party. The BWPP, renamed the BWP in 1957, joined in and dominated an alliance of left-wing groups formed in 1956 and known as the National United Front. When the UWPB was established, it included the BWP, while the NUF remained outside. Whereas the White Flags and their NDUF opposed Ne Win's second assumption of power, the NUF—and then the UWPB—supported it, apparently in accordance with the Soviet policy line they had been following.

"Burmese Way to Socialism" could be rationalized as belonging to that category. Thus, at the same time as the White Flags came out against the assumption of power by a military regime, as was to be expected, the CPR quickly recognized Ne Win's government (on March 6).

The heating up of the Sino-Soviet dispute during 1961 and 1962 seems to have intensified the longstanding rift within the CPB/White Flags over the question of negotiations with the Burmese government. As in the past, issues of personality as well as substance probably were involved. In any case, according to one newspaper account,[39] Soviet advocacy of peaceful coexistence found a supporter in Than Tun, but not in the majority of the CPB Central Committee and the party's leading theoretician, Goshal. But as before also, their differences were not so clear cut as between surrender and protracted warfare; rather, the chief bone of contention apparently was the terms on which to engage the government in peace talks.

With a number of senior White Flag cadres in China, Peking's leaders were obviously well situated to bring their influence to bear on the negotiations question. Their advice to the CPB, it seems, was based on a priority interest in Sino-Burmese relations. China's emphasis on armed revolution in the course of the theoretical debate with Moscow apparently did not keep Peking from advocating a GUB-CPB compromise. According to Chinese accounts published after the fall from grace of Liu Shao-ch'i, it was Liu who, in 1962, "wanted the Communist Party of Burma to 'bury its weapons, reorganize [i.e., integrate] its army into the "defense forces" [of the GUB] ; and cooperate with Ne Win in the building of socialism.' "[40] Red Guard writings accused Liu of having long been infatuated with "reactionary nationalists"; Liu was allegedly willing to see neutralists maintain dominant positions in their governments.[41] Perhaps it was also Liu's influence that led the CCP, in its theoretical dispute with the Soviets, to allow that while revolutionary movements should never sacrifice their goals, they could and should accept compromises when the revolutionary moment had not yet arrived.[42]

If China's policy of encouraging peace talks in Burma was Liu's policy, it probably was Mao's as well, for it fit with Peking's consistent low regard for the capabilities of the Burmese Communist movement. Only in mid-1967, when Peking turned against Ne Win, did Mao's supporters seek to foist upon Liu full responsibility for China's previous befriending of the Burmese government. It is, therefore, quite credible that China's leaders, in 1962 and 1963, advised the CPB to try again to reach a peaceful settlement with Ne Win, to deemphasize armed struggle in the meantime, and to work with the Burmese government in building a socialist Burma.

China's primary concern for continued good relations with the Ne Win government was symbolized by Liu Shao-ch'i's April visit to Burma in the course of a four-nation trip. The usual expressions of cordiality were exchanged. In addition, both parties agreed on the desirability of Laotian neutrality, free from foreign interference. Burma expressed approval of Chinese "initiatives" toward a negotiated settlement with India, and Liu thanked the GUB for its "sincere efforts" and "just attitude" in seeking to bring about a reconciliation. Interestingly, armed struggles for independence were also mentioned, but only as they were applicable to colonial countries and not as they might apply to "national liberation movements" of the type the CPB was supposed to be waging.[43] This last point dovetailed with the fact that Chinese statements in this period regarding liberation wars always omitted mention of Burma and the White Flags; after all, Sino-Burmese relations continued to be, as one commentary phrased it, "a glorious example for peaceful coexistence between nations with different social systems."[44]

Whether there was any connection between Burma's "just attitude" on the Sino-Indian border war and the return during the summer months to Burma from Peking of members of the White Flags is open to speculation.[45] Yet, during the same month (April) as Liu's visit, the GUB declared a general amnesty and called for unconditional negotiations with all insurgent groups. The 30-man White Flag mission headed by Ko Htay opened its phase of the talks on September 2, joined on October 4 by the KNUP leader, Mahn Ba Zan, representing the entire NDUF. Shortly beforehand, Ko Htay held a news conference to elucidate the party's national and international positions. For the establishment of internal peace, he said, the party's minimum conditions were the safeguarding of national independence, the development of national democracy, the legalization of all parties, and equal rights for all nationalities. Externally, Ko Htay announced support for China's position on the border war with India, disapproved of the Nuclear Test Ban Treaty—which the GUB had signed despite China's vociferous criticism of it—and said he could not understand Khrushchev's version of peaceful coexistence.[46]

The negotiations lasted from September 2 to November 15, at which time the GUB announced that they had collapsed without result. Throughout, Peking refrained from comment; and when they ended, *Jen-min jih-pao* published only the verbatim texts of the final statements made by the GUB, the CPB, and the NDUF.[47] Whether Peking had hoped (and persuaded the CPB to work) for Ne Win's accedence to a coalition government is unclear. Nor is it clear that Peking was behind the pressure for a coalition that the White Flags sought to exert by consolidating their territorial holdings and strengthening their administrative control over them during the talks. These, in any event, were the charges the Revolutionary Council leveled at the White Flags after breaking off the negotiations—without in any way implicating Peking in the Communists' maneuverings.

If those in the CPB hierarchy, like Than Tun, who had evidently again wanted to test Ne Win's firmness were not convinced of the government's tough line by the outcome of the peace talks, the ensuing roundup of Communist front members by the GUB should have confirmed the party's most militant members in their position. The (pro-Soviet) National United Front (NUF) was hardest hit, with over 400 of its members arrested. Leaders of the Red Flags and White Flags escaped arrest, however; 28 of the 30 White Flag representatives who had attended the peace talks fled into the jungles to spearhead a new campaign of violence, while the other two returned to Peking.[48] With the banning in March 1964 of all political parties in Burma except the Revolutionary Council's BSPP, moreover, the stage was set for another long round of armed confrontation.

Peking and Rangoon amid Rebellion in Burma

For the second time since the early 1950s, Peking was confronted with a friendly Burmese government at war with the pro-Chinese faction of the Communist Party. And once again, it appears, Peking placed a higher value on state-to-state relations than on party-to-party ties. Limited support of the CPB's political activities—through the party's representatives in Peking, in the news media, and probably via the CPR Embassy and consulates in Burma—were evidently judged sufficient to sustain its loyalty to China in the Sino-Soviet rift without damaging China's relationship with the Burma government.

The "Paukphaw" (Kinsmen) Spirit Continues

As before the failure of the peace talks, the GUB generally supported the major planks in China's foreign policy, but deviated enough to evidence that Rangoon prized its independence too much to become Peking's spokesman. Close examination of the points of agreement between Burmese and Chinese officials during visits by Chou and Ch'en Yi during February and July 1964, for instance, indicates that the two governments by no means held identical views. Specifically, despite the typical refrains about colonialism, China's rights in the United Nations, and the vitality of the five principles, the GUB was able to avoid condemning "United States imperialism," criticizing American policy in Laos or South Vietnam, and supporting the Chinese interest in a second Bandung conference.[49] To make up for these omissions, the Peking news media continued their habit of citing supporting comments in the left-wing Burmese press or by politically unimportant Burmese citizens.[50]

In other respects, the occasional news commentaries in *Jen-min jih-pao* were consistently friendly to Burma, citing aspects of Burmese life and Sino-Burmese cooperation that would later—in 1967—be sharply criticized. Cooperation between Chinese and Burmese technicians on a newly opened aid project was reported, for instance; and a review article on Burma's economy offered GUB statistics that presented a record of uneven progress, but hastened to point out that certain agricultural declines were due to bad weather and plague.[51]

On the other side of the coin, there were several substantive international issues concerning which the two governments did not see eye to eye; and several steps taken by the GUB in the name of socialism adversely affected the overseas Chinese as much as, if not more than, other foreigners. Aside from official silence about Vietnam and Laos, the GUB, as previously mentioned, signed the Test Ban Agreement in 1963, knowing full well China's hostile stand on it.[52]

Then, at the October 1964 Cairo Conference of Nonaligned Nations, Burma came out in favor of a resolution, sponsored by India, Yugoslavia, and the United Arab Republic, that, had it passed, would have represented criticism of China's nuclear testing.[53] Burma's concern over arms control and disarmament apparently predominated over consideration of China's stand on the necessity of testing—and Ne Win said as much in a letter to Chou En-lai in which the general replied to Chou's call for a heads-of-state conference to eliminate nuclear weapons by suggesting the greater practicality of China's participation in regionwide disarmament talks that would gradually evolve into a universal ban.[54]

Within Burma, meanwhile, the ban on political parties was only one of several measures during 1963 and 1964 that had the effect of consolidating control over the economy and communications in the Revolutionary Council. All banks were nationalized in February 1963, a measure that affected the Chinese Communist-run Bank of China and Bank of Communications and thus may have disturbed a traditional link between Peking and the overseas Chinese.[55] A second law in October 1963 paved the way for the nationalization of major industries. British and Indian nationals were primarily affected, but so were Chinese and Americans, and a good number of Chinese joined the exodus of foreigners from Burma.[56] Newspapers were also on the list. In September 1963, two pro-Peking journals—*Vanguard* and *Guardian*—were among those brought under government supervision. And although, by an agreement of August 1, 1963, the New China News Agency had been permitted to set up shop in Rangoon, during 1964 the number of channels for propaganda was limited by an agreement that closed the Chinese consulates in Lashio and Mandalay, and the Burma consulate in K'unming.[59] Not one of these events, it should be noted, was mentioned in the Peking news media.

The White Flags Adopt a War Line

The escape of nearly all the White Flag cadres—dubbed the Peking returnees—into the jungle preordained the party's gradual abandonment of the "peace line." Peking-trained cadres now dominated the party apparatus, which set up headquarters in the Prome district of central Burma. At a key meeting of the central committee that lasted from June to September 1964, the dominant influence of the Peking returnees was manifest in two related decisions: first, with respect to party strategy, adoption of the line of "winning the war, seizure of power, and total elimination" of the Revolutionary Council;[58] second, with respect to party members still interested in negotiations, preparation to launch a "great internecine plan of ousting, dismissing, and liquidation."[59] To some extent, of course, the inner-party struggle that these decisions foreshadowed reflected the Sino-Soviet dispute; but what they principally revealed, in the light of subsequent purges, was the start of a violent confrontation between supporters of Than Tun and Goshal that centered around personal and factional rivalry, and the degree to which the party should reflect Maoist doctrine and leadership style.

In line with its consistent official silence on the CPB's activities up to this point, Peking issued no reports on the Burmese party's central committee sessions. Indeed, even after the CPB received Peking's full support in the summer of 1967, party officials, looking back on the 1964 meetings, noted how the decisions reached then reflected adherence to Maoist precepts, but did not say that Communist China had at that time assisted the party in its domestic insurrection.[60] In view of the typically laudatory comments made, for instance, by the Viet Minh (Lao Dong Party) during the 1950s and the Communist Party of Thailand beginning in 1965 about China's valuable support for their movements, this omission from CPB statements may be important. It suggests that while the Peking returnees, loyal to Than Tun, successfully sought to remold the party into a thoroughly Maoist one, they did it without anything more than moral support from the Chinese leadership.

This apparent aloofness made Peking's publication of the CPB's greetings to the CCP on National Day, 1964, all the more surprising. Coming at a time of cordial official relations between the two governments, and when a Burmese government delegation was in Peking to attend the festivities, the CPB's message could only have embarrassed and disturbed the GUB. Yet, its contents left room for doubt just what motivated Peking to publish it. The message promised continued resistance to government attacks, accused "imperialism, internal reaction, and revisionism" of having sabotaged the 1963 peace talks, and said the party aimed "for the establishment of a new Burma of real independence, politically and economically...." The Revolutionary Council was not denounced by name, however, favorable mention was made of CPR-GUB relations, support was voiced for "the government's foreign policy of peace and neutrality," and continued interest was expressed in ending the civil war through negotiations. On balance, the message seemed quite defensive, almost compromising, in tone—quite different from the central committee's decisions of September—and, as published, actually may have been designed to *buttress* Sino-Burmese relations by praising the GUB's foreign policy and announcing that the "peace line" was not entirely dead. Thus, although the GUB had cause for dismay because the CPB had been given publicity by Peking, it also had some cause for relaxation over Peking's attitude as implied in the message's contents.[61]

Within the White Flag movement, however, China's attitude seemed less critical than that of the Peking returnees. From a variety of documents and interrogation reports that were captured by the Burmese Army and later appeared in the Burmese press, it is possible to piece together the story of the CPB's increasingly intense internal power struggle that began after the September central committee decisions. During 1965, the White Flags seemed primarily concerned with building up their strength at the district and lower levels, placing emphasis on bolstering their ranks through the recruitment and indoctrination of youth. For that purpose, a Marxist-Leninist Training School was set up in March at the party's main base area in the Prome district of the Pegu Yoma Mountains.[62] According to one defector,[63] party-building also entailed the elimination of older members whose fear of struggle made them unacceptable right deviationists. Finally, concomitant with the stress on strengthening the party, the politburo reportedly decided sometime during 1965 that cease-fire and peace talks would no longer be even secondary goals, and that henceforth the seizure of power by armed force was to be the party's sole line.[64]

It can only be guessed whether or not the stress on party-building from the bottom up and the cultivation of youthful successors to old-line cadres were influenced by the Socialist Education Movement then in progress on the China mainland. But there is no doubt that the movement's successor, the Great Proletarian Cultural Revolution, directly affected the style and content of the CPB's development after mid-1966. Actually, several months before the Cultural Revolution was officially inaugurated in August, first in China and then within the CPB, a "life forum movement" was launched among the Burmese party's youthful recruits (mainly students) to familiarize them with its history, the virtues of struggle, and the modes of criticism and self-criticism.[65] Then, on the basis of the CCP Central Committee's Sixteen-Point Decision of August 8, the Burmese party reportedly determined anew to develop a "new force" of youths who, under the direction of Peking returnees Aung Gyi and Tun Shein, would promote the 1964 line of violent tactics against party and foreign enemies.[66]

But the massive party purge in China that followed the August decision did not take place within the CPB until the spring of 1967. In speculating as to why this was so, the main reason may be that Than Tun's identification of the White Flags with Peking to the point of being ready to eradicate all vestiges of un-Maoist thought and conduct failed to generate sizable support. Unlike the leadership of the Thai Communists, that of the CPB was not dominated by ethnic Chinese, and considerable dissension may have been churned up by Than Tun's slavish emulation of a foreign leader's antiparty program.[S] Than Tun may have been forced to the conclusion that the time was not yet ripe to unleash the fanatical youths his Peking returnees were training against his rivals in the party.

The "ousting, dismissing, and liquidation" plan reached maturity about April 1967 when Than Tun is reported to have told his youthful followers that the Cultural Revolution had arrived in Burma.[67] Apparently without authorization from the Central Committee,[68] Than Tun ordered the execution of politburo members Goshal and Yebaw (Comrade) Htay on June 18, the two most prominent opponents of a Burmese Cultural Revolution.[69] These were only the first victims of a series of violent retributions that would continue into 1968 and

---

[S]One admittedly very indirect indication that Than Tun had not yet been able to lead the CPB down the road of total Maoization came during the Albanian Workers Party's Ninth Congress, which a CPB delegation, presumably from Peking, attended in November 1966. While avowing impeccably Maoist policies—antiimperialism, anti-Soviet revisionism, etc.—the unnamed CPB representative did not endorse Mao's thoughts or China's experiences as the ultimate guidelines for the Burmese party. The CPB's message was broadcast in full over ATA (Tirana) international service, November 6, 1966.

ultimately claim Than Tun himself (see Table 4-2)—manifestations, perhaps, of the kind of political violence that has many examples in Burmese history.

Having rid the party of two personal and policy antagonists, Than Tun evidently extended the purge down the line to regional and district party officials. In addition, the White Flags undertook important new military initiatives. Having made some headway toward rebuilding their strength—there may have been about 4,000 full- and part-time supporters by the end of 1966—the White Flags also stepped up their activity during the first half of 1967. Besides launching new attacks, including some large raids in the central delta, they also sought to exploit economic frustrations among the peasant farmers through familiar agitprop techniques. In coordination with this resurgence, moreover, a drive began to revitalize the National Democratic United Front, mainly by attracting the left-leaning Karens under Mahn Ba Zan. What was of acute concern to the GUB by mid-1967 was that the selected government targets that were successfully assaulted by Communist forces lay mostly in the delta, and thus seemed to indicate that the White Flags were gaining in their plan to coordinate with non-Communist dissidents.

Against the backdrop of the White Flags' evolution into a politically pure Maoist and militarily more active organization, Peking's attitude toward the party and the GUB needs to be traced. For if Peking's leaders were to be responsive to these changes in style and action of the CPB, when in past years the party had been largely ignored, a precondition was that Peking and Rangoon have a falling out.

Chill in the Wind: Peking and Rangoon, 1965-June 1967. Prior to 1965, Burma's foreign policy was sufficiently oriented toward Peking's interests so that China, far from being provoked, agreed to a border settlement, a friendship treaty, and a number of economic aid projects. Beginning in 1965, and in particular with America's intensive involvement in Vietnam, the GUB was harder pressed than before to maintain an independent policy line while still not offending China. Several developments, Vietnam being primary among them, may have caused a slight cooling of China's regard for the Burmese government. Yet, one must look elsewhere than to the content of Burma's foreign policy or developments in the CPB for the motivations behind Peking's break with Rangoon in June 1967.

If any single aspect of Burma's foreign policy began to disturb China, it undoubtedly was the GUB's silence on developments in Vietnam. During 1963 and 1964, with the exception of Diem's repression of the Buddhists, which drew vehement protests from the Burmese press, there was little publicity about Vietnam from official or quasiofficial sources.[t] Then and thereafter, in fact, the

---

[t]The only groups in Burma that harped on United States "intervention" and "aggression" in South Vietnam were certain leftist front organizations—the All-Burma Peace Committee, the Afro-Asian Solidarity Committee of Burma, and the National United Front—joined by the left-wing press, before it was nationalized.

Table 4-2

Impact of the "Cultural Revolution" on the White Flag Leadership, 1967-1970

A. Members of the Central Committee
(P)   Than Tun*
(P)   Ba Tin (Goshal)*
(P)   Thakin Zin
(P)   Thakin Chit
(P)   Yebaw Htay*

(R)   Aung Gyi**
(R)   Thakin Pu**
(R)   Bo Zeya**
        Thakin Tin Tun (CPB Secretary General)**
        Ko Mya (alias Tin U)***
        Ko Soe Than*
        Yebaw Toke
        Bo Myo Myint
        Yebaw Tun Maung
        Yebaw Kyaw Mya
        Ba Khet***
        Thakin Pe Tint
(R)   Yebaw Tun Sein
        Bo Yan Aung*
(K)   Thakin Ba Thein Tin
(K)   Thakin Than Myaing*
        Tun Hla (U Hla)**
        Naw Seng+

B. Non-Central Committee Peking Returnees
        Myo Tint**
        Col. Chit Kaung
        Tin Pe
        Tun Shein*
        Tun Nyein*
        Taik Aung
        Aung Nyein
        Soe Win**

(P)   = Member of the Politburo
(K)   = Resident in Peking
*   = Purged (and liquidated) or assassinated
**   = Killed in action
*** = Captured or surrendered
+   = Kachin rebel leader, appointed during 1968
(R)   = Peking returnee

GUB maintained relations with both Vietnams, but did not permit visiting delegations from either country to propagandize their respective causes while in Burma. Privately, the Burmese government apparently hoped to see the conflict ended through a negotiated agreement to hold elections for a national Vietnamese government.[70] But Ne Win was not prepared to go beyond that publicly, as was the case in the communiqués issued after visits by Chinese officials during 1964.

Peking, however, was determined by early 1965 to line up as many Afro-Asian nations as possible against the American effort. Burma's passivity in the face of the United States bombings of North Vietnam may have been unwelcome in Chinese eyes—and the extraordinary circumstance of three visits during April by Chou En-lai, accompanied by an impressive entourage of foreign affairs officials, is perhaps explainable only in the light of Burma's silence.[u] The almost equally unusual fact that no communiqués were issued after any of these visits may also confirm that, if Chou's purpose was to pressure Ne Win into adopting a strong anti-United States stance on Vietnam preparatory to the Algiers Conference, he failed. For the GUB to have climbed aboard a united-front bandwagon would not merely have been incompatible with its neutralist style. It would also have risked the loss of American military assistance (thereby forcing the government to look exclusively to Communist sources), and would have meant supporting an insurgent movement—the NLFSV—against a recognized government (thus indirectly legitimating the CPB's cause).

China's leaders did not fare much better when Ne Win visited Peking during late July and August, despite lavish publicity and praise of Burma's internal progress. The general deftly avoided responding to remarks such as those offered by Liu Shao-ch'i on the American threat and aggression in Vietnam. Although, as witnessed by the final communiqué,[71] Ne Win did join in condemning "foreign intervention" in Vietnam and supporting an all-Vietnamese solution of the war, the document was more significant for its omissions of specifically anti-American hortatory and backing of the Viet Cong or DRV programs. That position did not change, evidently, when, in late August, Ch'en Yi had a day of discussions in Rangoon with ranking Burmese government figures.[72] It was therefore probably with a sense of relief that the GUB greeted the postponement of the "second Bandung" conference in Algiers, a conference that Burma probably regarded as likely to serve Chinese propaganda interests rather than Afro-Asian harmony.[v]

---

[u]The first trip, April 3-4, came after Chou had visited Pakistan; *Jen-min jih-pao* offered no details. Assertedly "on the way" to Indonesia, Chou and Ch'en Yi landed in Rangoon a second time on April 6; again, the press gave no other details. Finally, en route home from Djakarta, Chou and Ch'en once more detoured to Rangoon for a three-day stopover (April 26-28); but, as before, whatever conversations took place were not reported.

[v]When the Algiers Conference was postponed for the first time in June 1965, Burma was not among the 19 delegations that favored Soviet participation. Yet, during Ne Win's July-August visit, nothing was mentioned publicly about the conference—and this, at a time when China was desperately trying to corral support for adopting an anti-United States agenda and excluding the Soviet Union.

The *nervenkrieg* that seems to have developed between Peking and Rangoon continued into 1966. A second statement of the CPB was reprinted in the Chinese news media. It was a denunciation of the United States and certain Indonesian "revisionists" and "reactionaries" for having assertedly collaborated to subvert the 1965 coup attempt. Conceivably—though not likely—the analysis may also have applied to the CPB's own situation.[w] Less ambiguous was the motivation for Liu Shao-ch'i's stopover in Burma during another round of state visits in the spring of 1966. (He also went to Afghanistan and Pakistan, countries whose position on Vietnam, like Burma's, was not openly critical of the United States.) Commenting on his trip, a *Jen-min jih-pao* editorial intoned that Asian nations had a special responsibility in the anti-United States struggle: "Because of their geographic closeness [to Vietnam and other trouble spots], Asian countries, in the struggle against the intervention, subversion, and aggression of imperialism and its running dogs, are even more intimately involved and even more must unite in common against the enemy." The Viet Cong, the editorial went on, were performing a special service for those countries by fighting the Americans; for that reason, the editorial strongly implied, Asian governments should actively work with China in support of the Viet Cong and, thereby, of eventual regional peace.[73] Presumably, Liu Shao-ch'i would be dropping by not merely to promote bilateral relations, but also and more importantly to collect political "contributions" to the common cause.

Liu carried his appeal to Burma, arguing that in the absence of unity of policy, "the national independence of Afro-Asian countries is unprotected and the achievements of economic construction cannot be preserved." He also reminded his audience that China and Burma were Vietnam's neighbors.[74] But Liu failed to convince the GUB leaders to commit themselves beyond what they had already said.[75] And with the onset of the Cultural Revolution soon after Liu's return to China, his trip turned out to be the last by a senior Chinese official to Burma.

The Burmese government's firmness in the face of what seems to have been a concerted Chinese effort to get its approval of the Communist position on Vietnam was not the only point of policy difference that separated Rangoon and Peking. Between late 1965 and mid-1967, Burmese neutralism became more expansive and less isolationist. Contacts of varying kinds were made with countries hostile to Peking, and certain agreements were concluded that Peking

---

[w]See the NCNA report from London, in *Jen-min jih-pao*, February 7, 1966, p. 3. The experience of the PKI, according to the CPB announcement, again demonstrated that "the Communist party and other democratic forces must be prepared at all times for every kind of unanticipated event. At the same time, in order to assure the ultimate victory of the people, there is the absolute necessity to carry through to the end the struggle against U.S. imperialism, the internal reactionaries, and the modern revisionists. . . ." One should not go too far in interpreting this report, however. It may merely have been published so that Peking could display evidence of solidarity with its view of the Indonesian disaster. Moreover, if Peking were trying to signal the GUB, it surely could have found a more direct means of doing so than a small backpage newspaper article.

may not have appreciated. These occurrences did not signal a departure from neutralism, let alone a shift to the West; but they did seem to denote the introduction of greater balance into Burma's foreign relations, and therefore were stylistically, as well as substantively, different from Ne Win's previous conduct of external affairs.

Among the more important events—a complete list is provided as Table 4-3—were the first visit by a ranking American since the 1962 coup (by Senator Mike Mansfield in December 1965); an exchange of visits between Ne Win and

Table 4-3

Burma's High-Level Diplomatic Activity, December 1965-June 1967

Date	Nature of Activity
Dec 1965	Sen. Mansfield visits Burma.
Dec 1965	India's Prime Minister Shastri visits Burma.
Mar 1966	Ne Win visits Prime Minister Indira Gandhi of India.
May 1966	Signing of Naaf River Boundary Agreement with Pakistan.
June-July 1966	Journalists' mission led by Information Secretary Col. Tin Tun visits United States, later China.
July-Sept 1966	Ne Win visits Great Britain for talks with the Prime Minister and the Queen.
Sept 1966	Ne Win visits Thailand, the United States, and Japan.
Oct 1966	Trade agreement reached with Poland.
Oct 1966	North Korean Deputy Prime Minister and Minister of Trade, Li Joo Yon, pays visit.
Nov 1966	Eugene Black of the World Bank is guest of state for discussions concerning regional cooperation.
Nov 1966	Premier Thanom and other Thai officials visit.
Dec 1966	Ne Win pays state visit to Nepal.
Jan 1967	Boundary negotiations with India, concluded with a treaty March 10.
Mar 1967	Visit of Israeli Foreign Minister Abba Eban.
Mar 1967	Agreement reported on first news exchange with the Republic of Vietnam.
Apr 1967	Trade agreement reached with Bulgaria.
May 1967	Demarcation of the Burma-Pakistan border.
May 1967	Visit of Indonesian Foreign Minister Adam Malik.
June 1967	Trade missions to Malaysia, Singapore, and Thailand.

the prime ministers of India; Ne Win's visit to the United States; reciprocal visits with Thailand's leaders; and the conclusion of a boundary agreement with India that "went beyond the territory that China claimed as its own, where the three boundaries meet."[76] What is striking about these activities is not that diplomatic exchanges declined significantly between Burma and the socialist countries, but that they *increased* significantly between Burma and the nonsocialist countries.

In addition to these aspects of Burma's external relations, during 1965 and 1966, the GUB added to the list of nationalized enterprises. In the spring of 1965, all private schools were nationalized, and while this order prevented neither private schools from continuing to operate nor the Chinese Embassy and the NCNA from financing many of them,[77] they did seek to control the Maoist indoctrination that had long been part of these schools' curricula. Furthermore, all foreign-owned, foreign-language newspapers were forced to suspend operations in January 1966,[78] an action that seems to have affected the left-wing Chinese publications more than any others.

But these clear signs of increased Burmese independence and flexibility in the conduct of foreign and domestic affairs do not seem to have been interpreted in Communist China either as hostility toward Peking or as departures from neutralism. Despite Burma's steadfast silence on Vietnam, despite her increasing confidence in dealing with a broader range of countries, and despite her nationalization program that adversely affected the interests of the overseas Chinese, Peking, although perhaps disappointed with Burma's behavior, revealed in a number of ways that it still valued Burma's friendship.

In the first place, the Peking press continued its favorable portrayal of relations with Burma. Articles appeared regularly in praise of Sino-Burmese ties,[79] the usual greetings were exchanged and official functions given on anniversary dates, and progress reports were issued on the CPR aid projects in Burma. This circumstance, moreover, prevailed not only during 1965 and 1966, but through the spring of 1967.[80] If Peking's policymakers were dismayed over Burma's attitude toward Vietnam, their concern was well-hidden where it might have been hinted.[81] Thus, for instance, a *Jen-min jih-pao* editorial evaluated Liu Shao-ch'i's trip as a major success for China's foreign policy and in no way alluded to Burmese stubbornness. The warmth of the welcomes given Liu was said to show that China's enemies had failed to create the "anti-China current" they planned.[82]

In addition to symbolic gestures of Sino-Burmese amity, the Peking press also published expressions of affection on the part of "Burmese friends" for Chairman Mao and his works. These were, of course, designed mainly to demonstrate how the revolutionary spirit bestirred by Mao's writings had penetrated to the common man. Yet, the quoted comments, typically from Burmese leftist (but not Communist Party) spokesmen, did not imply any Chinese hopes for a revolution in Burma.[83]

By June 1967, then, Communist China's leaders and press had given no warning or hint that Burma's foreign policy was moving in an unsatisfactory direction, or that the White Flags had become a legitimate contender for power.

Some of Burma's decisions, and nondecisions, may not have been entirely to Peking's liking; but they do not appear to have been considered as bringing into question China's basic interests in maintaining friendly relations, however cool those might have become, or demanding a reassessment of policy toward the CPB. Ch'en Yi's summarization of China's Burma policy on August 26, 1966, consequently still seemed to apply in June 1967. Observing that China was on friendly terms with several bourgeois-democratic governments that were combatting revolutionary movements, Ch'en pointed to the example of Burma:

We have friendly relations with the government of Burma, but as is generally known, Burma has a Communist party which, moreover, is in the midst of civil war against the government. The Burmese Government and the CPB have held several talks in the past, but all these have ended in failure. We naturally do not interfere in Burma's affairs.[84]

5 China's Cultural Revolution: Foreign Relations in Flux

The Struggle over the Foreign Ministry

The drastically changed political climate in Peking between mid-1966 and June 1967 occasioned by the Cultural Revolution had a corrosive impact on the foreign affairs bureaucracy.[a] Typifying the larger conflict of the Revolution between entrenched bureaucrats and Red Guards authorized to "revolutionize" Chinese social and political institutions, the struggle over the Ministry of Foreign Affairs and related agencies began and intensified primarily because of the Foreign Minister's adamant refusal to permit youthful zealots to establish themselves in his bureaucratic bailiwick. Although certain foreign policy issues were introduced into the contest—several months, significantly, after it had begun—the real matters in dispute arose out of Ch'en Yi's belief that the Cultural Revolution in general, and the Red Guards in particular, threatened his personal authority, the positions of experienced foreign affairs personnel, and the proper functioning of the foreign affairs machinery.

In retrospect, the confrontation occurred roughly in three stages. In the first, which took place during June and July 1966, Ch'en revealed his "conservative" position by dispatching "work teams" to certain institutions linked to the Foreign Ministry as a means of protecting besieged party and other officials from forcible removal and intimidation by Red Guards. This action put Ch'en in the same category as Liu Shao-ch'i and Teng Hsiao-p'ing, who bore primary responsibility for the work teams. The purge of Liu and Teng, which took place soon after the CCP Central Committee's Eleventh Plenum in August 1966, initiated the second stage. Although Ch'en's removal from office was not permitted, and although he managed to negotiate or dictate the retention of some key subordinates, Mao evidently approved an "investigation" of him, demands for his self-criticism, and the establishment by Red Guard groups of "liaison stations" within the ministry to oversee its work. A "confession" was extracted from Ch'en in January 1967; but he disavowed it in February, taking advantage of the army's entry into the Revolution, which temporarily put a damper on ultraleftist violence and disruption.

---

[a]Portions of this section have been adapted from the author's previously cited essay, "The Foreign Ministry and Foreign Affairs in the Chinese Cultural Revolution." The documentation, consisting mainly of original and translated Red Guard materials, has not been duplicated here.

But the trend of events turned around again beginning in March, and those Red Guard groups that had concentrated their attacks on the Foreign Ministry once more moved into high gear. They penetrated the ministry, upset files, and disrupted work; they demanded new confessions and self-criticisms of Ch'en (though his removal was still forbidden by the Central Committee); and they charged that Ch'en not only opposed introducing the Cultural Revolution into the Foreign Ministry, but also opposed correcting abuses in embassies abroad and forbade embassies from "making revolution" in the spirit of Mao's thoughts. Additional ground was cut from under Ch'en by the fact that the Red Guards subjected increasing numbers of officials loyal to Ch'en to criticism and physical abuse. Coming on top of the recall of all but one CPR ambassador to Peking for indoctrination (the recall had begun in December 1966), the widening of the Red Guards' assault against foreign affairs officials accomplished two things of relevance to the subsequent breaches in China's foreign relations: it probably facilitated the manipulation of several CPR embassies by fanatic followers of Mao left behind or subsequently sent abroad; it brought the foreign affairs machinery to a virtual standstill, a circumstance which, given the decision-making elite's preoccupation with domestic events, meant that foreign relations were simply not being systematically monitored. Just how critical these two developments were quickly became apparent in Burma.

The Rangoon Riots and the Collapse of Sino-Burmese Friendship

To understand the CPR's estrangement from the GUB and its encouragement of the White Flags to overthrow the Ne Win regime requires an examination of the circumstances and timing of those decisions. In January, China's ambassador to Burma, Keng Piao, and most of his staff had been recalled to Peking. When diplomatic personnel returned to Rangoon in March, the ambassador was not among them; the delegation was now headed by Hsiao Ming, a chargé d'affaires, who was reportedly accompanied by several Red Guards.[1] This entourage, undoubtedly inspired if not intoxicated by the Cultural Revolutionary fervor they had experienced during their stay on the mainland, either brought back or had shipped to them the usual assortment of Maoist propaganda: little red books, Mao badges and buttons, and films of the Cultural Revolution. Between April and June, a series of events occurred that were to be repeated with little variation in other countries: the transformation of the Chinese Embassy and the New China News Agency into centers for the propagation of Mao's thoughts; the distribution or attempted distribution of Mao badges and other symbols of the Cultural Revolution's personality cult; and the ensuing clash with local government authorities over Chinese insistence on the justifiability of distributing Maoist literature and badges without interference.[b]

The rioting broke out June 26 after four days during which some Chinese students, encouraged by Embassy cadres, defied the GUB's longstanding order banning such quasipolitical activities as badgewearing, refused to remove them on request, and conducted demonstrations to manifest their determination.[2] Also during that period, on June 23, Hsiao Ming protested the ban on badges;[3] but the GUB, while calling upon all citizens to eschew violence, reiterated the ban.[4] Instead, emotions became more inflamed and, on June 26 and 27, Burmese crowds took out their anger against Chinese residents, forced the closure of Chinese schools, and invaded the CPR Embassy, the Rangoon offices of the NCNA, and other official buildings.[5] On June 28, the Chinese Ministry of Foreign Affairs presented the first government protest demanding an end to anti-Chinese activities, compensation for damages to life and property, and punishment of the offenders. The GUB was charged with having "instigated" and "connived" in the incidents, and was warned that it "must bear full responsibility for all the serious consequences arising therefrom." (On the same day, Hsiao Ming also made an official protest that included similar demands.) Less official, but nonetheless indicative, comments via NCNA also pinned the blame for the "white terror" in Rangoon on the GUB but, similarly, stopped short of denouncing the government.[7]

Refusing to be intimidated by these threatening statements, the GUB sought only to contain rather than to prevent violence against local and official Chinese. On the 28th, the Revolutionary Council ordered parts of Rangoon placed under military administration.[8] But this action proved insufficient, for on the same day, according to a Rangoon radio account, two Burmese broke into the rear of the CPR Embassy, killing one person and wounding another.[9] The slain man, whom Peking later identified as an aid technician named Liu Yi (though whether he was an expert or not is unclear), became the focal point of renewed CPR protests. The second Chinese government statement was issued June 29, again warning of unspecified consequences should the GUB persist in its course of action.[10] And the Foreign Ministry demanded that a security cordon placed around the Rangoon embassy be lifted.[11]

This time the GUB replied in a memorandum delivered by a member of the Foreign Office to the Chinese chargé. Ignoring the bulk of China's demands, the GUB informed the Chinese government that it deemed the anti-Burma demonstrations then taking place in Peking an "unfortunate development" that

---

[b]In the particular case of Burma, the CPR Embassy during the spring was known to have shown propaganda films to Chinese youths, distributed Mao badges to Chinese students and teachers, and conducted indoctrination sessions on the Cultural Revolution. For a first-hand report on the distribution of badges and pamphlets from official CPR Embassy cars, see Jacques Decornoy's article in *Le Monde*, June 28, 1967.

"will adversely affect the sincere efforts of the Burmese government to restore a normal situation in Burma and to maintain and preserve the friendly relations between the two countries." The Chinese government was asked to step in to stop the demonstrations.[12] Peking rejected the memorandum; and, in Rangoon, Hsiao Ming presented a new list of demands to the Foreign Office concerning the lives and property of overseas Chinese affected by the riots.[13]

Despite the profusion of charges, rebuttals, protests, and demonstrations, Peking still held back from irrevocably condemning the Burmese government and throwing its support to the CPB. Evidently, Mao Tse-tung and his chief lieutenants, though perhaps taken aback by the forcefulness of Ne Win's response to the Chinese Embassy's actions, decided or were persuaded not to move too hastily toward a break with Rangoon. The CPR government statement of June 29 may have been the most crucial test of the GUB's intentions. Only when the GUB's reply evidenced no willingness to meet Chinese demands—and this at a time when a Chinese technician had been killed and the controlled Rangoon press had begun publishing unprecedently critical anti-China articles— might Mao have decided to push the confrontation further.

As additional mass demonstrations before the GUB Embassy in Peking reportedly were held, China's position changed radically on June 30 and July 1. On the former date, a *Jen-min jih-pao* editorial attacked the GUB as "reactionary," "fascist," and "counterrevolutionary." For the first time,[14] Peking cited the CPB's important revolutionary role:

In the last five years and more, the contradictions between the broad masses of the Burmese people and the Burmese ruling clique have grown increasingly acute. Strikes of workers and students have taken place one after another. After overcoming numerous difficulties, the revolutionary armed struggle led by the Burmese Communist Party is now developing successfully. In the last year in particular, the people's revolutionary armed forces have grown much stronger; they have expanded and consolidated their base areas and strengthened their ties with the broad masses. Burma's national-democratic revolution has taken a new and important step forward.[15]

Then, in a further illumination of the fact that a delayed shift in Peking had occurred, a statement of the CPB Central Committee assertedly delivered on June 28 was not broadcast (and thus given support) by NCNA until July 1. A sharp, uncompromising attack on the GUB, the statement called upon the Burmese people to reject Ne Win's breaking of Sino-Burmese bonds, urged them to back the White Flags' armed struggle, and spoke of establishing "a people's democratic and united front government." The National Democratic United Front was mentioned, along with the claim that "the nationalities of Burma are becoming more and more friendly and united under the leadership of the CPB."[16]

The break having now been made,[c] both sides took steps that effectively assured it would not quickly be repaired. In China, additional protests were issued from the Ministry of Foreign Affairs concerning restrictions on the activities of Chinese Embassy officials and treatment of local Chinese. One protest, delivered by the embassy, charged that Burma was trying to "sabotage" the Sino-Burmese aid agreement and hinted that the program might be discontinued.[17] Virulent verbal assaults on the person and government of Ne Win began on a daily basis: his anti-China posture was said to be the upshot of domestic troubles, association with imperialists and revisionists, and repressive rule; and previously applauded institutions in Burma, such as nationalization, military government, and socialist economic programs, were now debunked as part of a total rewriting of post-1962 CPR-GUB history. Finally, Peking became a public forum from which the resident CPB Central Committee vice-chairman, Ba Thein Tin, could air lavish claims of military success, denounce the GUB, and promise uncompromising obedience to the thoughts of Mao Tse-tung.[18]

For its part, the Burmese government sought to make the most of the anti-Chinese riots and the deterioration of relations with China. Demonstrations during July and August spread to a number of cities and towns in an outpouring of abuse, paralleled in newspaper articles, against China and the White Flags. These not only enabled the public to give vent to its anger; they also rallied support for the government at a time of flagging confidence in its economic programs, showed public backing for the government's firmness in the face of Chinese blandishments, and aroused mass awareness of the CPB threat. In addition, the government was given the opportunity to crack down on pro-Peking leftist leaders and silence propaganda outlets. At least 100 persons were arrested, while others were deported or went underground. They included officials of well-known Communist front organizations like the Burma-China Friendship Association and the Afro-Asian Solidarity Committee in Rangoon. The longtime Mandalay Communist newspaper, *Ludu*, was shut down.[19] On July 17, the NCNA correspondent in Rangoon was expelled from the country because the news agency had published the CPB's June 28 statement.[20]

What, in retrospect, had happened? In the context of developments on the China mainland, it appears that Peking's break with Rangoon over anti-Chinese incidents in the latter city was shaped by the actions of Chinese and Burmese officials on the spot. While it might be argued that Peking was simply looking for the appropriate pretext to denounce the GUB and align publicly with the revitalized White Flags, the previous discussions have shown that, until the Chinese student demonstrations and the rioting (June 22-27), state-to-state relations were sound and Peking was no more committed to the CPB's cause

---

[c]Officially, diplomatic relations were suspended after the events in Rangoon. The CPR government statement of June 27 indicated that the Chinese ambassador would not return to Burma. Dependents in the Burmese Embassy in Peking were withdrawn in late August, and the ambassador in September.

than before. The Chinese Foreign Ministry and government statements of June 28 and 29, in fact, were in certain respects belligerent but in others rather mild: in defending the interests of the overseas Chinese and sharply criticizing the Burmese government's actions, the statements refrained from categorizing the incidents in Rangoon as anti-China plots or signs of Ne Win's involvement with the Americans and the Soviets.

The phasing and timing of Peking's responses, in particular, the appearance of the *Jen-min jih-pao* editorial only on June 30 and the delayed broadcast of the CPB statement on July 1, suggest that the Maoist leadership finally supported the CPB not because of any new finding of strength in the Burmese Communist movement, but because the situation in Burma had developed to the point where Peking had to choose between backing down (by retracting or shelving its demands) or supporting its officials and overseas Chinese, some of whom had lost their lives. And Peking's choice seems in turn to have been compelled by the actions of those ultraleftists in the CPR Embassy and other agencies who considered themselves duty-bound not merely to fulfill the static function of representing Chinese interests abroad, but also to be active publicists of the thoughts and works of Mao Tse-tung. These zealots, when challenged in this latter role by the GUB, probably to their and Peking's surprise, responded as had their compeers on the mainland—by taking up the challenge and rejecting either retreat or compromise—and thus set in motion a chain reaction of increasingly intransigent statements and actions in Rangoon and Peking. Peking's choice of the second alternative may have been further influenced by the extremist tide that, by late June, had once more engulfed the Cultural Revolution.[d] Conceivably, the return of extremism further influenced Mao and the more radical members of the Central Committee not to let the crisis subside without backing China's warnings of "consequences" with deeds.

Cambodia's Confrontation with China: August-September 1967

The influence on events in Burma that may have been occasioned by the challenges to Ch'en Yi's authority was also to be felt decisively in relations between China and Cambodia. For in the aftermath of the Wuhan Incident and

---

[d]In general, factionalism within the Red Guard movement and often violent confrontations between leftist groups claiming Mao's support were the dominant themes of the Cultural Revolution throughout the summer of 1967. This situation was spotlighted when two members of the Cultural Revolution Group (Hsieh Fu-chih and Wang Li), dispatched to Wuhan late in July to resolve a dispute between two such groups, so outraged local military commanders by their decision that they were seized and held as political hostages. The Wuhan Incident was apparently precisely the kind of ammunition the more radical members of the Cultural Revolution Group needed to buttress their contention that only armed action and violence could root out party and military leaders opposed to Mao. See Philip Bridgham, "Mao's Cultural Revolution in 1967: The Struggle to Seize Power," *The China Quarterly*, No. 34, April-June 1968, pp. 24-25.

the signal by the senior policy-making unit under Mao, the Cultural Revolution Group, to "seize power," Ch'en Yi's opponents were excellently situated to make an open bid to replace him; and Chou En-lai's involvement in the Wuhan episode until at least August 4 probably prevented him from being able to protect Ch'en as he had in the preceding months.[21] In the interim, two men who seem to have been at the forefront of the anti-Ch'en forces—Wang Li, a member of the Cultural Revolution Group who had emerged from the Wuhan Incident something of a hero, and Yao Teng-shan, formerly the CPR chargé in Djakarta—apparently incited a final surge of the ultraleft.

According to one Red Guard account,[22] Yao Teng-shan functioned as foreign minister for fourteen days in August. Before his brief reign ended, apparently coincident with the sacking of the British chancery in Peking (see below), he had "wrested power from the Foreign Ministry's Party Center" and had "sent cables to the [Chinese] embassies in foreign countries without the permission of Chairman Mao and Premier Chou." In a subsequent interview report, Chou related that the power seizure in the ministry meant a direct challenge to his authority when the rebels went "beyond supervision" to actually making decisions, sending telegrams abroad, and defying the Central Committee's protection of Ch'en Yi.[23]

With respect to China's chaotic foreign relations during this period, two points stand out. First, the way in which the events leading to the power seizure in the Foreign Ministry unraveled tends to buttress the hypothesis that the promotion of the Cultural Revolution abroad was the handiwork of activists in Chinese embassies and was not initiated by policy decisions made in Peking. If Yao Teng-shan indeed "seized power"—or, perhaps more accurately, wreaked havoc while the Central Committee was too preoccupied with other matters to intervene—it was well after trouble had begun in Rangoon, Colombo, Phnom Penh, and Kathmandu. His short-lived tenure as foreign minister may have given added encouragement to ultraleftists overseas; but whether his telegrams and other hijinks caused real damage is debatable. Second, the turmoil within the ministry, and the regime's toleration of it, went far toward ensuring that foreign relations would get worse before they would improve.

Coming on top of continuing disagreement with the KCFA,[24] the events in Burma could only have been disturbing to the Cambodian leadership. Those events were a major reason for Sihanouk's dispatch of Prince Phurissara to Peking from August 15-18.[25] What the foreign minister had to report back was not at all encouraging.

The first signal that trouble was ahead for Phurissara's mission, according to Sihanouk, came at the Peking airport when the prince was not received by his opposite number, Foreign Minister Ch'en Yi. To the protocol-conscious Sihanouk, this was an important slight because when Phurissara had gone to Moscow earlier in the year, Andrei Gromyko had gone out of his way to be on hand to greet him on his arrival.[26] In Peking, Phurissara met twice with Chou En-lai and once with Ch'en Yi. He was quickly confronted with the accusations against China made by Cambodian journalists, who, he was told, were trying to

"blacken the friendship between China and Cambodia."[27] Chou asked Phurissara to transmit the request that Cambodia permit Chinese residents there to
display their affections for Mao, Chinese Communism, and the Cultural
Revolution. To Prince Sihanouk the request violated Chou's previous insistence
that the overseas Chinese be apolitical; it amounted to permission for the
Chinese "to commit subversion."[28]

Although Phurissara was assured by the Chinese leaders that Peking would
continue to respect Cambodian sovereignty and abide by the principle of
noninterference,[29] it was evident from the conduct of the Khmer-China
Friendship Association and the left-wing Cambodian press that Peking did not
have full control of the situation in Phnom Penh. With the KCFA clearly the
target, Sihanouk announced on September 1 that inasmuch as some friendship
associations had become subversive instruments, they would all be replaced by
national committees to be headed by government-appointed individuals.[30]
Putting the blame for this move on Cambodian nationals, the prince commented
that the propaganda activities of certain associations, if allowed to continue,
would surely lead to a "fatal rupture" in the nation's foreign relations, as had
already occurred in Indonesia, Nepal, Burma, and Ceylon.[31]

Refraining from specifically indicting Communist China or her supporters for
the troublemaking, Sihanouk also announced on September 1 that all news
associations would be dissolved and a new one formed only if all Khmer
journalists could agree on one. Again, the real target was the leftist press, as was
implicit in Sihanouk's warning that the continued service of "foreign ideologies"
by the newspapers would lead to nationalization.[32]

On September 4, the third anniversary of the now-defunct KCFA, the Peking
branch of the association cabled its Phnom Penh counterpart in a calculated
demonstration of disapproval of Sihanouk's action. Chau Seng's La Nouvelle
Dépêche published the telegram September 9. In it, the Chinese association's
attitude, which Sihanouk could only take to mean Peking's official attitude, was
made clear in a reference to the necessity of persistent struggle against
"imperialism, revisionism, and the reactionaries." The KCFA was praised for its
past efforts and urged to unite with "the Khmer people" against the common
enemies of China and Cambodia.[33] Not only had a banned organization been
recognized by Peking; in addition, so Sihanouk decided, he was being branded a
reactionary. The telegram, Sihanouk concluded, represented China's first official
attack on Cambodia and "an extraordinary interference in the internal affairs of
a sovereign state."[34]

Smarting from what he regarded as an insidious Chinese demarche, Sihanouk,
in succeeding days, kept up a steady barrage of criticism of Chinese Communist
activities in Phnom Penh but affirmed that he wished to remain China's friend.
But on September 13, the prince, speaking before a mass rally outside the royal
palace, said that the excitable climate in Peking might lead to incidents involving
his embassy. Evidently having in mind the destruction of the British chancery by
Red Guards on August 22, Sihanouk announced his intention to withdraw

Cambodian embassy personnel, leaving the embassy to one or two caretakers. He added, however, that he was not seeking to disrupt Sino-Cambodian relations.[35]

If the prince was trying, as he apparently had in June 1967 over the question of border recognition, to draw out China's position, he again proved successful. When Truong Cang, Cambodia's ambassador to Peking, conferred with vice-minister Han Nien-lung on September 13 about the prince's intention to withdraw all embassy officials, Han expressed surprise in view of the long-standing friendship and solidarity between the two countries. China, he told Truong Cang, had always considered aggression against Cambodia to be aggression against China—a policy in fact never before stated—and regretted that Cambodia had not chosen "other means" to convey her attitude on the September 4 cable.[36] The next day, September 14, Peking's desire to avoid any disruption in relations was reinforced when Truong Cang spoke with Chou En-lai.[37] Chou, the ambassador reported to Sihanouk, "considered that the new incident between our two peoples is an isolated problem and that China wishes to be able to maintain and develop our relations and our support." Chou expressed his high esteem for the prince and China's conviction that Cambodia's place in Indochina and Southeast Asia was important. Answering Truong Cang's statement that embassy personnel were being withdrawn to prevent the occurrence of unpleasant incidents, Chou said the prince's fear was "only an hypothesis" and that, in Truong Cang's words, "mass demonstrations against certain embassies have their reasons and are understandable acts because the Chinese people know who is the enemy and who is the friend." Chou foresaw no demonstrations against the Cambodian Embassy, and he noted that Sihanouk's September 13 speech concerning the withdrawal of personnel had not been published. (Actually, Chou reportedly had issued instructions soon after the violence at the British chancery that enjoined rebels from "beating, smashing, burning, invading, and obstructing" in their demonstrations before foreign missions.[38]) Concluding the hour-long interview, Chou appealed to Sihanouk to reconsider his decision so as not to push the affair to the point of a deterioration of relations.[e]

After reading Truong Cang's cables at his September 18 news conference, Sihanouk thanked his "old friend Chou En-lai" and, by way of response to Chou's personal involvement and appeal, retracted his decision to recall the Cambodian Embassy officials.[39] In so doing, the prince reemphasized that friendship with China had to be "on the basis of the five principles of Bandung, but not on the basis of the Cultural Revolution."[40] Sihanouk's follow-up actions to isolate the pro-Chinese left underlined that position. Whereas, externally, he sought to sustain an antiimperialist image, as by withdrawing

---

[e]In his telegram of September 15 in which Chou's remarks were reported, Truong Cang offered his "impression . . . that on the Chinese side there is no desire to envenom the situation. In conducting me to my car, Premier Chou En-lai, despite the late hour (about midnight), was smiling and we saluted in Cambodian style. . . ."

Cambodian participation in the Asian Development Bank,[41] internally he forbade the publication of NCNA news bulletins and replaced them with his own Chinese-language journal to be directed by his own appointee.[42] Moreover, he continued to harp on the differences between China's attitude toward Cambodia before and during the Cultural Revolution, and went so far as to say: "At the time of Liu Shao-ch'i, China was conducting itself in perfect fashion toward us."[43]

The Summer Crises with China:
A Comparative Evaluation

Why did Sino-Cambodian relations not reach the breakdown stage that was reached in Sino-Burmese relations? By looking at developments in China, and at the critical differences between the Cambodian and Burmese situations, some answers to this question can be attempted.

Perhaps the most decisive factor to account for China's hesitancy to push Sihanouk to the brink of an open confrontation was the shift of the Cultural Revolution by the first week of September 1967 to a stage of consolidation and an emphasis on unity over violence. Although the utility of Cambodia's relations with China was probably one factor, neither the prospect of a Sino-Cambodian break nor any other instance of adverse reaction abroad to the overflow of the Cultural Revolution may have been as significant as the regime's changed strategy for handling the Red Guards. The setting afire of the British mission by Red Guards on August 22 and the beating of the British chargé d'affaires and several of his staff when they rushed from the building may have been particularly influential on Mao and his lieutenants. Conceivably, the Red Guards had been authorized to carry out the act in retaliation for the failure of British authorities in Hong Kong to comply with Peking's demands concerning Communist newspapers and reporters.[f] But when the Red Guards went beyond all reasonable bounds by gutting the British chancery, moderates in the leadership like Chou En-lai may have impressed upon Mao that a number of other embassies in Peking were so distraught over the violence that they were seriously considering—as indeed seems to have been the case—closing up shop and returning home. Mao may finally have become convinced at that point of the overriding potential drawbacks to further violence, a conviction that may have been reinforced by the conclusion that violence had in any case served its purpose in the Cultural Revolution.

Various high-level decisions and instructions were issued soon afterwards to restrict Red Guard activities and to continue the Cultural Revolution by political means. In addition to the salutary effects these actions had on the Foreign Ministry,[44] they also may have made possible the conciliatory statements of

---

[f]The CPR government had issued an ultimatum on August 20 in which it demanded that the United Kingdom cancel a ban on three local pro-Communist newspapers and gave the Hong Kong authorities forty-eight hours to drop lawsuits against arrested newspapermen.

Han Nien-lung and Chou to the Cambodian ambassador on September 13 and 14. They and other foreign policy professionals might have pointed out, if they needed to, that the benefits of Cambodia's friendship, especially with respect to Vietnam policy, outweighed any advantages Peking might derive from ignoring Sihanouk's complaints and forcing him to go through with his announced intention to withdraw his representatives. They may also have argued, with reference to speculation in the Western press, that Sihanouk's anger could very well propel him into closer relations with the United States. This possibility was certainly being entertained by Chinese officials, to judge from Commentator's article in *Jen-min jih-pao* of September 10. Commentator actually seems to have had two purposes in mind: first, to stress the perfidious nature of what he perceived as "recent 'friendly' gestures by the Johnson Administration to Cambodia," gestures that people generally (and, by implication, Cambodia in particular) should not "harbor impractical illusions" about; second, to warn that the United States-Cambodia rapprochement would be incompatible with China's friendship.[45] Yet, the fact that he chose to comment on that possibility may have betokened China's high-level determination that it not come to pass.

Comparing these circumstances with the deterioration of Sino-Burmese relations, it becomes plain that the time factor worked against Rangoon whereas it proved beneficial for Phnom Penh. In the case of Burma, the disruption coincided with the onset of the most intense period of ultraleftist activity on the mainland; in the Cambodia case, the peak of anxiety in Phnom Penh was reached at a time when the trend of the Cultural Revolution was moving against the ultraleft. Secondly, the importance of personal relations should be stressed. Sihanouk's willingness to maintain his embassy in Peking, and China's interest in avoiding a further aggravation of relations, may have been significantly, though probably not critically, influenced by the rapport between the prince and Chou after numerous exchanges of visits over the years. Their mutual respect, so far as can be judged, seems to have gone much deeper than diplomatic niceties, which was quite different from Ne Win's personal standing with China's leaders.

Thirdly, the manner in which Sihanouk handled Chinese interference was firm but cautious, and hence quite different from the Burmese government's reaction. In Cambodia, subversive activity sponsored by the CPR Embassy was early and publicly identified, but without sparking anti-Chinese riots that, as in Burma, got out of hand. Nor did the Cambodian government emulate the Burmese government's restrictions on the movement of Chinese officials and technicians; instead, Sihanouk sought to isolate them through criticism and a distinction between their actions and Peking's official policy. Furthermore, Ne Win permitted, if he did not actually encourage, a crackdown on suspected Communist sympathizers (without taking correspondingly harsh legal steps against Burmese who were involved in the riots) and extensive criticism of Communist China in the press. One major consequence of these differences between Burma and Cambodia was that where developments in Rangoon fast came to a head and left little room for turning back, in Phnom Penh, they were spread out over more than four months and permitted time for maneuvering by both sides. Events in Rangoon narrowed Peking's choice of response; in Phnom Penh, the response was not decisively influenced by events beyond Peking's control.

Finally, Peking's decisionmakers may have calculated on the basis of the different values and opportunities in the two countries. If Cambodia's friendship was important to China because of Vietnam, Burma's refusal to denounce United States policy in Vietnam perhaps made Burma's friendship dispensable. In addition, Chinese leaders may have considered the alternatives to a change in policy. The Burmese Communist Party was always available once the decision to reject Ne Win's friendship had been made; but Peking had no meaningful Communist organization to turn to in Cambodia had it wanted to break with Sihanouk and throw its support to a dissident group. This is by no means to suggest that the availability of an alternative determined Peking's different responses; rather, it is to speculate that, if and when Peking's leaders asked themselves what recourse they had to maintaining good relations with their neutral neighbors, they could point to the CPB in Burma, but they could not do likewise in Cambodia.

Aftermath of the Summer 1967 Crises

The "return to normalcy" signalled by the Maoist Central Committee in September 1967 had a much more immediately salutary effect on China domestically than externally. Considerable damage had been done to China's proclaimed interest in basing foreign relations on the five principles. Foreign Minister Ch'en Yi, long identified with that policy, was quietly separated from his ministry.[a] The foreign service probably remained in confusion, having been infiltrated and criticized by Red Guards and still lacking ambassadors to head CPR missions. These were not circumstances that could quickly be set right by decisions from Peking; nor did the party center under Mao seem ready to give foreign relations the attention they had before the Cultural Revolution.

The Cultural Revolution's harmful effects on China's foreign relations and foreign affairs machinery do not, however, seem to have betokened a revolution in foreign policy. The overflow of the Cultural Revolution abroad is best understood as an aberrant episode that had its source in China's domestic upheaval, not in a predetermined foreign policy reassessment. For most of the Asian governments that experienced Cultural Revolutionary diplomacy, like Cambodia's, it proved possible slowly to repair the damage despite second thoughts about Chinese goodwill. In the Burmese case, where China's policy *had* changed, the GUB early decided to hold to a neutral course, correctly anticipating that a reconciliation with China would eventually again be of interest to Peking. The restoration of political and economic order in China probably contributed to Mao's interest in revitalizing diplomacy. But not until the spring of 1969—when Lin Piao declared China's determination to follow the five principles and to strive for peaceful coexistence, and when the Chinese government began to appoint ambassadors[b]—was that interest restated officially.

---

[a]Beginning in the summer of 1967, Ch'en was not referred to as vice-premier in Peking news dispatches. Then and thereafter, his protocol appearances and identification with Foreign Ministry statements declined dramatically, no doubt in part because of ill health. By April 1969, when the Ninth National Congress of the Chinese Communist Party was finally held, not only had Ch'en been dropped from the politburo (though he remained a member of the Central Committee), but also his foreign affairs functions were taken over by Chou En-lai, Li Hsien-nien, and Vice Foreign Ministers Chi P'eng-fei and Han Nien-lung. Early in 1971, Chi began to be referred to in the Chinese media as acting foreign minister.

[b]Lin Piao's reassertion of pre-Cultural Revolution foreign policy principles came in his Report to the Ninth National Congress of the Communist Party of China (April 1, 1969); text in *Peking Review*, No. 18, April 30, 1969, pp. 16-35. In May, the first two of eighteen ambassadors appointed during the year were sent abroad.

Uneasy Alliance: Cambodia and China

The events of the summer of 1967 apparently had a profound effect on Cambodian foreign policy thinking. Although they did not produce major policy shifts, they probably added to Sihanouk's doubts about Peking's influence with the Communist forces inside and on the borders of Cambodia. Sihanouk's reaction to intensified military operations near the border by American and South Vietnamese forces, especially when "hot pursuit" of the Viet Cong into Cambodia was widely reported to have been under consideration in Washington and Saigon, indicated that he also felt uncertain about the value of the Chinese deterrent. The upshot of these circumstances was that Sihanouk, while seeking to maintain good relations with Peking, showed willingness to improve relations with the United States.

Toward Peking, the prince offered reassurances of Cambodia's friendship as both sides took steps to remove the summer's events from the public arena. Announcing on November 1 that he had been informed by Chou En-lai of China's hopes for continued friendly relations, Sihanouk agreed and asked that his officials and the news media no longer refer to the crisis.[1] The prince had more difficulty quieting speculation concerning Cambodia-United States relations, however. The arrival of Mrs. Jacqueline Kennedy on what was billed as an unofficial visit touched off speculation that a United States-Cambodia reconciliation was in the offing. Mrs. Kennedy's visit clearly had a favorable impact on Sihanouk's view of Washington and seems to have smoothed over much of the bitterness that had developed from the Thlok Trach and other bombing incidents.[2] But Sihanouk insisted on several occasions before, during, and after Mrs. Kennedy's trip that his preconditions for reestablishing relations with the United States had not changed. Still, Mrs. Kennedy's arrival may have helped Sihanouk to signal Hanoi and Peking that Cambodia always had an "America option" in the event they became unfriendly.[3] In 1969, he would appear to use the same tactic to deal with the large-scale presence of Vietnamese Communist forces in eastern Cambodia.

China's renewed professions of friendship were emphasized in several specific ways. First, the Peking-based China-Cambodia Friendship Association, whose cable of September 4 had so provoked Sihanouk, sent a message of support to the national friendship committee under Penn Nouth.[4] Acceptance of Sihanouk's new organization was shortly followed by additional Chinese military assistance which, according to a letter of Prime Minister Son Sann to Chou En-lai, included training, reconnaissance planes, patrol boats, and ammunition.[5] Finally, the familiar themes regarding China's backing of Cambodian defense efforts reappeared in November in the Chinese press and broadcasts.[6] As before, these statements placed the responsibility on Cambodian forces; and when, beginning in December, the regularized entry of American troops into Cambodia on the heels of Viet Cong units became a distinct possibility, Commentator assailed hot pursuit as "gangster logic" but did not enlarge upon China's commitment to protect Cambodia from it.[7]

The threat of American moves into Cambodia prompted several new developments in Cambodian foreign policy: it produced the first explicit Cambodian admissions about a Viet Cong presence in the country; it led the Cambodian government to drop references to a Chinese deterrent against American-South Vietnamese incursions; it increased Cambodia's reliance on the Soviet Union's influence with Washington to deter hot pursuit; and it culminated in direct discussions with the United States on the security of Cambodia's frontier with South Vietnam.

The pressure Sihanouk was under from the American military led him to be more frank than previously about Viet Cong use of Cambodian territory. In a letter to an American newspaper,[8] the prince distinguished between occasional Viet Cong infiltrations into remote regions of Cambodia, which he did not deny, and Viet Cong "implantations," which he said had never occurred. He added that if Viet Cong happened to cross into Cambodia despite the efforts of his small army to keep them out, the fault lay with "the American and Saigon authorities who, with more than a million men, cannot hermetically seal the border on the Vietnamese side. . . ." But his claim that no Viet Cong units had established themselves for any length of time was brought into question in November. Two American journalists, permitted to investigate the charges of the United States military command in Saigon, came upon what they regarded as "unmistakable signs"—Viet Cong documents and medical supplies—that a major Communist unit had been encamped for several months near the village of Mimot in Kompong Cham province.[9]

Reacting to reports such as these as well as to others concerning possible direct American moves against Communist units and supply depots believed to be in Cambodia, the royal government chose not to stress Chinese "support." Phnom Penh referred only to the preparedness of its own armed forces to deal with intruders. The value of Soviet influence with the United States simultaneously increased. Sihanouk said Cambodia considered Soviet warnings more effective than Chinese warnings, since the United States might not as readily ignore what Moscow had to say as it had tended to ignore Peking's pronouncements. Although making clear that direct assistance from the Communist camp would be requested only if Khmer forces proved unable to rebuff an American attempt to occupy Cambodian territory—clearly, a very unlikely development—the prince said he was asking the Soviets for military trucks.[10] Coming in the wake of a concerted anti-China propaganda campaign by Moscow and laudatory Cambodian comments about the sincerity of Soviet friendship,[c] Sihanouk's statement represented a marked change in Cambodia's official evaluation of China.

---

[c]Soviet radio broadcasts and commentaries on Cambodia beginning in September 1967 played up Maoist interference in Cambodian affairs and related it to a general Chinese policy of pressuring smaller neighbors. At a time when Cambodia was said to be under imperialist attack, such Chinese actions were helpful to the United States. These comments went on to commend Cambodian neutralism and to pledge continuing Soviet support of Cambodia

In specifying that he was reluctant to call for external manpower support except as a last resort, the prince also said on December 27 that if foreign troops were ever needed, Cambodia would seek volunteers, whom it could control. This point was underscored when Sihanouk, responding to questions cabled him by Stanley Karnow of the *Washington Post*,[11] ruled out any request for Vietnamese Communist troops, said Chinese volunteers would be accepted only if they were "a vital necessity," and asserted that any troops sent to aid Cambodia "would be under Cambodian command." As to how he would deal with American hot pursuit, however, Sihanouk, perhaps wishing to forestall a precipitate American move, said Cambodia would consider United States incursions illegal but "would not intervene militarily" to rebuff them. He accepted in principle the concept of United States aid to reinforce the ICC—though he noted the opposition of the USSR and Poland to that step—and said he would "gladly" receive a United States representative accredited by the President.

The Bowles Mission

What may have appeared as Cambodian acquiescence in American troop movements into Cambodia actually may have been another delaying maneuver by Sihanouk to avoid further complicating his border security problems. As the prince stated, although Cambodian forces would not challenge United States border violations, the Americans did not have the right of pursuit into Cambodia.[12] This distinction between the illegality of hot pursuit and Cambodia's reluctance to counterattack was behind the different interpretations of the final communiqué signed at the conclusion of Ambassador Chester Bowles's visit on January 12, 1968.[13] Sihanouk said the United States had promised in the communiqué not to pursue Viet Cong into Cambodia; actually, Bowles had agreed that the United States would seek to avoid incidents that would violate Cambodian sovereignty. Both sides were surely aware that new incidents would occur, and that American forces would probably cross the

---

against domestic and external enemies. See, e.g., I. Loboda in *Izvestiia*, September 20, 1967, trans. in *Current Digest of the Soviet Press*, Vol. XIX, No. 38, October 11, 1967, pp. 26-27; *Pravda*, October 2, 1967; and A. Usvatov, "Cambodia: Between Two Fires," in *New Times*, No. 41, October 11, 1967, p. 17.

One of the most direct Cambodian responses to these Soviet remarks was made when a delegation of the Soviet-Cambodian Friendship Association arrived from Moscow in December 1967. A commentary of Radio Phnom Penh emphasized "the value and importance of peaceful coexistence between countries deciding to practice it *in all sincerity and without political considerations*. As the prince pointed out yesterday, Cambodia wants to show that peaceful coexistence between nations having different ideologies is *not an invention of propaganda* but can become a reality and even a success if the parties concerned entertain no ulterior motives. This is surely the case of the Soviet Union and Cambodia. . . ." Domestic service broadcast of December 15; italics added. The commentary undoubtedly was meant as much to criticize Chinese conduct the preceding summer as to praise the Soviet attitude.

border on occasion. Nevertheless, the meeting and communiqué served both countries' purposes. For Washington, they underscored the American contention that the Viet Cong were retreating into Cambodia, they demonstrated American restraint in the face of a Viet Cong sanctuary there, and they placed a certain political onus on the Communists for compromising Cambodia's territorial integrity. For Phnom Penh, the talks with Bowles helped relax Sihanouk's concern about a massive entry of American troops into inhabited areas. Moreover, by talking with a senior American representative, Sihanouk could demonstrate the ease with which diplomatic contact with the United States could be restored unless Cambodia's Communist friends were more respectful of the border.

Wary of going too far toward the United States, however, Sihanouk sought in a number of ways to assure Peking, Hanoi, and Moscow that he was not capitulating to American pressures. In the first place, Sihanouk did not exceed previous statements regarding use of the ICC to improve border surveillance. On January 12, the Cambodian foreign ministry requested the ICC, in accordance with the Bowles communiqué, to look into all border incidents and conduct investigations concerning foreign intervention.[14] But a radio broadcast the same day also reported the Soviet ambassador's comment that the standing American offer of two additional helicopters to the ICC was unacceptable, since any such aid required the approval of all the signatories to the Geneva accords.[15] Sihanouk, being sensitive to Soviet opposition, had on several occasions prior to Bowles's visit stated Cambodia's passive position with respect to the ICC. Cambodia would not object to, but also would not intervene to assure, a reinforcement of the Commission's capability. Only if the Soviet Union and Poland were willing would Cambodia accept American gifts and turn them over to the Indian head of the ICC[16]—which was the same as saying that enhancement of the ICC's ability to investigate American charges of Viet Cong incursions could not be facilitated.

Secondly, it may have been more than coincidental that Prince Phurissara was in Hanoi from December 31 to January 8. Although Sihanouk denied any connection between that visit and Bowles's, the foreign minister conceivably had the mission of reassuring the North Vietnamese leaders that Cambodia had no intention of changing her Vietnam policy despite conversations with Bowles. The final communiqué of Phurissara's visit was undramatic: Hanoi reiterated its recognition and respect of Cambodia's borders, while Cambodia reiterated criticisms of American policy in Vietnam and support of the DRV and NLF programs.[17]

The Domestic Crisis Renews

Perhaps based more on optimism than reality, the Cambodian government had declared the internal rebellion ended on June 18, 1967. But beginning in

January 1968, external issues once again became factors in domestic unrest and, as before, the government accused the Vietnamese and local Chinese Communists of having a hand in the disturbances. Like the previous unrest, that of early 1968 heightened Sihanouk's alarm over the intentions of his Communist neighbors toward his country.

The surface issues seized upon by the radicals once more concerned the future of Cambodia-United States relations. The visits of Mrs. Kennedy and Ambassador Bowles were cited by the left-wing as evidence of a slow drift of Cambodian foreign policy into the "imperialist" camp; so too was the arrival of Marshal Tito in January (just after Bowles).[18] Sihanouk, in fact, announced that a leftist plot to assassinate Tito had been broken up; later, he charged that local Chinese Communist agents had been involved.[19]

Below the surface, the question remained to what extent the dissidence that Sihanouk reported had erupted again in Battambang (and, subsequently, several other provinces) was externally instigated. The prince's position was that "Khmer Maoists," assisted by external Communist forces, were trying to bring about a change in government more acceptable to the interests of "Asian Communism." The radicals were assertedly in league with their fraternal Thai, Laotian, and Vietnamese Communist parties.[20] Far from being a jacquerie, as was reported by Jacques Decornoy in articles for Le Monde,[d] the rebellion lacked popular support or local causes, was taking place in areas that had benefited from the Sangkum's progressive programs, and was being abetted by propaganda tracts and weapons of foreign manufacture.[21] The prince refused to implicate Hanoi or Peking directly; but he did charge that Communist elements in Cambodia loyal to the Chinese and Vietnamese Communists were behind the turmoil, and he warned again that a pro-American regime under Lon Nol would succeed him if they persisted in their subversion.[22]

Beginning in March 1968, as dissidence that started in Battambang also broke out in most of the provinces bordering South Vietnam and Laos, the prince became more outspoken about the rebels' external ties. Where previously he had generalized about the Khmer Reds' reactivation of old Viet Minh cells, on March 7, he reported the capture of a motorboat with five men (three Vietnamese and two Cambodians) who had come from South Vietnam loaded with arms and ammunition destined for the rebels.[23] A week later, he said interrogated prisoners had revealed that six boatloads of arms and ammunition had already been sent into Cambodia.[24] Still later, Sihanouk accused Pathet Lao agents of giving arms to dissident Khmer Loeu montagnards and members of other minority tribal groups in Rattanakiri and Stung Treng; claimed the capture of 40

---

[d]E.g., February 2, 1968. In this and other articles, Decornoy held that while the dissidents may have been given revolutionary materials by outside elements, "The malaise seems above all due to local causes rapidly exploited by the 'reds' . . . " He pointed to the popularity of those leftist leaders who had disappeared, to the discontent of young unemployed intellectuals, to "the sometimes heavy burdens that fall on the rural population by virtue of the presence of the military, the arrests, [and] the absence of dialog between those in power and the governed. . . "

Pathet Lao troops; reported the participation of 20 Vietnamese Communists in an attack on several border outposts in Prey Veng; and allowed that some Viet Cong base camps and hideouts might exist in uninhabited, inaccessible, unadministered areas of Cambodia.[25]

Nor did local Chinese activists escape Sihanouk's sweeping indictment. The illegal currency activities of some overseas Chinese again were called into question, and required an explicit denial by an official of the CPR Embassy.[26] Printed matter from Peking was also reported to have been found in the hands of a radical student leader; the weapons on board the intercepted Vietnamese junk were of Chinese manufacture; and captured Battambang rebels carried Chinese documents.[27] In late November 1968, the Cambodian security police arrested two Chinese in Phnom Penh—the one, a plastics manufacturer; the other, a known leftist sympathizer who frequented the CPR Embassy—who were said to have been storing grenades and gas masks for use in a pro-left demonstration that never took place.[28] Here again, however, Sihanouk was careful to separate the activities of the leftist Chinese in Cambodia from China's official policy; but the implication of Peking's involvement remained, as it had in May 1967.

An important question is why Sihanouk went far beyond his accusations of the previous year to pinpoint the Communist use of Cambodian territory. Part of the answer may be Sihanouk's sensitivity to shifts in the balance of forces nearby. The Viet Cong, he may have decided, were no longer as close to victory as he had previously calculated. However distasteful the massive American involvement may have been to him, the United States showed a disposition to stick out its commitment rather than withdraw under circumstances that would be favorable to a Communist takeover. As a result, the see-saw military contest in Vietnam, which continued after President Johnson ordered a partial bombing halt in March 1968 and a complete suspension in October, perhaps gave Sihanouk new latitude to express his dissatisfaction with the Vietnamese Communists and to engage the Americans in direct discussions.

In focusing his verbal attacks on the Thai, Laotian, and Vietnamese Communists rather than on the Khmer Serai and Saigon, and in appearing to move closer to Washington, Sihanouk probably hoped that, as in mid-1967, Peking and Hanoi would react by reemphasizing their support and refraining from any form of interference in Cambodia's internal affairs. In part, this expectation was fulfilled. China's military and economic aid program continued.[e] In March 1968, Sihanouk announced that Peking, through Ch'en Yi,

---

[e]In January 1968, three MIG-17's arrived along with Chinese military personnel to assemble and train Cambodians to fly them. (Phnom Penh domestic service, January 4.) The glassware factory in Kandal was opened in June and, in October, an airport at Siem Reap built with Chinese aid was formally inaugurated. One official Cambodian newspaper—*Neak Cheat Niyum* (August 12, 1968)—charged, however, that the government's requests for spare parts to help repair and modernize a broadcast station built with Chinese assistance in 1959 had gone unanswered since 1967.

had reiterated its support of the prince and its policy of noninterference.[f] And, in September, Prince Phurissara's visit to Peking marked the renewal of high-level diplomatic exchanges. But these developments did not produce any sign that Peking was able to intervene on Sihanouk's behalf with the North Vietnamese.

Sihanouk's "signals" to Hanoi, if such they were, proved much less successful. While the prince may have been trying to tell the North Vietnamese and the NLF that they had overdrawn their account in Cambodia because of their subversive activities and extensive buildup, Hanoi and the Front may have interpreted Sihanouk's words and actions as hostile signs of a future change of policy that required supporting dissident groups in eastern and northern Cambodia to warn him. Thus, to judge from Cambodian accounts, the Vietnamese Communists were reacting to every threatening move in the Americans' direction by reinforcing their presence in Cambodia.[g]

Communist pressures continued despite an announcement in December 1968 that the Pathet Lao had finally agreed to recognize and respect the border,[29] and despite repeated professions of respect for Cambodian territorial integrity by NLF and DRV officials. In March 1969, for instance, Lieutenant General Nhiek Tioulong, commander-in-chief of the Cambodian army, reported to Sihanouk on the results of an investigation into armed incidents in Svay Rieng province. His report stated:

The investigations conducted . . . provided proof that several earlier incidents were largely provoked by the Viet Cong, who, unbeknown to us, used our border areas to carry out activities against the U.S.-South Vietnamese forces on the opposite side. These activities ultimately led to our clashing with the U.S.-South Vietnamese forces.[30]

One particular incident that had occurred on March 7, and that had prompted the investigation, also was "the work of the Viet Cong. . . ." When an explanation was demanded of the Viet Cong leader of the troops in the region—by itself, an interesting admission of direct contact between Cambodian and Viet Cong military authorities—he at first denied responsibility but "eventually admitted in writing that it was Viet Cong who conducted the

[f]Sihanouk stated at a March 28 news conference that his ambassador to Peking, Truong Cang, had conferred with Han Nien-lung on March 6 and with Ch'en Yi on March 16. Truong was assured of China's friendly intentions and of her hope to continue providing aid. To discuss the aid program, an invitation was extended to Son Sann, who had last visited the mainland in August 1965, to go to Peking. *Paroles, 1968,* p. 217.

[g]Sihanouk gave the Communists further ammunition when, in September 1968, Eugene Black, former head of the World Bank and special economic counselor to President Johnson, arrived in Phnom Penh accompanied by State Department officials. Ostensibly, the main topic was regional economic development, but United States-Cambodia relations were equally high on the agenda. According to an authoritative Cambodian report (in *Le Sangkum,* No. 40, November 1968), Prime Minister Penn Nouth, speaking for Sihanouk, accepted United States concern about a Viet Cong presence in Cambodia, denied that anything permanent had been uncovered, but agreed to exchange documents with Washington concerning the Khmer Serai and the Communist forces. Black took the occasion to renew American assurances of respect for Cambodia's territorial integrity.

shelling." General Tioulong's report concluded that every effort was being made to rid Svay Rieng of Viet Cong, but with only partial success.

Incidents such as these were brought before the NLF's representative in Phnom Penh, but produced no promises other than to look into them. Instead, during the spring of 1969, the Viet-Cong presence so deepened that Prince Sihanouk was compelled to acknowledge that he could no longer visit certain border regions because the Vietnamese completely controlled them. In late April, for the first time, Cambodian armed units were specifically ordered to attack the Viet Cong.[h]

Parallel and seemingly in response to these developments, Sihanouk indicated receptivity to reestablishing relations with the United States. The reasoning was that "the resumption of diplomatic relations . . . would make [U.S.] aggression along our frontiers more difficult and would facilitate compensations made to the victims."[31] Conceivably, though, the real reason was that Sihanouk considered he could no longer hold over the Communists the *threat* of a rapprochement with Washington but had to go further by actually beginning a dialogue with the Nixon Administration on the conditions for reopening the U.S. Embassy in Phnom Penh. A second factor that may have entered into Sihanouk's thinking was the Paris peace talks and Vietnam's future. By introducing greater balance into his foreign policy statements and actions, the prince may have hoped to get American support if Cambodian security were brought up in Paris. As Sihanouk said on several occasions during the spring, since the Communists were not reducing their internal and external pressures on Cambodia, he might as well have "a new card to play," one that might become increasingly useful in the future.[32] Typically, however, the prince moved cautiously toward reestablishing relations: in May, he put an end to talk of a reconciliation, charging that Washington had imposed new and unacceptable conditions;[i] but in June, after receiving further American assurances, he agreed

---

[h]In a special nationwide message on April 22, 1969, Sihanouk said that "in effect Rattanakiri is now in the hands of the Vietnamese." In July, he reported that the Vietnamese Communists had appointed a governor for the province and had succeeded at recruiting and equipping several units of Khmer Loeu. The following month, it was revealed by *Réalités cambodgiennes* (July 4, 1969, p. 11) that Lon Nol had conferred in late May with the DRV and NLF ambassadors about Communist forces in Rattanakiri and neighboring provinces. Reportedly, the Communist representatives expressed regret, restated their friendship policy, and proposed that the incidents were probably occasioned by the fighting in South Vietnam.

[i]In mid-April, the United States government had informed Sihanouk that it recognized Cambodia's existing frontiers. The prince accepted this statement and chose to drop one previous precondition to reestablishing relations, namely, that the United States also agree to respect the borders. Left unclear was the American attitude with regard to the offshore islands which, Sihanouk pointed out, were still marked on American maps as belonging to the Vietnamese. Later in April, an unfortunate elaboration of the United States position by a State Department spokesman implied that the United States still considered those islands Vietnamese. The prince responded on April 30 by rejecting the United States recognition statement on the grounds that "the United States now accompanies this recognition with reservations that we cannot accept." "If the United States desires a reconciliation," he added on May 3, "it must stipulate that our actual frontiers include our coastal islands, the temple of Preah Vihear, and the several Khmer villages claimed by Saigon." Quotations from *Le Monde*, May 3 and 6, 1969.

to the reopening of the American Embassy with a chargé d'affaires at its head. At the same time, Sihanouk apparently continued to cooperate with the Communists to keep their forces supplied.[j] He also took steps to mollify the Vietnamese Communists politically: on May 9, the Cambodian government announced that the NLF mission had been elevated to embassy level; in mid-June, Cambodia recognized the NLF-dominated Provisional Revolutionary Government of South Vietnam; and late in June, the newly-declared president of the Provisional Government, Huynh Tan Phat, arrived in Cambodia on a "state" visit. When Ho Chi Minh died in September, Sihanouk, probably with reference to these manifestations of his support, sought to pry new assurances from Ho's successors of their respect for Cambodia's territorial integrity.[33]

China and the Future of Cambodian Foreign Policy

Cambodia's dependence for security on the actions and promises of the major powers in Asia, and the constraints on Cambodia's foreign policy choices because of this dependence, accounted for the shifting nature of Cambodian neutralism under Sihanouk. Neutralism was a source of political unity and external strength by itself. Like other countries in Southeast Asia, however, Sihanouk's Cambodia had to make foreign policy conform to political and geographical realities; Sihanouk was constantly reappraising the components of neutralism to assure their appropriateness to prevailing circumstances inside and outside the country. Gradually during 1967 and clearly by 1968, Phnom Penh was compelled by events in Vietnam, by dissidence and subversion at home, and by experiences in its diplomacy toward another reevaluation, one that spelled a pessimistic future with limited alternatives.

Sihanouk's Perspective

The political and military situation that had evolved in Indochina late in the 1960s may have made the earlier part of the decade seem placid by comparison. Many of the assumptions that had been behind Cambodian diplomatic closeness to Peking and Hanoi had to be discarded, tacitly or openly. Between 1960 and

---

[j]Apparently based on documents seized during the United States-South Vietnamese ground operations in eastern Cambodia in the spring of 1970, "official sources" in Washington reported that the port of Sihanoukville had been a major supply route for Communist forces in the sanctuaries and in the Mekong delta between early 1969 and the overthrow of Sihanouk. During that period, the sources asserted, Sihanouk consented to the docking of Chinese ships laden with food, ammunition, and weapons intended for four North Vietnamese divisions that operated along the Cambodia-South Vietnam border. A local Chinese-owned company trucked the supplies to these forces. Confronted with evidence of these deliveries by United States officials, Sihanouk is said to have had the traffic reduced. See *Los Angeles Times*, October 29, 1970, p. 1.

1965, peace had not been restored in Laos, the United States had not directly intervened against Pathet Lao-North Vietnamese forces there, the Viet Cong were well down the road to a military victory against a Saigon government riddled by factionalism and *coups d'état*, and China's friendship seemed to be the only means of assuring limited Viet Cong involvement in Cambodia. By 1969, the *de facto* division of Laos was in danger of being upset, the United States had completed a major buildup in Thailand, and American and GVN forces had brought the Vietnam fighting to a military standoff and negotiations. Communist China's willingness, much less ability, to restrain the Vietnamese Communists was subject to serious doubts. In the words of the semiofficial *Réalités cambodgiennes*, Asian Communists were playing a "double game" with Cambodia: while professions of friendship and respect for the borders had come from the North Vietnamese, the NLF, and the Pathet Lao, these same forces were said to be supporting dissidence in Cambodia. American bombing and strafing along the Vietnam-Cambodia border were meanwhile exacting a mounting toll on Cambodian lives and property; the United States still backed the Thai-controlled Khmer Serai, and Saigon remained as hostile as ever to Cambodia.[34] From the Cambodian point of view, the dangers to independence had multiplied over the years; and Cambodian leaders had begun to develop an encirclement psychosis that could be justified by the turmoil surrounding the country.

The large-scale involvement of the United States in Vietnam had become a critical element in Sihanouk's calculations about the future. Although hesitant to say so specifically, he seems to have come to the conclusion that the American effort there, for all its faults, was in some ways advantageous to Cambodian security. A settlement that might lower the level of violence in South Vietnam, he apparently decided, was preferable to a precipitate American withdrawal. This changed perception fit, however, with Sihanouk's longstanding conviction that Cambodia benefited most when conflict in Vietnam was confined to the contending Vietnamese factions in a divided country.[35] Since the Americans *had* become deeply committed in Vietnam, their hasty withdrawal would surely yield up the country to the Communists and significantly increase Cambodia's vulnerability to Vietnamese intrigues. Sihanouk's view in 1968 therefore was that the United States should turn from attempting a military victory, which could only eventuate in defeat, to influencing an accommodation between Communists and non-Communists in South Vietnam that would stabilize the situation and perhaps give Cambodia a breathing spell. Once an accommodation had been effected, the United States could honorably withdraw and continue to play a broad security role in Southeast Asia that would be denied it if it were compelled to withdraw under military pressure.[36] Vietnam might indeed remain locked in civil war after an American withdrawal under any circumstances; but America's prestige would no longer be involved, and a Communist victory might be considerably delayed (and Cambodia's security at least temporarily assured) while the energies of the Vietnamese were directed toward control of Saigon and reunification.

Sihanouk's apparent feeling that the United States was buying time for Cambodia in Vietnam reflected his vastly diminished confidence in Communist China. Having estranged Cambodia from the United States in the first half of the 1960s because China's value to Cambodian interests seemed so much higher, Sihanouk by 1967 found reason to question China's sincerity and usefulness. The fact that Peking had been so deliberate in its statements about Cambodia's defense probably was not at issue, since Sihanouk manipulated them to suit his needs anyway. But Peking's hesitancy in 1967 to take the lead in recognizing and respecting Cambodia's existing borders meant to him that China's leaders were unwilling to stand beside Cambodia against the North Vietnamese. And the ensuing difficulties with the Chinese Embassy in Phnom Penh had a traumatic effect: they amounted to an attempt by representatives of Peking to propagate Maoism and stir up leftist sentiment at a time when the Cambodian government was embroiled in a domestic crisis; and they contradicted Chou En-lai's avowed policy of restraint on the overseas Chinese.

Although a break with China was avoided, Sihanouk could no longer be certain how much sincerity he could attach to China's praise of him or even how much reliability he could put on the friendship treaty of 1960.[37] His past view of China as a valuable ally who would prevail against the Vietnamese Communists seems to have been quietly dropped. In its place, Sihanouk stated outright in 1968 that one of the chief benefits of an accommodation in South Vietnam would be to frustrate China's hopes for a protracted military conflict that would humiliate the United States and bring about a complete American withdrawal from Asia. In contrast to China, which in his view was urging against a negotiated Vietnam settlement out of preference for ending the war by military means, he favored accommodation partly in order to maintain American influence in Asia and, at a minimum, delay the day of Chinese control of the entire area.[k] These views were in line with Sihanouk's oft-stated projection of eventual Chinese domination of Asia; but they differed markedly from his previous evaluations that China, not the United States, was the best hope for stabilizing Cambodia's eastern frontier.

Against this background of mistrust, uncertainty, and pessimism about the future, Cambodia's foreign policy alternatives narrowed considerably. The promises Cambodia received from Asian Communist governments and parties

---

[k]See the *Mainichi* interview previously cited. In an interview with Attwood (op. cit.), Sihanouk remarked that in the event of a United States withdrawal from Asia, the Chinese "will become more active all over the area through their own agents and local Communist parties." He expressed confidence, however, that Asian nationalism would be able to deal with any subversion. The prince's premonitions of trouble from China may also have influenced his comments about the Soviet invasion of Czechoslovakia in August 1968. In condemning the invasion, he said it was an example of how vulnerable even a country pledged to Communism becomes after having been made a satellite. And he went on to ask whether Cambodia, once having become red, could ever escape a similar fate at the hands of the Vietnamese or Chinese. Speech of August 27, in Phnom Penh domestic service broadcast of the same day.

had either been proven baseless or, after the Paris talks, might prove irrelevant.[1] Yet no promises at all regarding Cambodia's security were obtained from the West. What, then, were Cambodia's options?

Caught "between the hammer and the anvil," as a Cambodian editorial put it,[38] Sihanouk apparently concluded that no international or regional mechanism could effectively prevent the application of pressures, political and military, from the Vietnamese Communists. Alignment with the United States, South Vietnam, and Thailand, through the conclusion of aid agreements or the acceptance of direct military help, would only prolong and widen Communist involvement in Cambodia. Active association with the Western powers would have to remain a useful threat rather than an available alternative. The only real choice Sihanouk seemed to think he had was the continuation of old policies that would count heavily on his personal ingenuity. Adroit diplomacy, not a dramatic foreign policy shift or resort to military power, was still the most positive way to cope with the spillover of the Vietnam war, the demands of Peking and Hanoi on Sihanouk's conduct of foreign relations, and the uncertainties of domestic politics.

Sihanouk's Overthrow and the End of Neutralism

On March 18, 1970, while Prince Sihanouk was en route from Moscow to Peking, the Cambodian National Assembly voted to remove him as chief of state. Full power was vested in Premier General Lon Nol and his first deputy premier, Prince (and General) Sirik Matak. In the next several weeks, Cambodia's politics and foreign policy underwent several dramatic transformations. Politically, Sihanouk's allies in Phnom Penh were removed from office, the prince was accused by the new government of crimes ranging from nepotism and corruption to misguided handling of foreign and economic problems, and the institutions of

---

[1]In the latter category were said to be the promises of respect and recognition made by the NLF. Since the Front is now nominally part of the so-called Alliance of National, Democratic, and Peace Forces, it can claim after a Vietnam settlement or United States withdrawal that it is no longer bound by statements made in the name of the Front alone. This possibility was mentioned by Sihanouk in a press conference of May 23, 1968 (broadcast by Phnom Penh domestic service, May 24). See also *Réalités cambodgiennes*, July 26, 1968, p. 4. Thus, even when Sihanouk reported in June 1969 that the NLF's (later, the Provisional Revolutionary Government's) ambassador in Phnom Penh had signed a pledge to withdraw all Viet Cong troops in Cambodia after the war, the prince, in a speech on June 19, commented that he did not fully trust any Vietnamese promises.

Hanoi's pledge of June 1967—reiterated several times since, including after Sihanouk's overthrow—also contains loopholes that could be exploited in the future. Since that pledge, like the ones granted by other nations, recognizes Cambodia's present frontiers but does not specify where they are, the basis for a dispute still exists. What Cambodia regards as her borders are not so well demarcated that disputes cannot arise with countries that have recognized them.

monarchy were replaced by the trappings of a republic.[m] Externally, cooperation along the border with South Vietnamese military commanders began soon after the "coup," the Vietnamese Communist forces retaliated by widening their areas of control in Cambodia and withdrawing their embassy staffs, and the Lon Nol government appealed for (and received) military assistance from the United States, South Vietnam, and Thailand. From Sihanouk's "oasis of peace," Cambodia turned into part of the Vietnam battleground; the new regime, exchanging enemies and friends, became informally allied with the Thai and South Vietnamese governments and rejected Chinese Communist overtures for continued friendly relations based on support of the Communist effort in South Vietnam.

The Removal of Sihanouk

To the extent that policy differences, as distinct from the distribution of political authority, were behind Lon Nol's move against Sihanouk, they probably concerned, above all, alternative methods for dealing with the growing Vietnamese Communist presence. While Lon Nol, to judge only from subsequent events, may have favored publicly and formally protesting to Hanoi and committing more men to secure the border areas, the prince was not prepared to go to such lengths. In October 1969 he had announced an increase in the Cambodian armed forces to 37,000 men, but he continued to assert in broadcasts that any major effort to oust the Communists from Cambodia would require alignment with the United States and the overturning of his neutralist approach—and these were steps he refused to take.

Problems with the Vietnamese Communists were compounded by economic troubles. Sihanouk-style socialism, with its emphasis on state-run enterprises and its rejection of international financing, had resulted in stagnation. Sirik Matak emerged as a leader of reform, and his programs gained adoption despite the prince's apparent opposition.[39] But it was Sihanouk who had installed Lon Nol and Sirik Matak in August 1969 as the head of the "Salvation Government." When the prince departed in January 1970 for a vacation in France, he could not have expected that his subordinates, any more then than in previous years, would seize the opportunity to remove him.

On March 8 in Svay Rieng province and again on March 11 in the capital, public demonstrations against the Viet Cong were reported. Doubtless planned by the army under Lon Nol, the demonstrations resulted in the sacking of the DRV and NLF embassies. More important was the political inspiration behind them: the demonstrations were the opposition's way of telling Sihanouk, with the advantage of long distance, that public feelings were running high in favor of a firmer government stance against the Communists. Sihanouk may actually not have opposed, and possibly even ordered, protests in front of the embassies, but

---

[m]Since October 9, 1970, Cambodia has been officially called the Khmer Republic.

as his angry remarks from Paris made clear, he would not tolerate the violence to which they had led and the implication that the military rightists were running the government.[40]

The Lon Nol government showed its control of the situation in succeeding days. On March 11, the National Assembly, without criticizing Sihanouk or his policies, voted unanimously to support the demonstrations and urged the government to do everything possible—including increases in the budget and the army—to defend the country. Lon Nol's office also voiced approval of the demonstrations the next day. And on March 13, after receiving a rather mild protest from the Communist embassies, Cambodia delivered notes to them regretting the incidents but requesting that their armed forces "kindly" be withdrawn from Cambodia by dawn of the fifteenth.

It appears that while the demonstrations were probably premeditated, the removal of Sihanouk was not.[n] Lon Nol and Sirik Matak apparently wanted to capitalize on Sihanouk's absence to compel his acceptance of new policies, foreign and domestic, that would have amounted to increased authority for themselves and their supporters in the army, the National Assembly, and intellectual circles. Instead, Sihanouk denounced their actions and sought to regain command of the situation—not by returning to Phnom Penh but by flying to Moscow. There, he hoped to convince the Russians, and following them the Chinese, that the future of neutral Cambodia depended on their preparedness to influence the North Vietnamese to reduce their presence in his country. The alternative, he would tell Soviet and Chinese leaders, would be a pro-American Cambodia.[41]

The failure of Sihanouk's mission to Moscow was evidenced not only in the weak wording of a Soviet statement (March 16), which spoke only of "respect for the neutrality and territorial integrity of Cambodia,"[42] but also in the continued presence of Communist forces after March 15, Lon Nol's deadline. On that date, the two sides agreed to negotiations, which opened on March 16. But it soon became apparent that the Communists' objective was to gain Lon Nol's acceptance of Sihanouk's *laissez-faire* policy, not to bargain on the withdrawal of their troops. When that happened, Lon Nol and Sirik Matak, supported by an angry National Assembly and public, probably decided that a takeover was necessary and indeed possible. The fact that the entire 92-member assembly voted "no confidence" in the prince on March 18 showed that much more than army pressure was involved in the overthrow.

---

[n]Among the indirect indications that Sihanouk's overthrow was not planned are, first, that Radio Phnom Penh twice (on March 12 and March 16) announced Sihanouk's impending return to Cambodia, and second, that Lon Nol, addressing Sihanouk as prince and chief of state, sent a telegram to Sihanouk in Peking to keep him informed of developments (broadcast by Radio Phnom Penh on March 17). T.D. Allman observes that Phnom Penh's airport route was decked out in preparation for the prince's return. He speculates that had Sihanouk returned on March 18 as originally planned rather than gone on to Moscow, the coup might never have occurred. In an interview with an Italian journalist (*L'Espresso* [Rome], December 27, 1970), however, Sihanouk said he was advised by the Russians to return but did not because he feared he would be arrested by loyalists of Lon Nol.

China's Reaction

As in February 1966, when Ghana's Kwame Nkrumah was ousted while he was en route to Peking, the Chinese leaders again found themselves hosting a deposed head of state when Sihanouk landed on March 19. Although Sihanouk was greeted as though nothing had happened and immediately had broadcasting facilities put at his disposal to assail the coup leaders and defend his policies, Peking revealed in several ways that its main objective was to preserve China's political interests in Cambodia, not to regain power for Sihanouk.

The first of China's two-pronged policy toward the new Cambodian leadership was to allow Sihanouk to establish his entourage in Peking, thereby making Phnom Penh aware that the prince *might* have Communist support in attempting a comeback. On March 20, Sihanouk made the first of many statements for transmission to Cambodia and the world in which he called the coup unconstitutional, defended his foreign and domestic policies, rejected various charges of corruption, and warned of the dangers to Cambodia in a realignment with the West.[43] He vowed to fight to overthrow the coup group, but said he would never again hold the reins of government.[44] As to the means of his return, Sihanouk, in a March 23 message,[45] said he would set up a "new government of national unity" and a "national liberation army" organized, with broad popular participation, under a "National United Front of Kampuchea" (NUFK).

While dutifully publishing the prince's statements, the Chinese did not associate themselves with them. In the first week after the deposition, the Chinese media issued only two reports. An NCNA broadcast of March 20 cited the "grave situation" created by "premeditated" public assaults on the homes and property of overseas Chinese and Vietnamese. On March 23, NCNA mentioned the Lon Nol government for the first time, but relied on foreign reports that called the overthrow United States-planned and its leader pro-American. The article concluded that the Cambodia situation "is still developing" and that "people are closely watching the development and changes of the Cambodia situation."[46] By contrast, during the same period, the North Vietnamese official media directly labeled the overthrow an aggressive American move and vowed that the threat to Cambodia's independence would be met by further Vietnamese "solidarity" with the Cambodian "people's struggle."[47] Well in advance of Peking, Hanoi, by March 22, was already calling resistance to Lon Nol part of "the Indochinese people's fight" against U.S. imperialism.[48] And on March 25, the day the Vietnamese Communist embassies (but not China's) advised the Cambodian government of the recall of their diplomatic staffs, the DRV officially announced its support of Prince Sihanouk, his program, and "the just struggle of the Khmer people till final victory."[49]

China's hesitancy to break with Lon Nol and join the North Vietnamese in supporting Sihanouk's "struggle" was probably motivated mainly by the consideration that the extension of the Vietnam fighting into Cambodia might overextend the Communists' capabilities, might lead to American intervention, and, even if successful, would only benefit Vietnamese Communist interests. Rather than accede immediately to Hanoi's initiative, Peking preferred to try to persuade Lon Nol that the continuation of Sihanouk's policies was in Cambodia's (as it was certainly in China's) best interests. That this was Peking's approach has been attested to by Lon Nol himself, who said that from the time of the deposition until May 5 (when Peking recognized Sihanouk's exile regime), Chinese representatives "several times" told him that if Cambodia maintained her political and material support of the Communist effort in South Vietnam, the overthrow of Sihanouk would be accepted as an internal Cambodian affair.[o] Presumably, the Chinese would no more have objected then than previously to the improvement of Cambodian diplomatic relations with the United States, or even to statements and armed actions (of the limited kind Sihanouk began) against Communist-occupied base areas deep inside Cambodia.

But Lon Nol proved uncooperative. On March 25, his government closed Sihanoukville (renamed Kompong Som) to Communist-flag ships, thus cutting off an important source of supplies for Communist forces in the lower half of South Vietnam. The same day, a trade agreement that had been concluded with the NLF in September 1969, chiefly concerned with rice sales, was abrogated.[50] Of greater significance for the Communists' war effort were several reported instances of Cambodian, South Vietnamese, and American cooperation in assaults on Communist sanctuaries along the border.[51] Beginning late in March, South Vietnamese units launched attacks into Cambodia.[52] (At this time, the White House disclosed that American troops could also cross the border in "protective reaction" to Communist fire from Cambodia.) These actions challenged the credibility of Phnom Penh officials who kept maintaining that Cambodia was still neutral and who protested United States-South Vietnamese penetrations of the frontier. On March 27, when the Cambodian defense ministry ordered a mobilization of the military reserve, the first step was taken toward a government appeal for foreign, including American, military assistance.[p]

The Chinese leadership responded to these developments by toughening its portrayal of the possible consequences. An NCNA article on March 26 accused the United States of having instigated the overthrow and predicted victory for

---

[o]Nationwide appeal by Lon Nol, broadcast over Phnom Penh domestic service, May 11, 1970. The three conditions of Cambodian support of the Communists were: (1) that Cambodia "permit the supply of arms and medicine from China to North Vietnamese and Viet Cong troops"; (2) that Cambodia continue "to allow North Vietnamese and Viet Cong troops to rest in Khmer territory"; (3) that Cambodian propaganda continue to be friendly toward China and North Vietnam.

[p]At a press conference on March 30, Lon Nol, Sirik Matak and the new foreign minister, Yem Sambaur, were questioned about the availability of manpower and weapons in the event Viet Cong forces did not withdraw. The response was that 200,000 to 300,000 men could be mobilized, and that weapons would be accepted from Indonesia and other "friendly nations," including the United States. Ibid., March 31, 1970, pp. 1, 6; Phnom Penh domestic service radio, April 2, 1970.

"the Cambodian people" in their struggle against United States intervention.[53] Articles in succeeding days cited demonstrations against Lon Nol outside Phnom Penh, his "collusion" with United States, Thai, and South Vietnamese authorities to obtain military aid and to fight Vietnamese (Communist) forces, and his government's steadily eroding authority.[54] Active resistance to the government was said to be rapidly spreading.[55] A new stage in China's identification with the fighting in Cambodia was reached when Chou En-lai, in a speech in Pyongyang, lent support to Sihanouk's appeals and voiced confidence that the Cambodians, "fighting shoulder to shoulder" with the Vietnamese and Laotians, would be victorious.[56]

With all this, China's embassy in Phnom Penh remained open and, if Lon Nol's statement is to be believed, CPR officials continued to approach him about changing his policies. But China's hand was forced by events during April: the fighting in Cambodia intensified as increased South Vietnamese involvement in the sanctuary areas was met by deeper North Vietnamese penetrations westward, threatening Phnom Penh. On April 14, the Cambodian government appealed for foreign military aid, to which the United States responded with an initial shipment of several thousand automatic rifles captured from the Viet Cong.[57] The first combined Cambodian-ARVN operation was also reported.[58]

In view of these developments, it was not surprising that Chinese commentaries and press reports began emphasizing the military successes of organized "patriotic armed forces" in Cambodia. Prospects for "people's war" and protracted struggle under the NUFK were now mentioned;[q] the Cambodian government's massacres of Vietnamese residents were highlighted;[r] and, perhaps, because of Chinese objections, a Soviet proposal in the United Nations to hold a new Geneva Conference on Cambodia was quickly watered down.[s] Peking seemed to be moving closer to the North Vietnamese position, as was dramatized when it was announced that an Indochinese People's Summit Conference, called

---

[q]Jen-min jih-pao, April 16, 1970, p. 5; April 17, p. 6; April 19, p. 6; April 25, p. 5. Among the participants in the "people's struggle" were Sihanouk's leftist foes of a few years earlier, the ex-assemblymen Khieu Samphan, Hu Nim, and Hou Youn. They were said (ibid., April 11, 1970, p. 5) to have issued a statement supporting the prince's movement. Later, they were announced as being members of his exile government.

[r]Article by Commentator, ibid., April 22, 1970, p. 5. At least several hundred Vietnamese in Cambodia were slain in the first month after the deposition. The Cambodian government may not have been directly responsible, but its encouragement of hatred against Vietnamese (which needed little prompting), the involvement of Cambodian troops in some of the killings, and the belatedness in calling a halt to them give the government a major share in the blame. For some reports, see New York Times, April 14 and 16, 1970, p. 1.

[s]The proposal, made by Soviet representative Yakov A. Malik, was especially interesting because it was made when Le Duc Tho, the chief North Vietnamese negotiator at the Paris talks, was in Moscow. One interpretation might be that at least a faction of the North Vietnamese leadership supported a new international conference. Two days after Malik's overture, however, on April 18, it was dropped with the suggestion that too much emphasis had been placed on the idea by Western observers. See ibid., April 17, 1970, p. 10 and the Chinese criticism in Jen-min jih-pao, April 25, 1970, p. 5.

by Sihanouk, had been held on April 24-25. The conference, attended by Viet Cong, Hanoi, and Laotian Communist leaders (and, at the close, by Chou En-lai), did not announce any concrete agreements; but it did underscore North Vietnam's contention that the three anti-American struggles in Indochina were now interrelated.[59]

Still, statements in the Chinese press or by Chinese officials did not promise or imply—unlike North Vietnamese statements[t]—material support for the Communist movement in Cambodia to overthrow the Lon Nol government. That threshold was not passed until after President Nixon's decision of April 30 to send American troops into the sanctuaries. While Chinese statements prior to the President's speech suggest that the new American action did not take Peking by surprise,[60] the fact that the CPR waited until after the event to announce the founding of Sihanouk's regime and China's backing of its aims may show just how reluctant it was to embrace a Vietnamese Communist strategy for Cambodia. The President's decision left Peking with little choice. On May 3, a speech by Chou En-lai delivered over a week earlier was published in which Chou asserted that Chinese territory is "the reliable rear area of the people of the three Indochinese countries. The brotherly people of the three Indochinese states can believe that in the common struggle against U.S. imperialism, the Chinese people will forever be with them."[61] A Chinese government statement and a *People's Daily* editorial the next day offered similar assurances in recognizing Sihanouk's Royal Government of National Union.

Once having lined up behind North Vietnam, the Chinese leadership then seemed to look for opportunities to expand its influence over developments in Indochina, with respect both to Moscow and Hanoi. The Soviet government presented one opportunity when it refused to recognize Sihanouk's regime, probably because Moscow saw no advantage to supporting an exile regime based in Peking.[u] This attitude could not have won many friends in Hanoi; and it gave Peking a chance to publicize Soviet unreliability in helping revolutionary movements.[62] China's leaders may also have hoped to capitalize on the prospect of reduced Soviet aid to North Vietnam, although Moscow, at least initially, responded positively to North Vietnamese aid requests, perhaps in order to

---

[t]North Vietnamese statements throughout April vowed to punish the Lon Nol government for massacring Vietnamese and collaborating with South Vietnamese and American military forces. One commentary in the North Vietnamese army newspaper, *Quan Doi Nhan Dan (People's Army)*, said on April 11: "It [the Lon Nol regime] is on the verge of turning Cambodia into a second South Vietnam or Laos, and of placing Cambodia in front of the danger of a barbarous U.S. aggression." Broadcast by Hanoi domestic service, same date.

[u]Following Chinese and North Vietnamese recognition, Soviet Premier Kosygin sent Sihanouk a congratulatory message that promised "sympathy and support" to the prince's struggle but did not grant recognition. (*New York Times*, May 13, 1970, p. 13.) Later, Soviet diplomats in Laos hinted (*Los Angeles Times*, June 8, 1970, p. 1) that Communist operations in Cambodia were also viewed with disfavor, probably because they encouraged U.S.-allied intervention, would require additional Soviet aid to Hanoi's forces, and increased the possibility of new Soviet commitments if, for instance, Communist forces were to seize Phnom Penh.

counterbalance China's increased assistance.[v] If Hanoi's dependency on China for political and military support should increase, it might compel greater adherence than in the past to Chinese advice on strategy—and beginning early in May, Peking made clear its strategic preferences, implicitly ruling out the large-scale commitment of Communist forces to the capture and control of Cambodian territory and cities.[w] China's consistent opposition to the Paris talks and to a negotiated settlement with the United States on less than optimum terms could also be expected to have Hanoi's continued endorsement under the new circumstances in Cambodia.

Sihanouk's continued presence in Peking was also a source of Chinese influence over developments in Cambodia, though not a powerful one. The Chinese could hope to control the style and content of the prince's pronouncements and to influence (though much less than the Vietnamese) the political complexion of the Cambodian insurgent movement. In Sihanouk, Peking had the equivalent of the Laotian "Red Prince," Souphanouvong—the acknowledged leader of the "resistance forces" whose support, in the event of the establishment in Cambodia of a pro-Communist government, might prove indispensable to any groups attempting to consolidate their rule, expand their authority, or establish their legitimacy. With the passage of time, however,

---

[v] A "supplementary" military and economic aid agreement was signed in Moscow on June 11, 1970. Details were not announced (VNA [Hanoi] international service, same date.) The agreement was preceded by a statement of Sihanouk that Mao had personally offered the Cambodian Communist movement a long-term loan and free arms and transport. *New York Times*, June 7, 1970, p. 3.

[w] In the government statement of May 4, cited previously, and in a message of the CCP Central Committee to the Lao Dong Party on the anniversary of Ho Chi Minh's death (*Peking Review*, No. 21, May 22, 1970, p. 3), Peking stressed the necessity of conducting a protracted guerrilla war based on the principle of self-reliance. In the latter document, this strategy was urged "no matter whether U.S. imperialism continues to enlarge the war, or makes use of the service of its accomplices and running dogs, or carries out intervention and sabotage through the United Nations or any international conference."

The Chinese seemed to be advising the North Vietnamese to build up an indigenous (Cambodian) antigovernment force, presumably around the Khmer Rouges, for a long-term struggle rather than rely overwhelmingly on Vietnamese forces and attempt a rapid conquest. Perhaps in line with that advice, the three former assemblymen in Cambodia, according to Sihanouk himself in a broadcast of May 12, were said to be leading the national resistance movement. (See *New York Times*, May 24, 1970, p. 6.) North Vietnamese forces in Cambodia conducted themselves in accordance with that strategy, moreover, at least in northeast Cambodia where they began to hold pro-Sihanouk political meetings, train guerrillas, and set up village councils. (Ibid., May 29, 1970, p. 3.) Relatively few North Vietnamese troops—no more than several thousand—were directly committed to actions in Cambodia, according to most news reports.

Sihanouk may become a wasting asset to the Chinese if the insurgents are able to increase their control of territory and population.[x]

The Outlook for Cambodia in 1971

For the Lon Nol regime, the extension of the Vietnam fighting into its homeland was hardly the mark of a successful foreign policy. At the same time as substantial foreign assistance had been received with which to attempt to expel the Communist occupation forces, the country also faced a prolonged war against a previously impotent Communist rebel force now buttressed and dominated by veteran Vietnamese Communist troops. Ground and air support had been received from South Vietnam and air support from Thailand; but in the process, both countries had to be granted access to historically disputed territory, with no assurance that old claims might not be revived or simply staked out as compensation. Finally, perhaps contrary to its expectation, the Lon Nol government had gotten American troops to attack the sanctuaries, but had failed to obtain an explicit American commitment to Cambodia's security. The survival of the new government, precarious from the start, would have to depend largely on United States air power and assistance from the South Vietnamese and the Thai.[y]

Sihanouk's neutralism had been traded for quasialliances with Cambodia's traditional enemies; but little had been gained in long-term security, and perhaps much would be lost. Sihanouk had not politely stepped from the stage of power; the myth of his indispensability punctured, he had defiantly lent his name to a resistance movement and thus legitimized a Communist rebellion under the guise of a nationalist uprising. North Vietnamese military forces were widely dispersed across Cambodia, controlling all of the northern provinces from the border of

---

[x]Sihanouk admitted as much when he told newsmen in Peking that the Khmer Communists in Cambodia (of whom Khieu Samphan seems to be the leader) are not subject to his authority, constitute the real alternative to the Lon Nol government, and, should they come to power, would have no need of him. (Ibid., September 26, 1970, p. 5.) Although the Khmer Communists lack Sihanouk's national appeal, they are probably anxious to reduce their reliance on his prestige and charisma as quickly as possible. Hanoi's leaders are probably equally as willing to make the prince dispensable in view of his past behavior. Sihanouk's chances of returning to Cambodia thus appear extremely slim.

[y]On May 12, 1970, Cambodia and Thailand agreed to reestablish diplomatic relations. Cambodia and South Vietnam reestablished relations on May 26. A statement by Yem Sambaur and President Nguyen Van Thieu authorized the presence of South Vietnamese armed forces until Communist troops had been removed from Cambodia. Also in May, the first indications came to light of a reconciliation between the Cambodian government and Son Ngoc Thanh's Khmer Serai. These were confirmed in August 1970 when Thanh was named adviser to Lon Nol.

South Vietnam to Battambang at the Thai border. In response to the United States-South Vietnamese incursions, the North Vietnamese Army also strengthened its grip on southern Laos east of the Mekong. The Laos-Cambodia border region thus became a new sanctuary and redoubt from which to supply Communist forces in South Vietnam and attempt to reactivate the lost base areas in eastern Cambodia. South Vietnamese pressure from the east and Thai air attacks in the west, instead of squeezing the Communist forces in the middle, had succeeded only in widening their area of military responsibility and dividing Cambodia into zones of foreign occupation.

As 1971 began, the outlook for Lon Nol's regime was for continued fighting, Thai and South Vietnamese involvement in the western and eastern border provinces, and the expansion of Communist-controlled territory. In many respects, Sihanouk's prediction in Paris that Cambodia under military rule would become "a second Laos" had come true. Even if the new regime could manage, with an army planned for over 200,000 men, to fight the Communist forces on even terms, it, like the government of Souvanna Phouma, would probably have to contend with large areas under Communist control and a Communist capability to disrupt the economy[63] and to mobilize indigenous manpower. Eventually, depending on developments in South Vietnam, North Vietnamese- and Chinese-supported demands for the establishment of a coalition government to end the "civil war" may also materialize.

Burma's China Problem: Firmness and Flexibility

Although the riots in Rangoon may have had the effect of decompressing the tension in Burmese society that had been building because of economic setbacks, intellectual unemployment, and administrative difficulties in the rural areas, the government was not about to use the groundswell of public support to reorient foreign policy. Despite speculation in the Western press that the Revolutionary Council was contracting with the United States and the Soviet Union for counterinsurgency weapons and advisory personnel,[64] in actuality, the GUB seems to have been determined not to compromise the possibility of a future reconciliation with Peking by turning to China's main enemies for military assistance. Similarly with economic aid, the GUB apparently politely rebuffed Soviet offers to step into the breach created by the withdrawal of China's technicians in October.[65] The government newspaper *Mirror* put the Council's thinking succinctly when it stated:

After the recent anti-Chinese disorders, it has been asked whether Burma would submit and yield or would choose to depend on other countries. If the 700 million Chinese are armed with the thought of Mao Tse-tung, the 25 million Burmese are armed with sincerity and love. Burma will not renounce her neutrality.[66]

The GUB was apparently calculating that so long as neutralism was maintained, China might eventually again soften her support of insurgency in Burma. By 1971, the calculation was proving accurate.

China's response during the first three years after the summer crisis was less consistent. Burmese Communists were given access to China's radio and news facilities, but were apparently not given much material assistance. Chinese contacts with other rebel groups in Burma did increase beginning in 1968. But Peking seems to have kept clear of commitments to any anti-GUB movement. Its own statements concerning the Burmese government blew hot and cold, reflecting, perhaps, China's indecision as to the procedure and terms for effecting a reconciliation.

China and the GUB

In August 1967, at the height of confusion in the Cultural Revolution and tension between Peking and Rangoon, the chances were probably as great as at any time before the border treaty that a border incident might occur and risk dangerously escalating the confrontation. In fact, although Peking did make a number of charges concerning Burmese border violations and attacks on Chinese villagers,[67] these did not become pretexts for Chinese retaliation. Nor, significantly, did Peking go to the extreme of breaking diplomatic relations; as with Indonesia after the abortive PKI coup attempt, relations were suspended.

Instead, Peking chose to retaliate, first, by publicizing the CPB, and second, by terminating its aid program. As already stated, the first hints that the aid program was on the way out came in August; at that time, its continuation was linked to Burmese satisfaction of the five demands contained in CPR protest notes. Rather than initiate the break, Peking apparently wanted to have Ne Win do so. On October 6, the GUB complied, demanding the withdrawal of all CPR workers and technicians; and, not surprisingly, a Chinese government statement acknowledging the GUB's demand sought to make it appear that China was acquiescing despite great forbearance and only because her demands had not been met.[68] During November, three groups of technicians totaling 412 men left Burma.[69] Considering that many projects had taken a long time to get started, and that the most important ones were either completed or could be completed by the Burmese, the withdrawal of China's aid teams was not a severe blow to Burma's economy.

Burma's treatment of the overseas Chinese remained a major sore spot in the absence of friendly state-to-state relations. CPR protests persisted through 1967 and into 1968 on the subject; but Burmese authorities continued to try local Chinese accused of subversion and conspiracy in civil courts.[70] The problem was somewhat alleviated when, beginning in 1968, China agreed to accept local nationals who wished to leave Burma. According to the Rangoon *Working People's Daily* (May 23, 1968), about 1500 Chinese left Burma during the first five months of 1968. Additional flights to the mainland for returning Chinese took place that summer. In Burma as in Indonesia, China's grudging acceptance of her overseas nationals probably helped reduce the possibility that new incidents might occur to further aggravate relations.

The repatriation was one of several signs during 1968 of a possible change of attitude in Peking, one that held out hope for an eventual reconciliation. Statements about Burma from Peking were noticeably less vituperative than before; the GUB was referred to critically, but without the addition of expletives like "reactionary" and "fascist." More substantively, the Chinese Red Cross donated 10,000 *yuan* to the Burmese Red Cross to assist in the relief of hurricane victims (May); the Chinese chargé participated in the July 19 Martyrs' Day ceremony honoring Aung San; and Burmese officials attended a reception held by the Chinese military attaché in Rangoon commemorating the founding of the Chinese Army (August 1).[71]

Other Chinese statements later in 1968 and during early 1969 indicated, however, that Sino-Burmese tensions would not quickly be resolved. Whether because of continued political uncertainty in China, or because of Burma's hesitancy to respond to China's gestures, comments by the Peking media again assumed a strident tone. In mid-August, Radio Peking broadcast a vigorous denunciation of Ne Win by the CPB's first vice-chairman, Ba Thein Tin.[72] New protests concerning treatment of the overseas Chinese were sent to Rangoon.[73] CPB officials attended China's National Day reception in Peking even as Chinese Embassy personnel were hosting Burmese officials in Rangoon. Several direct Chinese diatribes against Ne Win's "reactionary clique" also were published or broadcast.[74]

The peculiar situation in which the proprieties of diplomacy continued to be respected at official functions but not always in news commentaries reached another plateau late in 1969. The burden of hostile remarks directed at the GUB fell to Burmese Communist sources; Chinese statements were sharply reduced in frequency and stridency. This time Ne Win did respond publicly. In an address of November 6 to a BSPP seminar, he reported heavy losses during the first eight months of the year in fighting with Communist insurgents near the China border. But instead of implicating China, he expressed a desire to "heal the wound of the 1967 incidents. Despite the clashes at the borders and the present situation," Ne Win said, "we shall do whatever we can on our part to restore the old friendship."[75] In the first half of 1970, when new clashes occurred in the northern Shan state that probably did have Chinese encouragement, no formal accusations were made by Rangoon, whose forces were withdrawn in March rather than engage the insurgents too close to the border.[76]

These events proved to be the forerunners of a diplomatic rapprochement. In addition to the attendance of both countries' officials at important ceremonies, Ne Win sent National Day greetings to Chou En-lai in October 1970. A new Burmese ambassador was appointed to China and took up his post in November. For the first time since 1967, a Burmese delegation attended the Canton

Autumn Trade Fair. The appointment of a Chinese ambassador to Rangoon seemed imminent.[z]

China and the CPB

The disruption of Sino-Burmese relations in 1967 set the stage for an acceleration of three trends in the Communist movement that had already begun earlier in the year: violence and destruction by Communist forces in the rural areas; inner-party purges; and the party's identification with Chinese military theories, political doctrine, and foreign policy.

Under the direction of Bo Tun Nyein, the White Flags carried out raids on villages and Buddhist monasteries in an attempt to strike fear into the peasant population, upset government administration, and produce rice shortages. One captured directive to a Peking returnee who apparently had charge of the vital Prome District party committee quoted Mao's dictum, "Political power grows out of the barrel of a gun," and demanded the "building of 'Red Power'" by killing.[77]

The call for greater violence was accompanied by a stepped-up assault on "revisionists" still believed to be in the CPB's ranks. In much the same way as, in China, criticism of the so-called Liu Shao-ch'i-Teng Hsiao-p'ing clique gradually expanded into a purge of other senior party officials,[78] Than Tun added to the Goshal-Htay group the name of Bo Yan Aung, a member of the central committee and one of the original leaders during Burma's drive for independence. Bo Yan Aung was executed December 26; and on December 31, Than Tun decided to extend the struggle against the "Ba Tin [Goshal]-Nga Htay-Yan Aung gang" down to the district level.[79]

On a third level, the CPB naturally had an interest in fully exploiting CPR-GUB tensions to propagandize its cause and establish its legitimacy. Giving full vent to the Maoist cult, party officials announced their unfettered devotion to the chairman's thoughts and precepts. One Burmese exile in Peking displayed his loyalty by stipulating that the party's armed struggle was bound to succeed so long as it adhered to Mao's thoughts, possessed an armed force under the party's leadership, and relied on the masses and a "worker-peasant alliance."[80] It was, of course, the traditional Chinese "tripod" formulation for protracted war, now embellished by professed obedience to Mao's proven prescriptions.

China's international position likewise received the CPB's approval—on the encouragement of armed struggle in India, condemnation of the pro-Soviet wing of the Indian Communist Party, support of Albania's anti-Soviet posture, Vietnam, the rebellion in Thailand, opposition to both Soviet aggression and Czech "capitulation" following the Russian invasion of August 1968, and Soviet responsibility for the border clashes with China in 1969. At least in Peking,

---

[z]In March 1971, Ch'en Chao-yüan, previously a chargé d'affaires of the CPR in India, was appointed to the Rangoon embassy as ambassador.

whichever Burmese Communist exiles lived there were apparently willing to countenance China's authority, for no splits, such as may have occurred within the Thai exile group, were hinted or reported. The earlier purge of "revisionist" elements among the exiles no doubt goes far toward explaining the apparent absence of splittism.

Overriding all these circumstances, however, is the fact that increased military activity, consolidation of the party's ranks, and adherence to Maoism neither significantly improved the White Flags' stature or power in Burma, nor tangibly changed China's involvement in their behalf. As in past years, the factors that had consistently inhibited the White Flags persisted late in 1967 and thereafter: (1) lack of cohesion at all leadership levels, furthered by the purges; (2) depletions of strength through defections and government attacks on the vulnerable Pegu Yoma base area; (3) alienation of the population, making the party unable to form either a mass base or a workable alliance with the rebel ethnic groups; and (4) isolation from the international Communist movement.

Than Tun's rectification program seems to have "purified" the party at the expense of its stability. The CPB Politburo was left with three men—and then two when, on September 24, 1968, Than Tun was assassinated by one of his own men, who thereafter surrendered to the government.[81] (Acknowledgement of Than Tun's death did not come from the CPB or Peking until late March 1969, at which time it was also announced that Thakin Zin had become the new party chairman.) Moreover, among the Peking returnees and central committee figures, some key supporters of Than Tun were either executed or died in battle.[a] Sizable losses were also sustained through battle casualties and defections. As a result of the Burmese Army's spring and summer 1968 offensives, four other members of the Prome District Party Committee reportedly perished besides Bo Zeya, and several others surrendered.[82]

In the party's campaign for popular and ethnic minority support, other serious weaknesses remained. Despite an ability to move freely about the more sparsely populated sections of the country, the White Flag irregulars could neither establish firm territorial control nor achieve sustained peasant support.[83] The White Flags apparently defied Mao's most elementary instructions concerning the troops' conduct in dealing with and winning over the masses. The peasants' grievances against the government, mainly of an economic nature, were probably deflected rather than exacerbated by the burning, killing, and pillaging of the White Flags.

---

[a]Among them were Bo Zeya, the principal military field leader, who was killed in a raid by the Burmese Army on the party's Prome headquarters (April 1968); Bo Tun Nyein, director of the Marxist-Leninist Training School and one of Than Tun's henchmen, whom Than Tun ordered executed after the Army's raid; and Tun Shein, who lost his life in 1968 for alledgedly trying to subvert the "Burmese Cultural Revolution" he had once ardently championed. A Burmese newspaper (*Botataung*, April 12, 1969) reported that of the 27 party members who had returned from Peking for the 1963 peace talks, only 12 remained at large.

Nor were the White Flags successful at invigorating the NDUF; as before, dissident factions of the nationalities were as inclined to reject alliance with the Communists as to spurn government entreaties. Among the Karens, for instance, Mahn Ba Zan's KNUP (the so-called "Red Karens," who had split with the more moderate KNDO) reportedly ended its ties to the White Flags in December 1967 and rejoined forces with other Karen rebels in a previously established non-Communist National Liberation Council.[84] In 1970, the KNUP backed U Nu in his bid to regain power.[b] The Maoist character of the CPB was also an important deterrent to cooperation with the Kachins. Although Naw Seng, the KIA leader, was elevated to the CPB Central Committee during 1968, other Kachin rebel groups remained divided on alliance with the Communists, Burmese and Chinese. And how dependable Naw Seng's forces will be as the Communists' ally is arguable based on the past record.

Another source of weakness was the isolation of the CPB within the international Communist movement. No less after the Sino-Burmese break than before, the CPB failed to attract the political support of other Asian and non-Asian parties and socialist countries. Only the Chinese and Albanian parties were behind the CPB after July 1967. For its part, the Soviet Union vigorously denounced the Maoist take-over of the CPB and appealed to the Burmese Communists to throw off the Chinese yoke, reestablish their independence, and join in some form of coalition with the GUB.[c] Other socialist countries and parties also maintained friendly ties to Burma, including North Vietnam, East Germany, and North Korea.

[b]Former Premier Nu, released from detention in the fall of 1966, left Burma and traveled extensively during 1969 in search of support for a new political alliance that would overthrow Ne Win. In October 1969, U Nu was granted political asylum in Thailand on condition that he not engage in activities against the GUB. But he set up a Parliamentary Democracy Party in Bangkok whose opposition program—although not identified as such—began to be broadcast in April 1970 to Burma by a group calling itself the Patriotic Youth Front. Late in May 1970, U Nu's party, the KNUP, and the New Mon State Party agreed to collaborate to bring down Ne Win, establish a "federal union republic," and restructure state lines to allow all ethnic peoples greater autonomy. Since then, U Nu's headquarters have reportedly been shifted to the Thai-Burma border in Tak province, from which he directs his partisans and broadcasts his messages. See *Botataung*, October 22, 1970 (a report on U Nu's activities by a Burmese defense ministry official); *Bangkok World*, February 24, 1971 (an interview with Mahn Ba Zan); and *New York Times*, January 31, 1971, p. 3.

[c]Well before the purges in the CPB, Moscow's commentaries on the Burmese political scene had revealed concern that the transition to socialism required much more than socialist programs—it demanded the formation of a worker-peasant united front of "anti-imperialist, anti-feudal, and anti-capitalist forces . . . " (*Izvestiia*, December 26, 1967.) After Than Tun's rectification campaign and the falling out between Peking and Rangoon, Moscow addressed itself to the Burmese Communist rank-and-file, arguing that identification with China would spell disaster for the party and that "the 1955 line" of peaceful coexistence with Burma's anti-capitalist leaders remained the best alternative. Radio Moscow Burmese-language broadcasts of July 7, 1967 and March 26, 1969, and English-language broadcast of March 27, 1969.

The CPB's failure to make headway against the Burmese government probably helps to explain China's continued refrainment from providing the White Flags with significant material assistance. Taking a hard look at the political and military ineffectiveness of the Burmese party, Chinese leaders may have decided that, beyond political support, only limited supplies were warranted.[d] Not only would it be difficult to transfer aid to the White Flags' central Burma base area; based on the party's performance, the aid may have been judged unlikely to be used efficiently. The infrequent reports from Burma concerning Chinese-made weapons captured from the insurgents seem in this instance accurately to reflect the limitations of Chinese aid.[85]

China's stinginess has been alluded to indirectly by the occasional reference in CPB propaganda to self-reliance. A speech by Ba Thein Tin in August 1967 suggested that restrictions on the amount of aid the White Flags could expect was decided upon in Peking soon after the rupture with Rangoon. Perhaps addressing concern in the party ranks about China's active support, Ba Thein Tin said the insurgents needed to adhere to Mao's doctrine of self-reliance and discounted the view of "some people" that successful warfare depended on being "geographically contiguous to a socialist country."[86]

Chinese reports on White Flag activities have been much more liberally infused with talk of self-reliance, although the same reports have expressed confidence in the ultimate success of the Communist revolution in Burma. In a message to the CPB on March 28, 1968, for example, the CCP Central Committee twice praised Than Tun's followers for relying on their own efforts in having "pushed the Burmese people's revolutionary armed struggle to a completely new stage."[87] When Than Tun's death was reported, the Chinese Central Committee noted that he had led the CPB "on the basis of self-reliance and a protracted armed struggle against imperialism and the Ne Win military group's dictatorial rule."[e] Typical of her advice to Communist parties leading

---

[d]One indication, though not from a high-level Chinese source, that by late 1967 some Chinese Communist cadres were aware of the White Flags' deficiencies appears in a speech on the international situation by Feng Piao, Director of the Information Department of *Jen-min jih-pao*. As quoted in a Red Guard tabloid, Feng noted that some Communist parties had made mistakes in implementing Mao's thoughts with respect to such specific questions as "how to arouse the peasants, how to carry out agrarian reform, how to carry out the new democratic revolution.... Some places have not even solved the most fundamental question—the question of Party leadership. Because of this, there are bound to be twists and turns. For example, [the Communist party in] Burma has also not solved these problems." *Hung-se tsao-fan-che* (*Red Rebel*, Chiangmen), December 13, 1967; trans. in American Consulate-General, Hong Kong, *Current Background*, No. 850, April 3, 1968, p. 4.

[e]In a message of March 16, 1969; text in *Jen-min jih-pao*, March 19, 1969, p. 1. The CPB's statement on Than Tun's death did not stress self-reliance. The party's central committee listed its assets as being the integration of Marxism-Leninism and Maoism with Burmese conditions; its experienced leadership; a party-led army; a mass base; a united-front organization; and worldwide, but especially Chinese, support and guidance. *Peking Review*, No. 13, March 28, 1969, p. 6.

rebellions under adverse indigenous circumstances, the CPR has belabored the point that the Burmese Communists, despite over twenty years of struggle, must overcome still more difficulties and expect additional "twists and turns" before they can win the revolution. "Persistence is victory" has been the standard Chinese advice to the CPB.[88] The Burmese Communist broadcasts from south China that were inaugurated in March 1971, at the time of the Chinese ambassador's return to Rangoon, were Peking's way of reinforcing self-reliance while retaining influence over CPB strategy.*f*

Increased Chinese contact with some elements of rebellious minority forces beginning in 1968 may have been Peking's alternative means of applying pressure on the GUB. To what extent Chinese assistance that previously went to the White Flags was channeled elsewhere is not known. It does appear that after a "North-East Command" under Naw Seng was established in the far north, along the China border, some military supplies and equipment were provided from Yünnan Province.[89] Naw Seng's forces, recruited from several tribal groups but not under the CPB, were probably responsible for the serious fighting along the border in 1969 and in the first half of 1970. These actions posed no threat to central Burma; but they did keep the Burmese Army occupied and thus may have served China's purpose of demonstrating that, with limited assistance, the border area could be kept insecure.*g*

A second explanation for China's willingness to supply minority and White Flag rebels with arms but limit their availability may be that Peking's leaders, particularly those who wished to mend fences abroad (as Chou En-lai had been able to do with Cambodia), did not want to close out the possibility of an eventual normalization of relations with Rangoon. Had the CPR openly and substantially assisted Burma's rebellious groups, Ne Win might have come under pressure internally to respond publicly to China's interference and begin to move toward closer political and military ties with the United States and the Soviet Union. China's fluctuating public statements about Burma, her maintenance of diplomatic relations with the GUB, and her self-limited role in support of the insurgents were all consistent with the aim of keeping an open line to Rangoon and avoiding provoking a reorientation of Burma's foreign policy.

*f*A "Voice of the People of Burma" began broadcasting March 28, 1971, the anniversary date of the start of the White Flag rebellion. By giving the CPB its own radio outlet, Chinese leaders avoided having to identify with Burmese Communist propaganda attacks on the GUB that formerly were carried over Radio Peking.

*g*Another purpose of Chinese assistance to rebels in Burma's far north may have been to facilitate contact with dissident Naga tribesmen in India's Nagaland State. The Nagas have been in revolt against the Indian government since 1955, and in mid-1967, Peking began speaking of their "liberation struggle." There have been reports of Chinese training and supplies for some Naga factions willing to accept outside assistance. See *New York Times*, April 4, 1968, p. 3, and Crane, p. 12. In an effort to cut down illegal border crossings by the Nagas into Kachin territory, Burmese government officials have conferred regularly with Indian officials. Much to Peking's displeasure—as indicated in an NCNA broadcast of March 29, 1968, for instance—Ne Win has met with Mrs. Gandhi to improve border patrolling, and demarcation of the common boundary has been achieved.

China's Place in Burmese Neutralism

Despite the many stylistic and substantive differences between Burmese and Cambodian neutralism (under Sihanouk), both may be judged successful foreign policies if the test of success is the maintenance of territorial and decisionmaking sovereignty, not strict nonpartisanism. Neutralism alone cannot account for that success, nor will neutralism necessarily remain a viable foreign policy. But thus far, the kind of neutralism Burma has practiced has probably best served Burma's interests—as Sihanouk's policies served Cambodia's—in terms of security and independent decisionmaking.

Security

In orienting neutralism toward certain of the unspoken (political) demands of Peking, Burmese governments aimed at enhancing, not sacrificing, national security. Rangoon had to take into account soon after independence was achieved that, in the event of an external threat, the prospects of Western assistance were low. Burma, under both U Nu and Ne Win, had to remove herself as an arena of possible big-power confrontation and seek to stabilize the border region abutting on the most likely security threat, Communist China. Neutralism accomplished these objectives: through circumscribed aid and diplomatic ties, Burmese governments were able to avoid compromising entanglements with any one power bloc; through friendship, nonaggression, and border treaties with Peking, they reduced substantially the likelihood of major Chinese penetrations and, beyond that, added to China's valuation of Burma and helped minimize CPR contacts with Burma's Communist and non-Communist rebels.

An argument could be made that in adopting these policies, Burma handicapped herself: in the name of neutralism, she became heavily indebted to the aid of the Communist countries and lost opportunities for economic help that would have been available through Western, and especially, American, sources; by appearing to side more often with the Communist countries than with the West on outstanding international questions, she limited her freedom of diplomatic action; and by concluding the friendship and nonaggression treaty with China, she foreclosed outside assistance to meet aggression. Yet, none of these objections stands up well under close examination. Soviet and Chinese aid may not have been the most suitable for Burma's long-term growth, and perhaps a greater infusion of Western aid, or Burma's greater and earlier reliance on internationally administered assistance programs, would have made a difference. But in security terms—and Burma's aid policy was based on security considerations, not economic calculations—it is difficult to see how Soviet and Chinese loans and credits impinged upon Burma's foreign or domestic policies. In fact, Burma's attitude toward China was largely irrelevant to the size or composition of the aid of the Communist countries, which in any case accounted for below 20 percent of all monetary commitments to Burma (through 1966)[90] and has been almost exclusively economic.

Secondly, while Burma more often sided with or did not oppose the policies of the Communist countries than those of the non-Communist countries, this is not evidence of Burma's vulnerability to coercion by foreign powers. Burma has had to make allowances for the fact that China is best situated to apply sanctions against her "unfriendly" behavior. But Burma has not become a Communist base, given Communist countries special access or occupation privileges on or through Burmese territory, nor become a Chinese dependency. Should aggression against Burma occur, she would not be impeded by the treaty with China from exercising her right of self-defense, bringing the matter before the United Nations, or calling for assistance from other nations.

Nor has internal security been undercut by the character of Burma's foreign policy. One of the principal aims of Burma's friendly policy toward China was to reduce or eliminate any pretext for China's direct involvement with the White Flags or the ethnic rebels. Prior to the events of June-July 1967, that goal was fairly well achieved; Peking stood aloof from the White Flags and restricted its contacts with them and the Kachins to low-level training and indoctrination. Even thereafter, Peking's material support of rebel groups in Burma, the White Flags included, remained modest—it was not of a level or calibre to indicate a Chinese interest in generating a revolution.

Of importance in Peking's disposition was an awareness of the inherent difficulties in promoting the interests of clients, Communist and non-Communist, who are of doubtful reliability and cohesiveness. The Burmese government thus has a built-in defense against Chinese influence over the White Flags and the minorities: the White Flags' emphasis on violence, problems of leadership, and organizational weaknesses have alienated them from the population and from other rebellious factions; the minority nationalities, whose basic demands concern increased or absolute political, cultural, and economic autonomy,[h] have by and large rejected alliance with the Communists (who are Burmans, not minority peoples), especially since the CPB's identification with the Maoist cult. These two complementary factors—Peking's revocable commitment to the Burmese rebels of all persuasions, and the vulnerabilities, mutual suspicions, and parochial nationalisms common to the rebels—have given the Burmese government many opportunities to put down or come to terms with internal opposition. The GUB's failure to take advantage of the absence of a

---

[h]On the tactical and transient nature of alignments between ethnic minority rebels and the Communists, see Badgley, "The Communist Parties of Burma," p. 305. Regarding the issues that generally persist between the GUB and the minorities—notably, the composition and functions of the Burmese Army within the states, and the degree of control by the states over their own economic resources—see *Far Eastern Economic Review*, January 16, 1969, p. 107. Crane (p. 15) contends that the minorities, far from merely resisting "Burmanization," are moving in the direction of "communal nationalism," that is, a common sense of separatism from the Burmans. This trend, he suggests, transcends national boundaries to encompass minority peoples along Burma's frontiers who would prefer "decentralized, confederative regionalism" to belonging to a nation whose boundaries were determined in the colonial past. But whether the loyalties of the Karens, Kachins, Shans, and other peoples living within Burma are in fact expanding to communal scope seems debatable in view of their strong tribal attachments and suspicion of outsiders (see following note).

united front among the dissident forces may be attributed mainly to its own tactics and attitudes, and to the multifaceted character of the "minority problem,"[i] not to external interference or any shackles imposed by foreign policy considerations.

Decisionmaking

Foreign and domestic policymaking generally has not been as encumbered by Burma's relations with China as is sometimes supposed. Burma, unlike Sihanouk's Cambodia, has taken account of China's international position by maintaining a discreet silence concerning key events such as the Tibet invasion, the Sino-Indian border war, the Laotian and Vietnam conflicts, and the U.S.-South Vietnamese incursions in Cambodia. But in other cases—including Burma's signing of the Test Ban Agreement, her refusal to condemn American involvement in Vietnam, her maintenance of friendly relations with India, South Vietnam, South Korea, Thailand, and the post-Sihanouk Cambodian government, and her reluctance to criticize the United States or the Soviet Union—Burma's foreign policy has not reflected Chinese preferences. Burma has not been, or claimed to be, a passive neutral; but neither has she permitted the interests of other powers, such as China, to take preference over her own.

Well before the break with China, and continuing thereafter, the Burmese government became increasingly confident and assertive in foreign affairs. Burma improved border cooperation with neighboring countries (India, Thailand, and Pakistan), broadened diplomatic contacts with the major powers, and, hesitantly, expressed interest in expanded trade and other ties with three of the "offshore" Southeast Asian countries (Malaysia, Singapore, and Indonesia). Like Cambodia under Sihanouk, however, Burma was wary of involvement in any regional organizations. With the exception of the Colombo Plan, which is not an organization but a forum for aid agreements and programming, the GUB preferred bilateral to multilateral activities;[j] the latter risk not only compromis-

---

[i]As several writers have observed, the Burmese government needs not one but many minority policies in view of the numerous distinctions—in language, customs, religion, habitations, and methods of cultivation, to name a few—among and within the minority nationalities. Each minority is distinguishable by the fact that it considers itself different from the others and that, within each, there exist subminorities which regard themselves as somewhat unique. Moreover, although the minorities share a desire for greater autonomy, some of them do not reject inclusion in the Burman civilization and the Burmese Union. For further discussion, see F.K. Lehman, "Ethnic Categories in Burma and the Theory of Social Systems," and Maran La Raw, "Toward a Basis for Understanding the Minorities in Burma: The Kachin Example," in Kunstadter, ed., I, chs. 2 and 3; and E.R. Leach, *Political Systems of Highland Burma: A Study of Kachin Social Structure*, Harvard University Press, Cambridge, Mass., 1954.

[j]Burma has received grants and loans from the World Bank, the International Monetary Fund, and the United Nations Specialized Agencies and Expanded Technical Assistance Fund. (The GUB is not, however, a member of the Asian Development Bank.) Since 1952, moreover, Burma has received about $16 million of $2 billion dispensed under the Colombo Plan's auspices in capital aid and technical assistance. The Plan has been praised by the Burmese government for its "totally nonpolitical character." See *Forward*, Vol. VI, No. 8, December 1, 1967, pp. 1 and 6.

ing Burmese neutralism by their political and/or military character, but also incurring China's displeasure.[91] It is also questionable whether, politics aside, any existing regional body in Southeast Asia would prove economically beneficial. For all these reasons, Burma has not been receptive to membership proposals in organizations such as ASEAN, whose members (Thailand, Indonesia, Philippines, Singapore, and Malaysia) have only limited trade relations with Burma and are on unfriendly terms with China. Still, Ne Win has not ruled out eventual participation in ASEAN or some other group; and, during state visits to Malaysia and Singapore in April 1968, he expressed Burma's full support and cooperation for regional undertakings.[92]

Nor, finally, have the requirements of Burma's relationship with China predisposed decisionmaking in the domestic context. The poor record of Burma's economy in recent years, particularly in rice production and industrial output under state ownership, has to do with the ineffectiveness in management, planning, and operation of the "Burmese Way to Socialism." These problems are traceable in great part to the military's domination of politics and administration at the national and local levels. Whether Ne Win proves able to cope with them—for instance, by improving the supply, distribution, and price systems, by permitting the revival of private and semiprivate enterprises, and by broadening the government's political constituency—will be determined by changes in his own thinking, not by external developments. The GUB's success or failure in its economic and political programs, as in its handling of dissidence, is chiefly a function of its own capacity, confidence, and compassion.

The China Tangle

Neutralism in Burma has kept the "China problem" out of domestic politics. But the successful resolution of Burma's internal difficulties is relevant to her relations with China, for the persistence of economic chaos, political stagnation, and rebellion can only weaken the government, encourage China's undoubted preference for seeing the removal of Ne Win (who stands as a symbol of the 1967 riots), and, if sufficiently intense, dissuade China from coming to terms with the Revolutionary Council. Burma's bargaining position with respect to Peking improves with the amelioration of internal tensions, and weakens as those tensions increase.

Like Rangoon, Peking can play a waiting game, allowing relations to remain tense but tolerable for both sides. In this case, China would probably continue her low-level support of the CPB and other dissidents while maintaining close watch over Ne Win's actions and political future. Friendly relations could then either be gradually restored (as seemed to be the trend as 1971 began) or dangled as bait before any Burmese with good prospects for replacing him. For China, the absence of friendly relations does not mean the loss of influence over the GUB's foreign policy, only the loss of the political advantages that were derived in the past from having normal, uncomplicated ties with a neutral government. The Burmese leaders, while recognizing that Peking can afford to be cautious in approaching a reconciliation, will certainly want to encourage it, not because China's friendship is valued in itself, but because it is instrumental to assuring China's continued restraint toward the White Flags and the minority rebels. But whatever China's policy, the GUB is bound to persist in attempting to destroy the Communists' military and political organization in Burma.

7

China and Southeast Asia:
A Concluding Assessment

China's Policies Toward Southeast Asia

An assessment of China's relations with Thailand, Cambodia, and Burma provides a useful basis for analyzing the motivations, instruments, and objectives of China's foreign policy in Southeast Asia generally. In particular, the case studies make it possible to identify, or at least speculate about, the respective roles of ideology (the Maoist world view) and practicality in foreign policymaking, the conditions under which some policy instruments are used and others rejected or deemphasized, and the elements that comprise China's regional objectives.

The Motivating Forces in Chinese Foreign Policy

Every Chinese foreign policy decision has probably involved both ideological presumptions and practical evaluations. Indeed, it would be difficult to imagine any policy in any government as having evolved solely on the basis of "realistic" judgment, without having been influenced by the philosophical inclinations of the decisionmakers. In the Chinese Communist case, because the ideology stems from the similar experiences as revolutionaries of an extraordinarily cohesive group of decisionmakers,[a] it is sufficiently distinctive to be identified in its functions.

In foreign policymaking, the Chinese Communist ideology performs three different functions. First, the ideology orients the leadership to a particular perspective on international affairs. The concept of struggle is of central importance here. Conflict within individual societies and between nations derives, in Mao's view, from inherent contradictions involving contending

---

[a]The guerrilla war experiences of Chinese Communist leaders have been particularly influential on their perceptions of international events. (See Tang Tsou and Morton H. Halperin, "Mao Tse-tung's Revolutionary Strategy and Peking's International Behavior," *American Political Science Review*, Vol. LIX, No. 1, March 1965, pp. 80-99.) These and other commonalities in the backgrounds of senior Chinese officials have not produced agreement on every foreign policy issue; but they probably have contributed to some kind of perceptual consensus. Even though Cultural Revolutionary documents indicate that Mao's role in foreign policy formulation may have been significantly restricted between 1958 and 1965, other leaders (including Liu Shao-ch'i and Chou En-lai) probably carried on foreign policy discussions and framed decisions in the Maoist litany.

political, economic, and social forces. Within societies, such conflicts broaden and sharpen to the point where external intervention by imperialism invariably occurs at the behest of "reactionary" rulers, thus transforming a revolutionary civil war into a local war.[1] Between nations, including Communist ones, such conflicts may not lead to war, but they do produce serious tensions. In both cases, the Chinese Communist ideology demands unremitting struggle: in the first, a relationship of "oppressed" to "oppressor" exists that demands "a sympathetic and supporting attitude" by China and other genuinely socialist nations toward their revolutionary ally, "the people" (as represented in the Marxist-Leninist party);[2] in the second, a matter of principle is at stake that is tied to the future direction of the world Communist movement and that consequently rules out compromise and capitulation. The more these two forms of struggle continue, the more are the Chinese Communists confirmed in the correctness of their appraisal that contradictions existed and that struggle was inevitable.[3]

The concept of struggle not only helps us to understand why the Chinese Communists, because of their ideology, have an interest in revolutionary change. It also affords an explanation of the importance to them of having an adversary relationship with hostile forces. Struggle is said to give "evidence [of the enemies'] weakness and their fear of the increasingly developing revolution."[4] Because it involves conflict between revolutionary and anti-Communist, anti-China forces, struggle that pits "oppressed" against "oppressor" also reflects the strength of China's influence. "The more anti-Chinese U.S. imperialism, modern revisionism, and the reactionaries of all countries are, the greater will be the influence of the Chinese Revolution."[5] Only through struggle and the resistance it meets can China's distinctive international position be clearly established.[b] Thus, in a very real sense, China (like other powers, big and small) needs an enemy: it enables Peking to draw a clear line between itself and its ideological or military opponent; it "proves" that China has not exaggerated her claims to being surrounded by hostile forces; it enables the Chinese to focus their

---

[b]As put by Commentator, "If they [U.S. imperialism, Soviet revisionism, and the reactionaries] did not oppose us but praised us and supported us, that would ruin everything; wouldn't we then have become one of them? . . . " In "The Enemy's Being Anti-China is a Good Thing for Us," *Jen-min jih-pao*, August 17, 1967, p. 5. Lin Piao, in his Report to the CCP of April 1, 1969, following the border clash with Soviet troops, said that Russian and American attempts to "isolate" China do China an "honor." Not only are the Chinese given greater incentives to achieve; Soviet-American hostility also "serves to prove to the whole world that China has drawn a clear line between herself on the one hand and U.S. imperialism and Soviet revisionism on the other." *Peking Review*, No. 18, April 30, 1969, p. 34.

When Sihanouk was being tried *in absentia* for treason by the Lon Nol government, Mao was quoted as having said: "If we are opposed by the enemy, that is good, since it proves that we have drawn a clear line of demarcation between the enemy and ourselves. If the enemy strongly opposes us and calls us utterly stupid and without a single virtue, that is even better; it proves not only that we have drawn a clear line of demarcation between the enemy and ourselves but also that we have been very successful in our work." Commentator, *Jen-min jih-pao*, July 8, 1970, p. 4.

propaganda effort, domestic and international, on a particular target; and it may help the regime to rationalize keeping the Chinese society and armed forces in a prolonged state of tension.[6]

Aspects of the concept of struggle in Chinese Communist ideology have been observed in China's perceptions of the three Southeast Asian countries. China's open hostility toward Thailand in 1965, Burma in 1967, and Cambodia in 1970 was in each case explained as having resulted from the contradictions between their governments and the people, and from their subservience to United States neocolonialism. In effect, at those times the three governments had come into an "antagonistic" relationship with China; and this kind of contradiction required that China proclaim support for the ideologically most suitable, if not the most reliable or effective, revolutionary ally, the Communist movement in each country. From the Chinese Communist viewpoint, when the United States thereafter continued to build up its military resources in Thailand and to increase counterinsurgency assistance to the RTG, this was an inevitable American reaction that was bound to intensify and expand the Communist-led rebellion. The RTG's cooperation with the Americans and its "oppressive" tactics could only deepen the contradictions, not only between it and its people, but also between it and China, and between China and the United States. China's adversary relationship with the United States was probably further cemented. Increased American involvement in Thailand, coincident with fighting in Vietnam and Laos, lent substance to official Chinese appraisals that the American threat was not only real, but also useful in demonstrating the potency of China's revolutionary influence and in spurring the Chinese population to alertness and war-preparedness.[7]

A second function of ideology is to inform policy. It dictates that struggle requires time and persistence—the "protracted fighting"—in order that new opportunities for advance may arise and that contradictions may be successfully resolved. It does not rule out flexibility and compromise where basic goals and principles are not at stake,[8] but it does contend that lasting accommodations with hostile forces—imperialism, reactionaries, neocolonialism, and modern revisionism—should not be expected. It sees the worldwide revolutionary process as unfolding in a way favorable to the forces of socialism; but it regards setbacks to the revolution as being not only inevitable and reversible, but also as acceptable and sometimes even beneficial, stages in the overall advance.[9] With respect to policy toward revolutionary movements, the ideology asserts the desirability of situations of flux and turmoil over static, tensionless situations; a controllable amount of "agitation" is the sine qua non of revolutionary progress.[10] Ideology also influences the Maoist insistence on a tripartite united front, including the Communist party in the vanguard, a Red Army to win its military objectives, and a temporary alliance of "all those classes that are capable of being united."[11] Finally, Maoist ideology, because it represents "practical" doctrine rather than "pure" Marxism-Leninism,[12] acts to limit the extent of Chinese involvement in, and responsibility for, revolutions China supports. Other revolutionary parties must evolve their own "practical ideologies" while accepting Peking's version of Marxism-Leninism. Ultimately, success in revolution depends on the ability of those in rebellion to adapt relevant Chinese experiences to their own struggle; the Chinese Communist Revolution is not an exact blueprint for success, and hence China's support, no matter how great, cannot determine how well the revolutionaries perform.[13]

These concepts, which have become part of Communist China's revolutionary ideology but also derive from the leadership's own experiences, guided China's policy toward Southeast Asia. Protracted struggle and self-reliance were consistent themes in Chinese statements—and were reflected in Chinese actions—concerning revolutionary movements in Burma, Thailand, and post-Sihanouk Cambodia. The Communist parties and fronts there were said to be following the Maoist road and were praised for their adaptations of the Chinese Communist revolutionary experience. But Chinese commentaries were quick to caution the Communist movements that they faced a long, uphill battle, that there would be setbacks along the way, and that the outcome of their struggle would depend in the final analysis on their own capabilities. Compromises with antagonistic forces were evidently also advised, as in the 1963 peace negotiations between the Burmese government and the CPB; but the fact of negotiations did not mean capitulation on any terms, nor the termination of China's moral and limited material support of the White Flags. If only to maintain the saliency of their ideology at a time of sharp differences with the Soviet Union over revolutionary doctrine, the Chinese Communists had to (and still must) impress upon Communist movements like the CPB that tactical accommodations with the enemy are always acceptable, that temporary reversals are to be expected, but that victory in the long run is assured so long as they adhere to Maoist political and strategic principles. Ideology thus influences the political orientation and military strategy of local parties, explains why China's involvement in support of revolutions abroad cannot be decisive, and rationalizes failure.

The third function of ideology is to provide foreign policy statements and, presumably, foreign policy discussions, with theoretical underpinning. The characterization of friends and enemies, of developing situations, and of alternative strategies reflects, and is reflected in, the ideological vocabulary that frames every statement of the Chinese Communist standpoint. Here again, the concept of struggle is crucial. In their public statements, the Chinese Communists, whether addressing the global situation or specific events, consistently phrase their interest in terms of contending (contradictory) forces. Revolutionary movements that China chose to support, such as in Burma and Thailand, were said to be engaged in struggle (political and military) against domestic reactionaries and their imperialist allies. Neutral Cambodia, when she was friendly toward China, was always depicted as engaged in intense struggle (resistance) against American, Thai, and South Vietnamese aggression. And Burma, before the summer of 1967, was portrayed as having scored impressive economic gains and attained increased political stability by struggling against the adversities of nature, political fragmentation, and the unfavorable legacy of a colonial past.

The Maoist revolutionary ideology, by emphasizing situations of conflict, probably leads to an exaggeration of external threats and may distort the intentions of nations unfriendly to China. But the ideology does not bias the leadership in favor of incautious policies, as evidenced in the stress on flexibility, self-reliance, and perseverance. Nor does the ideology predetermine the choice of conciliatory or hostile policies. The leadership's evaluations of specific events, and the content of China's relations with specific governments, here interact with ideology in Chinese decisionmaking.

During most of the period from 1950 to 1970 in Southeast Asia, Communist China proved capable of coexisting with neutral governments at the same time as she supported revolutionary movements in various ways against hostile regimes. So long as relations with Cambodian and Burmese governments were friendly, dissident organizations in those two countries were either ignored or given just enough support to maintain their allegiance and viability. This consistency of policy cut across so-called "hard" and "soft" periods in China's foreign policy as a whole. When support of the Thai Communists was announced in 1965, the Burmese Communists were still left without meaningful Chinese backing. That situation changed in mid-1967, after Sino-Burmese relations deteriorated. Yet, the ideological frenzy in China that had played a major part in the events leading to the rupture—as it did in the Sino-Cambodian confrontation—did not blind Peking's leaders to the weaknesses of the Thai Communist movement or lead them to support a North Vietnamese-sponsored insurgency in Cambodia.

In each of the three cases, China's decisions to support the antigovernment forces were calculated responses to specific events. The influence of ideology probably lay in the selection of weak Communist parties (in Thailand and Burma) as the recipients of China's political and material support. Even then, the apparent shift of some of China's limited assistance from the Communist parties to dissident ethnic minorities (the Meo in north Thailand, the Kachin and Shan rebels in Burma) late in the 1960s—accompanied by the claim, however, that the activities of these groups were those of the Communist party—showed the predominance of practical over ideological considerations. Chinese leaders apparently decided that they could exert leverage over unfriendly neighboring governments more effectively through groups anxious to defend their traditional, parochial interests than through Communist revolutionaries.

If practical considerations have significantly shaped China's policies in Southeast Asia, it might be argued that China's decision whether to support a government or a revolutionary group opposed to it has depended on Peking's evaluation of the strengths and weaknesses of each. Where the prospects for rebellion were good, China responded with an increased investment without regard to the complexion of state-to-state relations. The case studies, however, do not support this explanation. Revolutionary prospects in Burma were reasonably favorable in 1949-1950 and again in 1966-1967, when the White Flags were militarily strongest and the government was beset by economic problems and peasant discontent. Yet, China's attitude and actions were guided by those of the GUB. On the other hand, China has supported the Communists and other dissident groups in Thailand because, even though revolutionary prospects are dismal, outside support is probably deemed an economical and risk-free way of inhibiting the Thai government's involvement in Indochina and undermining its authority in the northern rural areas by demonstrating that the government cannot deal effectively and decisively with the rebels. In mid-1967, the Peking leadership may have considered a break with Rangoon acceptable because the stability and effectiveness of the GUB, in contrast to the Cambodian government, could be more easily undermined through support of the Communist party. Here again, however, China was apparently motivated to disrupt friendly relations with Burma not because the CPB was getting stronger and the GUB weaker, but because the quality of Sino-Burmese relations had changed. Similarly in Cambodia, the change in Chinese policy in 1970 was precipitated by the local government's shift from friendly to hostile neutralism, not by a shift in the balance of Communist and non-Communist forces in the country. Opportunism in China's policy followed the breakdown of diplomacy. Once the three governments turned against China, their strengths and weaknesses then became relevant to China's choice of policy and tactics.[c]

The Instruments of Foreign Policy

Insofar as practicality motivates Chinese foreign policy, China's statements and actions indicate that policy toward revolutionary movements in Southeast Asia is primarily a function of state-to-state relations rather than a function of domestic Chinese politics, the receptivity of insurrectionaries to Chinese ideology and material aid, or China's capacity to provide assistance. Where the content of state-to-state relations was acceptable to Peking, as in Burma (except for 1967 to mid-1970, when Chinese politics *was* a critical factor), and in Cambodia under Sihanouk, China compensated friendly governments through proclamations and demonstrations of support. In the first category, the Chinese media offered words of praise and encouragement, Chinese diplomats exchanged visits and reaffirmed a policy of friendship, and Peking officials constantly stressed the reality of the "five principles of peaceful coexistence." In the second category, the low-level partnership of Peking and dissidents in friendly countries was meant to show China's adherence to a policy of noninterference. That is, in return for a government's avoidance of provocative relations with China's enemies, China pledged no subversive coordination with anti-regime

[c]One comment by a Chinese Communist official suggests that Peking may consider political order a *desirable* characteristic of developing societies because it can become the first step toward a friendly policy toward China. Feng Piao, the previously quoted information director of *Jen-min jih-pao*, said in 1967 that the anti-China attitude of a government reflects its domestic contradictions, its political weakness, and its vulnerability to revolution. He cited the examples of Burma and India. If the government is stable, unified, and effective, he implied, it should have no reason to fear revolution and every reason to be friendly toward China—and to have that friendship reciprocated. *Current Background*, p. 7.

elements, including overseas Chinese.[d] Aid and trade, as well as friendship and border treaties, were also instruments of state policy toward cooperative governments, in the first two cases to reward compliant behavior,[e] in the latter two, to perpetuate it.

Whether toward friendly governments or toward unfriendly ones, like Thailand, Peking consistently maintained at least low-level, unobtrusive ties to native Communists and leftists. In doing so, Peking seems to have had two distinct purposes: first, to exert some control over the public and underground activities of these potential allies, the value of whose outspoken loyalty to Peking in the ideological dispute with Moscow had to be balanced against the embarrassment they could cause to China's foreign relations with smaller powers; second, to possess leverage that *could* be used (but still controlled) against the legitimate governments should they turn *un*friendly or, once unfriendly, should they not be responsive to Peking's initial warnings.[f] In the Thailand case, for example, unfriendly relations were, until 1965, evidently not sufficiently inimical to Chinese interests to justify Peking's open identification with the Thai Communists' cause. But when circumstances changed beginning late in 1964, the CPT leaders in China were readied to receive moral and material support. The *level* of Chinese support of Communist movements was intimately related to the status of governmental relations, as illustrated in Table 7-1.

---

[d]Only a small percentage of the overseas Chinese (in Burma and Cambodia) were probably ever in touch with Chinese Communist representatives, despite the 1967 incidents. This does not mean that the three governments regarded the overseas Chinese as politically inconsequential; to the contrary, they seem to have retained the old fear of a Peking fifth column. In fact, however, China never openly sought to exploit that fear, contrary to the assertion of Williams (p. 69) that "the Chinese in countries hostile to the People's Republic . . . are called upon to be disobedient to their governments" whereas, in other countries, "Chinese are encouraged to be inconspicuous, decent settlers." Peking probably was aware that to return hostility toward China with the encouragement of local Chinese agitation would dilute the appeal of indigenous Communists and bring quick reprisals down on the entire overseas Chinese community. For an excellent analysis that portrays Peking's aloofness from the overseas Chinese, see Stephen FitzGerald, "China and the Overseas Chinese: Perceptions and Policies," *The China Quarterly*, No. 44, October-December 1970, pp. 1-37.

[e]Chinese economic aid to Burma (in loans) and Cambodia (mostly grants) was never more than 20 percent of the aid actually disbursed by all countries. Similarly, the China trade was important, but not critical, to either Burma or Cambodia: in most years it was under 10 percent of the imports and exports of both countries. As a result, withdrawal of China's aid or trade could not be an imposing threat—as became evident when all Chinese technical personnel left Burma and Cambodia without impairing either country's economy or progress toward completing the unfinished projects.

[f]Unlike the Soviet Union, Peking thus could exploit its associations with insurgent groups in Southeast Asia to gain leverage either against friendly governments, which had to be aware of China's activatable ties to indigenous dissidents, or against unfriendly governments, which would have to contend with Chinese support of rebel movements. But the level of that support was controllable from Peking; even in the cases of Burma (from 1967 on) and Thailand, it stopped considerably short of significant material assistance.

Table 7-1

China and Communist Movements: Levels of Support and Objectives*

Support Activity	Objectives
I: Contact. Revolutionary party personnel in Peking; limited cadre training in China; occasional attendance of party representatives at pro-CCP meetings; contact with local Communists/leftists through CPR Embassy or NCNA (if any).	Hedge against disruption of friendly ties to regime; show of solidarity with "pro-Chinese" party; some, perhaps fairly complete, control over revolutionary party's ideological line, military doctrine, and leadership activities.
II: Minimal Propaganda. Mention of revolutionary party in Peking media (though without identifying with its objectives).	In addition to above, possibly providing soundings to indicate concern over regime's foreign/domestic policy.
III: High-level Propaganda. More consistent mention in Peking media, coupled with (indirect) identification with revolutionary movement's objectives; news exposure of movement's leaders at Communist front gatherings, and use of Peking forums by them for propaganda.	Calling attention to CPR disturbance over regime's foreign/domestic policy course, and indicating availability of alternative to continued support of the legitimate government.
IV: Low-level Involvement. Disruption of friendly relations, though without necessarily precipitating complete diplomatic break; increased, though still limited logistical support to rebels; vocal support of rebels' objectives and denunciation of regime.	Warning of CPR's capability to aggravate regime's internal security problems; indication that commitment to revolutionary movement is contingent upon changes in regime's foreign/domestic policies or its leadership.
V: High-level Involvement. China assumes sanctuary or "rear-base" status, putting range of logistical and political resources at the disposal of revolutionary movement; ties to regime completely severed; some logistical and training personnel may be put at ally's disposal.	Overthrow of the regime and commitment to assisting the movement "to the end" against "lackeys of the imperialists and revisionists" in power.

*This table does not attempt to portray a finite set of alternatives or an automatic progression of events. It merely suggests, on the basis of the three case studies, the uses China has made (and is capable of making) of revolutionary movements for publicizing and if necessary promoting CPR objectives abroad.

The ways in which Chinese decisionmakers used these policy instruments—in particular, the careful coordination of propaganda and action—suggest that what have until now in this study been called "China's" or "Peking's" policies should be considered shorthand for decisions that primarily reflected the views of foreign affairs professionals. With the exception of part of the Cultural Revolution period (August 1966-August 1967), when foreign policy virtually ceased to function, the policymaking process in Peking seems to have been dominated by relatively "conservative" or "traditional" influences. Personalities like Liu Shao-ch'i and Chou En-lai, and probably most offices and agencies of the foreign affairs bureaucracy under the State Council, may have developed vested interests in policies that emphasized diplomacy, aid programs, treaties, trade, and restricted resource allocations to (unreliable) revolutionary exiles.[g] Tensions between these individuals and factions and others in the party, the government, and the military probably arose over different evaluations of the policies of foreign governments and different preferences for dealing with foreign revolutionary movements. But, to judge from the results of policy, the less moderate elements were almost consistently defeated by professional diplomats and bureaucrats.

China's Objectives

Broadly speaking, the case studies indicate that China's objective in Southeast Asia is the promotion of a militarily quiescent, politically accessible region occupied by weaker (noncompetitive) states that are "friendly" and "non-hostile." China's concern seems to be highest when, especially on the Southeast Asia mainland, hostile armed power or political influences establish footholds that enable them to threaten China's security, disturb the balance of forces in nearby countries, or impede China's capacity to publicize her revolutionary ideology.

In promoting *friendly* relations, Peking's interest is not in the development of genuinely sentimental and emotional attachments—although, *pro forma*, maudlin

---

[g]This is not to say, however, that the charges made against Liu during the Cultural Revolution—alleging that he consistently advised antirevolutionary, accommodationist policies, in opposition to Mao's views—should be considered accurate. Rather than having been Mao's antagonist on foreign policy, Liu may have been indicted for policy preferences and decisions with which Mao was once in agreement, which were appropriate at one time, but which lost their relevance because of subsequent events. The resumption of high-level diplomacy, the ambassadorial appointments, and the revival of foreign aid programs that occurred after the Ninth CCP Congress in April 1969 are among the indications that "Liu-ist" influence over Chinese foreign policy has survived Liu's purge. Lin Piao as much as admitted this when, in his previously cited Report to the party congress, he said: "Our proletarian foreign policy is not based on expediency; it is a policy in which we have long persisted. *This is what we did in the past* and we will persist in doing the same in the future." Nevertheless, a good case can be made that, with respect to nearby revolutionary movements, Liu for several years was consistently able to outvote Mao in politburo meetings. For the latter hypothesis, see David Mozingo, *China's Foreign Policy and the Cultural Revolution*, I.R.E.A. Interim Report No. 1, Cornell University, Ithaca, New York, March 1970, pp. 14-16.

appeals have been part of China's diplomacy.[14] The CPR seems to want countries to recognize her legitimacy and support, or at least not oppose, her policy positions of international consequence. Peking has not insisted on total conformity; to judge from the Burmese and Cambodian studies, "deviant" behavior is tolerated so long as it does not become dominant or continuous.

China values friendly relations for their utility—negatively, against third parties; positively, in promoting Peking's regional and international interests. Thus, Burma's friendship was valuable to China in part because of the tensions in Sino-Indian relations, as became clearest when Peking decided to conclude an equitable border settlement with Rangoon. In a larger perspective, China found friendship with Burma and Cambodia useful as examples of her ability to coexist with smaller nations in accordance with the five principles. Cambodia's agreement with China's global anti-American stance, including China's position on Vietnam and on an international united front, further manifested Sihanouk's friendship.

In seeking to encourage the nations of Southeast Asia to adopt policies that are *not hostile* to her, Communist China apparently has the objective that they reject provocative or antagonistic associations with other countries or organizations that China opposes. Specifically, although these nations might accept aid from and maintain other economic and political relations with the United States and the Soviet Union, they should not permit the establishment of "foreign" (i.e., United States or Soviet) bases on their soil, not join (or, alternatively, be active in) military alliances that are or may be directed against China, not afford China's enemies privileged diplomatic or economic positions, and not join third-world (Titoist) blocs. The fact that Thailand became an active jumping-off point for American military efforts in Laos and Vietnam put the RTG in the "hostile" category; but both Burma and Cambodia signed friendship and nonaggression treaties with Peking that removed them as potential bases for or allies of Moscow or Washington. In Peking's lexicon, Thailand had compromised her status as an independent state, whereas the agreement by Burma and Cambodia to the treaties proved their rejection of American or Soviet domination and hence the genuineness of their independence.

China's objectives to have friendly and nonhostile states on the Southeast Asia mainland reveal a special interest in encouraging neutralist sentiment. Although having pretensions to worldwide revolutionary leadership, the CPR probably considers neutralism a trend much less costly and potentially more beneficial to promote than the emplacement of Communist regimes. Neutral countries are not likely to become forceful policy antagonists, are antiimperialist, are off-limits to American or Soviet military establishments, and yet are accessible to Chinese aid programs, diplomatic agencies, and propaganda. Moreover, the cultivation of a sound relationship with the neutrals helps China's image in the underdeveloped community as an anticolonialist, nonimperialistic big power. Where neutralism has evolved in a friendly, nonhostile direction, China has ignored the fact that neutral governments might be headed by ideologically suspect personalities ("bourgeois" types, royalty, or military men), might be engaged in nonsocialist or semisocialist domestic programs, and might suppress leftist insurrectionaries, parties, or propaganda outlets.[h] What therefore made the events of mid-1967 in Burma and Cambodia significant for China's foreign policy was not that China had swung to a new period of belligerency, but that China's self-proclaimed and demonstrated tolerance of friendly neutrals, and her adherence to noninterference in their internal affairs, were brought into serious question by the actions of some of her representatives abroad.

China's Impact in Southeast Asia

Foreign Policy in Southeast Asia:
Flexibility and Resistance

Thai, Cambodian, and Burmese governments, despite the differences in their political style and policies, have long shared a determination to keep foreign and domestic affairs separate. The formulation and implementation of domestic policies have been kept apart from the requirements, as these have sometimes been cast, of policymaking in China's shadow. This differentiation, which lies at the heart of the successful practice of the politics of survival, may best be accounted for by the durability, cohesiveness, and seclusiveness of ruling elites, and by the legitimacy and authority they have among at least a majority of their people. These conditions have generally produced a broad elite consensus about foreign policy priorities that has given policy coherence and consistency. (Events in Cambodia since Sihanouk's removal show, however, how quickly differences within the ruling elite over foreign policy tactics and the distribution of power, among other things, can bring about a complete turnaround in foreign policy.) Local governments have thereby often had room to use their ingenuity to take advantage of major-power rivalry.

The foreign policy differences of these three countries may be considered differences of procedure rather than premise: they have made their choice whether, how, and when to align or not align on the basis of different, and

---

[h]An oft-mentioned disproof of these conclusions is the attempted coup in Indonesia by the Communist party (PKI) and allied army officers in 1965, which Peking allegedly pushed along by shipping arms to the Communists. (See, e.g., Gordon, *Toward Disengagement in Asia*, p. 77, n. 11.) Authoritative accounts of the coup attempt show otherwise. There were no secret Chinese arms shipments. The weight of the evidence favors the interpretation that an increasingly militant PKI leadership, aware of Sukarno's failing health, conspired with sympathetic army officers (and probably with Sukarno himself) to seize power and form a new revolutionary coalition, thus preempting an anticipated or possible initiative by the army's anti-Communist leadership. Peking may have known of the PKI's plans; but there is no indication that the PKI's repetition of previous revolutionary misadventures was due to decisions made or approved in China. See Guy J. Pauker, "The Rise and Fall of the Communist Party of Indonesia," in Scalapino, ed., 2d ed., pp. 274-308, and Justus M. van der Kroef, "Interpretations of the 1965 Indonesian Coup: A Review of the Literature," *Pacific Affairs*, Vol. XLIII, No. 4, Winter 1970-71, pp. 557-577.

differently perceived, political and military realities and prospects in Asia, as well as in the light of internal politics and security. In all three cases, the general orientation of foreign policy has undergone important transformations and was not predetermined or constrained by philosophical or ideological commitments. Their governments have retained a capacity to redirect foreign policy when necessary. Thus, policy statements are often symbolic, and foreign policy alignments or "postures," such as neutralism or self-reliance, are flexible national interest formulations born of responses to the existing power relationships among the major actors in Asia.

Experience with alliances and a realistic appraisal of their value have also influenced this foreign policy adaptability. Despite concern about China's intentions and despite an environment of conflict and confrontation, these nations have strong reservations about security alliances. The Burmese and (at least in Sihanouk's time) Cambodian view has been that political or military alliances with non-Communist Asian countries risk provoking China and becoming pawns in the Sino-American rivalry[i] rather than providing added protection. Their nonaggression treaties with China, far from having sacrificed their policy independence, were sensible political acts that testified to their nonaligned status. Thailand, on the other hand, early looked to SEATO for security; but, like Burma and Cambodia, the Thai leaders have often and openly expressed their skepticism that paper treaties or promises amount to solid commitments. Moreover, Thailand's interest in all-Asian, nonsecurity organizations may reveal how far her leaders have moved toward the position of Rangoon and Phnom Penh. The leaderships of all three countries seem to agree that because the major powers in Asia act out of self-interest, never out of altruism, professions of friendship, let alone defense pledges, will prove meaningful only when their internal security interests happen to coincide with the global security interests of the major powers.[j]

Suspicion about the reliability of the major powers, Communist and non-Communist, has prompted these Southeast Asian governments to be alert to

---

[i]Not having security associations with the United States, Ne Win and Sihanouk lessened China's interest in using the threat of supporting insurgency in their countries as a lever against United States policies elsewhere in Southeast Asia. Since the United States had made no commitments to Burma or Cambodia, and hence had no stake in the maintenance of Ne Win or Sihanouk in power, China could not have expected to deflect United States action in, say, Thailand or Vietnam by taking hostile actions toward Burma or Cambodia. United States commitments to Thailand, on the other hand, have provided China with the alternative of assisting dissidence there in response to United States policies in Indochina.

[j]Hostility to the Vietnam war and foreign commitments among the American public and in the Congress have added to doubts in Southeast Asia about United States reliability. As Thanat Khoman told members of the American press in an interview in Bangkok, a foreign country's desire to help is always "subject to the vagaries of [its] domestic politics. . . . In other words, outside nations may have the military capability to accept and assume military responsibility, but they may not have the psychological adequacy to shoulder such a responsibility." Thai Permanent Mission, Press Release No. 13, March 12, 1969.

shifts in the policies of the major powers. This has helped them to avoid being caught off guard by initiating policy changes of their own. Such was the case when U Nu and Sihanouk traded pro-Westernism for neutralism, when Sihanouk supported the Viet Cong but later condemned their territorial violations and reestablished relations with the United States, and when Thai leaders began emphasizing regional involvement, self-reliance, and the improvement of opportunities for friendly relations with the Communist world.

The Southeast Asian governments have also proven adept at exploiting their similar *dis*advantages in size, military resources, and position in the midst of major-power rivalry. Weakness, as Thomas C. Schelling has observed,[15] can often prove an asset in international political "bargaining"—often a better one than bluffing strength. Thus, Burma's vulnerability along the border with China and her fairly restricted diplomacy may be more of an asset to Burma's security than would active border patrolling and unfettered contacts with all nations. Sihanouk's publicizing of Cambodia's weakness, and especially of her encirclement by hostile forces, was designed to focus world attention on his country and hopefully to deflect the predatory ambitions of Cambodia's neighbors and their allies. Thai governments, finally, have played on threats arising from nearness to conflicts in Indochina, as well as their anti-Communist position, to extract economic and military resources and security promises from the United States.

References to Southeast Asia as a "power vacuum" open to Chinese penetration consequently need to be sharply qualified. Those who have used the term, mainly with respect to the neutrals, assume that, individually, Southeast Asian governments, because of China's potential to threaten their independence,[k] have had a limited capacity to resist or deflect Chinese influence upon their political systems.[16] The assumption, however, is questionable on several counts. Besides neglecting the distinction between China's capability and performance, it also ignores or underestimates the ways in which these governments have effectively coped with China, and the limitations on China's revolutionary capacity that are posed by the region's political tradition, ethnic and geographic fragmentation, and the character of its dissidence.

China has sought to exert influence in these Southeast Asian countries in four ways. Chinese nationals have been directly involved in the politics of other countries—for example, Chinese Communist banks and official CPR missions, agencies, or technicians. Secondly, the behavior of Southeast Asian nations has been in response to Chinese actions. Examples are the public statements of Burmese leaders and Sihanouk lauding Chinese technical or economic achievements, or supporting Chinese international positions. The conciliatory gestures of Thai leaders toward China beginning in 1968, and their talk of self-reliance,

---

[k]To be clear, the kind of threat is commonly believed to be support of subversive movements, not unprovoked aggression or nuclear devastation. And this perception adds to the shared belief mentioned above that security guarantees, insofar as they cover outright aggression or nuclear threats, are of little relevance to the most probable form of outside involvement, namely, political and logistical assistance to indigenous rebels.

might also be considered an example, as might the adoption of neutralism by Burma and Cambodia in order to avoid antagonizing China. Thirdly, Communist movements in all three countries have sought to pattern their tactics, organization, party programs, doctrine, and international stance after those of Maoist China. In terms of practical support, finally, China has at various times offered Thai, Burmese, and Cambodian Communists residence in exile, trained cadres, and surreptitiously provided material assistance.

How much influence these forms of penetration have actually had on the security and independence of the Southeast Asian countries is a different matter. The activities of Chinese officials, agencies, and some overseas Chinese were successfully controlled by the Burmese and Cambodian (Sihanouk) governments. They kept Chinese offices and representatives under surveillance, nationalized the pro-Chinese Communist press, banks, and commercial establishments, deported undesirable Chinese resident aliens, and eliminated opportunities for legal pro-Chinese parties to flourish. As to "pro-Chinese" official statements by Southeast Asian governments, these were often symbolic. They did not open the door to Chinese manipulation of domestic affairs (e.g., during the Cultural Revolution period), compel governments to espouse unsupportable policies (e.g., Burma's silence on events in Indochina), or deter governments from various international associations (e.g., Cambodian and Burmese trade, aid, and diplomatic relations with the United States and the Soviet Union).

Emulation of Maoism by the Communist movements in all three countries on balance was not as politically destablizing as it might have been. One reason is that emulation was not rewarded with significant Chinese material support. But the more important reason, strongly implied in China's statements and actions concerning the Burmese and Thai Communist movements, is that these revolutionary groups failed in their attempts to adapt Chinese Communist principles of ideology and organization to their own circumstances. Moreover, emulation of Maoist ways and programs to some extent compromised these groups' nationalistic, antineocolonialist appeals.

Actual and potential Chinese aid to dissident groups compelled the three governments to consider the consequences of adopting foreign policies inimical to Chinese interests. There was considerable domestic and foreign policymaking leeway for those governments, like Burma and Cambodia, that chose one or another way of accommodating to Peking. For those (like Thailand) that did not, policymaking leeway was great, but so was the uncertainty about Chinese activities.

Security and Revolution

The most immediate dangers to national survival suggested by the case studies do not stem directly from China. Rather, they come from antagonistic indigenous elements and rival neighbors. Both revolutionary and traditional dissidence[1] are widespread in Southeast Asia: the former (examples are the CPB, the CPT, and the so-called Khmer Viet Minh) relies mainly on organizational discipline, radical reformist programs that aim at overthrowing the established order, and violence; the latter (e.g., the rebellious elements of the national minorities in Burma; bandits and non-Communist, non-Thai antigovernment elements in the regions surrounding central Thailand, and disaffected or unintegrated minorities in the border provinces of Cambodia) is at best loosely organized, aims at resisting rather than overthrowing central authority, is ethnically or tribally oriented, and is rooted in local grievances or threats to customary ways of life.

Security is also endangered, as the leaders of these countries perceive it, by hostile neighbors. Cambodia's fears of the Thai and the Vietnamese may, as proposed earlier, have some domestic political motivation, but remain real nonetheless, especially since Sihanouk's removal. The armed presence of Viet Cong units in Cambodia is of more immediate concern to Phnom Penh than the future hegemony of China in Southeast Asia that Sihanouk foresaw. Similarly for Thailand, North Vietnamese involvement through the Pathet Lao in the northeast has posed a graver threat than has China's political and very limited logistical support of the Thai Communists. Burma's improved relations with India and Thailand in recent years make her an exception; but that cooperative spirit has probably not completely eliminated a deepseated Burmese suspicion about Indian and Thai interests (especially since U Nu, in his comeback attempt, established a base along the border with Thailand) in or respect for Burma's territory.

Whether the principal source of subversion is internal or transnational, the challenge to the Southeast Asian governments is to create conditions that will keep traditional dissidence localized and ineffective (at most), and that will make revolutionary dissidence unsuccessful internally and unattractive to hostile forces beyond the borders. China's role in both these security problems is secondary: the factors that contribute to dissidence cannot be externally manufactured, though they may be externally exploited. They include the insufficiency of administrative contact between the government center and outlying areas; the absence of reliable police or army protection of rural populated areas; an attitude of superiority on the part of government officials toward rural peoples and local cultures; and long-standing neglect of the well-being of rural areas by the center. These inhibiting features of central-rural relations are accentuated by the parochial loyalties of tribal and ethnic minorities (not to mention overseas Chinese or Vietnamese) who have chanced to be living within the boundaries of nations whose authority they may not

---

[1]On the distinction between revolutionary and traditional dissidence, I am indebted to discussions with Richard Maullin, who has made the distinction in dealing with antigovernment violence in Colombia.

always acknowledge. Racially, linguistically, and culturally different from the majority people, these minorities often regard them with suspicion. To date many minority groups have rejected, either by resort to hostilities or by noncooperation, a politically or culturally subordinate role within the larger system of the dominant majority.

Some of the same factors that undermine national security and the integration of diverse populations in a single political system, however, also have proven formidable barriers to Communist movements, whether or not externally supported. A revolutionary potential exists to some extent in each of the three countries inasmuch as their governments have not yet achieved a level of institutionalization that permits the absorption of various social forces into the political process and into government.[17] Government has been highly personalistic, narrowly based, and authoritarian. But successful revolutions in underdeveloped Asian countries have also consisted of an alliance of alienated social groups, of which the peasantry is the most numerous; a foreign presence or intervention that acts as a catalyst of nationalist resentments against the government, and a disciplined organization that can harness nationalism and provide revolutionary leadership.[18] (Examples are the Chinese Communist and Viet Minh revolutions.) Communist movements in Thailand, Cambodia,[m] and Burma have thus far failed to fulfill these conditions and have been frustrated by others. Circumstances may change, of course; but for them to change would require radical transformations in the historical and political landscape of mainland Southeast Asia.

First, minority-majority, urban-rural, and intellectual-peasant alliances have not been forged. Minority opposition has undercut central government authority (to the greatest extent in Burma), but Communist appeals to the minorities, as well as to the majority peoples, have largely fallen on deaf ears. The Communists, especially in Burma, have made few inroads into the ranks of rebel minority groups; where they have succeeded, it has been because such groups found them useful for the achievement of their own limited (nonrevolutionary) objectives. Moreover, the parochialism characteristic of hill tribesmen, whether in rebellion or not, has posed a major obstacle to Communist manipulation, either separately or under a "united front." Finally, though more in Thailand than in the other two countries, which were formerly Western colonies, intellectuals have disdained Marxist-Leninist appeals; and in all three, unemployed urban intellectuals have not been attracted by the notion of a peasant-based revolution.

---

[m]Here and in the following paragraphs I have in mind the Cambodian Communist movement as it existed before it received Sihanouk's endorsement, came under North Vietnam's direct control, and sought to capitalize on the Lon Nol government's collaboration with the United States, Thailand, and South Vietnam. The combination of these new factors since March 1970 may before too long make the Cambodian Communist movement a powerful political and military force in its own right though, like the Pathet Lao, with substantial North Vietnamese assistance.

Second, in the one country in which a foreign presence might have had a catalytic effect on peasant nationalism (Thailand), the absence of a colonial experience has substantially diminished the chances for the Communist party to arouse popular support against the government. Thai Communist propaganda has devoted considerable attention to the American presence, but with little success. As the United States presence is reduced, moreover, any propaganda advantage the Communists have derived will probably vanish.

Above all, the weaknesses of the Communist dissidents limit their ability to become vanguards of a revolution and also lessen their attractiveness to the Chinese, should the Chinese be inclined to support their cause. The Communist movements in the three countries have been hampered by lack of popular support, fractured leaderships, difficulties in obtaining supplies and coordinating strategy, inability to form workable alliances with other disenchanted groups, limited backing from Communist governments, and damaging relations with nonindigenous Communist parties. These factors have seriously detracted from the effectiveness of these movements. To judge from Peking's qualified support of them, moreover, and its emphasis on their need to practice self-reliance, Communist China's leaders are skeptical that they are realistic alternatives to the regimes they oppose. As successful students of revolution, China's leaders may recognize that their identification with and support of a rebellion against a hostile government—as in Burma until recently and Thailand—cannot compensate for the deficiencies of the local Communist party that must lead it.

Among the other factors in Southeast Asia that present difficulties for Communist movements is geography. In certain circumstances, geographical features of the three countries have been as disadvantageous to Communist forces as to central governments. The weakness or absence of a border control capability for these countries has facilitated rebel communications with nonindigenous supporters and has enabled the rebels to have a sanctuary across the open frontiers. But the dispersed, disconnected nature of the Communist and other rebel forces (in Thailand and, before March 1970, Cambodia), or the distance of their headquarters from the China border (the White Flags), has hindered outside assistance and reduced its effectiveness. Just as the Burmese Army, for instance, has been prevented by distance and terrain from launching sustained drives on the White Flags, so have the White Flags been kept from establishing reliable liaisons with the Chinese Communists.

The barriers to Communist influence posed by the nature of politics in Southeast Asia are perhaps the most imposing of all. Marxist doctrine, and the issues it has raised to mobilize popular support, have had limited appeal in countries where politics is essentially nonideological, nonprogrammatic, and personalistic. Although these features can make politics highly unstable, as in Burma, Communist parties have not been able to exploit that situation because, among other things, they have been as susceptible as the non-Communist groups (including the military and political parties) to factionalism and cliquism. Beyond that, the emphasis in Communist theory and practice on violence, discipline, and loyalty to foreign powers has made Marxist and Maoist parties suspect. Their emulation of and public identification with foreign parties have been alien to countries where political thought and practice are influenced by the Buddhist stress on right action and individualism, by the primacy of personality or ethnic identity in determining political loyalty, and by the nationalistic assertion of freedom from external manipulation. In Sihanouk's Cambodia and Thailand, these values were embodied in the monarchy, which is a powerful unifying symbol and a source of governmental legitimacy. But even where, as in Burma and Lon Nol's Cambodia, the traditional monarchy has disappeared, an autocratic tradition has survived to give continuity and centralized direction to policymaking.

A "Balance of Power" in Southeast Asia?

The motivations and objectives of Chinese foreign policy toward the three Southeast Asian countries cast doubt on the applicability of a traditional balance-of-power analysis of Asian security. Influence, not the use of military power, and threats, but no actual use of force, have most consistently characterized China's relations with Burma and Cambodia.[n] With respect to Thailand, China's leaders have seemed to want a relationship of influence, not power or force. Yet, advocates of United States policies to maintain a "balance of power" in Southeast Asia, and writers who describe a regional balance of power system or the potential for one, treat China's military capabilities—her potential for directly subverting weak governments—as the key element in China's relations with Southeast Asia.[19] They argue the need for the United States and its allies to orchestrate military power so as to deter Peking from its supposed goal of regional "dominance" or "hegemony." The role of external force—America's retaliatory capability—is useful and necessary: it deters (highly unlikely) Chinese aggression and thus contributes to reduced anxiety among Southeast Asian nations about the potential threat from China. But external force cannot "balance" or contain the principal sources of China's power in Southeast Asia, namely, her psychological and political influence, and her capacity to assist indigenous rebellions.

Despite the confusion over power, diplomats in Southeast Asia such as Thanat Khoman have alluded to different kinds of balancing arrangements, and

---

[n]The careful distinctions between power and influence that have been made by Peter Bachrach and Morton S. Baratz (in "Decisions and Nondecisions: An Analytical Framework," *American Political Science Review*, Vol. LVII, No. 3, September 1963, pp. 632-642) do not readily fit in the China-Southeast Asia context. Influence, in their view, is mainly distinguishable from power by the absence of threats to impose sanctions. But Peking was often able to obtain compliant behavior from the Cambodian and Burmese governments by making them aware, *without* having to communicate direct threats, that China was in a position to impose (unspecified) sanctions for noncompliance. Sino-Cambodian and Sino-Burmese relations thus illustrate the difficulty, which Bachrach and Baratz remark upon, of differentiating influence from power, especially since one may lead to the other.

all the region's governments agree that no single nation should be allowed to "dominate" the region. But a balance of power that would bring Southeast Asian states together against China, with or without American participation, does not seem to be uniformly desired or capable of being created.

Vital to the performance of any balance of power system is that the states in it be willing to form alliances and coalitions that can enforce an equilibrium.[20] In Southeast Asia, however, interest in an anti-China alliance is not widespread. There is little confidence, moreover, that the nations in alliance would be able or willing automatically to act to preserve the balance. Common cultural traditions have not removed or reduced mutual suspicions, influenced the formulation of similar foreign policies, or given concern about extraregional (i.e., Chinese) domination priority over concern about expansionist neighbors. Relations among the region's nations will probably be marked for some time to come by shifting alliances with different major powers, political warfare, and uneasy peace along common borders.[21]

In view of the different foreign policies of the Southeast Asian nations, the United States could not expect to have conferred upon it a major balancing role.[o] As much as Communist China's policies and behavior have generated concern about Peking's intentions in Southeast Asia, the region's governments have not concluded that the United States should intervene whenever signs of expansionism appear. While the value of an American military presence in the region has been acknowledged (openly by the Thai and Cambodian governments, tacitly by the Burmese) for its deterrence of major attack, its location and means and conditions of employment have not been generally agreed upon. Like all other security systems that depend on the promises and actions of the major powers—such as alliance systems and guaranteed neutralization—a balance-of-power arrangement in Southeast Asia based on the United States (or any other major power) would not be uniformly accepted by its small-power constituents as a reliable guarantor of security.

Is the only alternative to a balance-of-power system the eventual "forcible establishment of a unified power system centered on China"?[22] The cautiousness and reactiveness of Chinese policy in Southeast Asia, which is the result of their leaders' appreciation of American power and the conservatism of their own ideology put into practice, argue otherwise. So does the experience of Southeast Asian governments. By placing their own interests and calculations foremost, they have avoided making irrevocable commitments to major powers or allowing major powers to exercise dominant influence over policymaking. Southeast Asia, as a result, might best be characterized by an imbalance of "power," which the region's governments, determined to control their own fate, may prefer to any balance system dominated by the major military powers.

---

[o]Nor does the United States government seem interested in being automatically committed to intervening whenever any nation might seek to disturb the "balance."

Notes

Notes

Notes to Chapter 1

1. This point is well made by Michael Brecher, *The New States of Asia: A Political Analysis*, Oxford University Press, New York, 1963, p. 92.

2. Ibid., pp. 98, 104, 110 and Bernard K. Gordon, *Toward Disengagement in Asia: A Strategy for American Foreign Policy*, Prentice-Hall, Englewood Cliffs, N.J., 1969, p. 76.

3. The profusion of meanings that have been given by writers on the balance of power is remarked upon by John H. Herz, *International Politics in the Atomic Age*, Columbia University Press, New York, 1959, p. 65, and by Inis L. Claude, Jr., *Power and International Relations*, Random House, New York, 1962, Chapter 2. For use of all three meanings of balance of power in a discussion of Asia, see Fred Greene, *U.S. Policy and the Security of Asia*, McGraw-Hill, New York, 1968, especially pp. 40-41.

Notes to Chapter 2

1. For an extensive discussion of these points, see David A. Wilson, "Thailand and Marxism," in Frank N. Trager, ed., *Marxism in Southeast Asia: A Study of Four Countries*, Stanford University Press, Stanford, California, 1959.

2. The party's publication of a pamphlet in 1935 is offered in evidence by Wilson, ibid., p. 92. J.S. Brimmell (*Communism in South East Asia: A Political Analysis*, Oxford University Press, London, 1959, p. 242.) indicates that the party first came into the open following a general meeting on December 6, 1946, when its program was announced, leaflets were distributed, and Chinese were recruited.

3. Brimmell, p. 244; Skinner, p. 291. A party member interviewed by Thompson and Adloff in May 1947 asserted that his group of Chinese had no connection with the Siamese party. See Virginia Thompson and Richard Adloff, *The Left Wing in Southeast Asia*, Wm. Sloane Associates, Institute of Pacific Relations, New York, 1950, p. 60.

4. Brimmell, pp. 242-245, 352; Skinner, pp. 325-328.

5. Brimmell, p. 346.

6. Ibid., p. 351.

7. The ten-point program is quoted in full in Wilson, "Thailand and Marxism," pp. 92-93.

8. Quoted in Wilson, *China, Thailand and the Spirit of Bandung*, The RAND Corporation, P-2607, Santa Monica, California, July 1962, pp. 71-73. The message was publicized and discussed approvingly by the New China News Agency.

9. On the early history of organized opposition to the Thai government, see Pierre Fistié, "Minorités ethniques, opposition et subversion en Thailande," *Politique étrangére*, No. 3, 1967, pp. 295-324. Fistié's account seems to err in attributing separatist aims to the Free Thai and later antigovernment movements in the northeast.

10. Robert Karr McCabe, *Storm over Asia: China and Southeast Asia, Thrust and Response*, The New American Library, New York, 1967, p. 105.

11. George Modelski, "The Viet Minh Complex," in Cyril E. Black and Thomas P. Thornton, eds., *Communism and Revolution: The Strategic Uses of Political Violence*, Princeton University Press, Princeton, N.J., 1964, pp. 199-200.

12. See Fistié, pp. 309-310.

13. Peter A. Poole, "Thailand's Vietnamese Minority," *Asian Survey*, Vol. VII, No. 12, December 1967, p. 886; Vietnam News Agency (VNA, Hanoi), October 28, 1967, broadcast.

14. Poole, p. 888.

15. Poole, pp. 890-891.

16. NCNA Daily Bulletin No. 640, October 2, 1959, p. 41.

17. Comments of a CPT member broadcast in Thai over Radio Peking, December 5, 1967. The same date (1961) is referred to in an NCNA international service broadcast of September 4, 1966.

18. Quoted in D. Insor, *Thailand: A Political, Social and Economic Analysis*, Praeger, New York, 1963, p. 75, footnote.

19. For surveys of world-wide revolutions, cf. Kuei Mao, "Struggle to Strengthen Afro-Asian Unity and Oppose Imperialism and Neocolonialism," *Shih-chieh chih-shih (World Knowledge)*, No. 8, April 25, 1963, p. 5 (in which Thailand is omitted); Mei Chih-chin, "The United States Vainly Struggles on in Southeast Asia," *Shih-chieh chih-shih*, No. 5, March 10, 1964, p. 9 (in which "people's armed struggle" is said to be "also developing" in Thailand); and "People of the World Unite under the Fighting Banner of Opposing U.S. Imperialism!" by the Editorial Department, *Shih-chieh chih-shih*, No. 1, January 10, 1965, pp. 4-8 (in which Thailand is again not mentioned).

20. *Jen-min jih-pao (People's Daily*, Peking), June 20, 1964, p. 4.

21. NCNA Daily Bulletin No. 2435, October 3, 1964, pp. 75-77.

22. Harvey H. Smith, et al., *Area Handbook for Thailand*, 2d rev. ed., U.S. Government Printing Office, Washington, D.C., 1968, p. 299.

23. VTP broadcast of December 8, 1964; published in *Jen-min jih-pao*, December 14, 1964, p. 3.

24. Broadcast January 22, 1965, by VTP; published in NCNA Daily Bulletin No. 2587, February 5, 1965, pp. 11-12.

25. The merger was announced by NCNA on December 14, 1965, exactly one year after *Jen-min jih-pao* had published the proclamation of the TIM. The

NCNA announcement included word of the Front's leading role in the alliance. See *New York Times*, December 16, 1965, p. 5.

26. *The Communist Threat to Thailand*, Thai Sambhand Press, Bangkok, August 1967, pp. 22, 24; VTP broadcast of June 1, 1965; NCNA international service broadcast of June 25, 1965.

27. McCabe, p. 107.

28. McCabe, p. 107.

29. See *Jen-min jih-pao*, April 17, 1965, p. 2.

30. McCabe, p. 107.

31. For a brief biography of Pridi, see Wilson, *Politics in Thailand*, Cornell University Press, Ithaca, N.Y., 1962, pp. 121-124.

32. J.L.S. Girling makes a similar point in his "Northeast Thailand: Tomorrow's Viet Nam?" *Foreign Affairs*, Vol. XLVI, No. 2, January 1968, p. 394.

33. See Wilson, *China, Thailand and the Spirit of Bandung*, p. 39.

34. *The Communist Threat to Thailand*, p. 15.

35. Girling, p. 396.

36. Note, for example, the comments of Communist defectors who had gone through the Hoa Binh training regimen: Bangkok domestic service broadcast of October 13, 1966; *Bangkok Post*, March 10, 1967.

37. Speech by Marshall Green, then Deputy Assistant Secretary of State for Far Eastern Affairs, March 14, 1965, in *Department of State Bulletin*, Vol. LII, No. 1345, April 5, 1965, p. 490.

38. A State Department estimate which stipulates, however, that not all those trained may still be active. See U.S. Senate, Committee on Foreign Relations, Subcommittee on United States Security Agreements and Commitments Abroad, *Hearings, Kingdom of Thailand*, part 3, November 10-17, 1969, 91st Cong., 1st Sess., Government Printing Office, Washington, D.C., 1970, p. 754 (Hereafter cited as *Senate Hearings on Thailand*).

39. From the speech by Secretary Green, cited above.

40. In the summer of 1968, for instance, it was claimed that a North Vietnamese captain had been taken prisoner in Uttaradit province, which borders on Laos, while engaged in action with the CTs. See *Bangkok Post*, Supplement, July 31, 1968, and *Le Monde* (Paris), August 2, 1968.

41. See, in particular, Nuechterlein, *Thailand and the Struggle for Southeast Asia*, Cornell University Press, Ithaca, N.Y., 1965, Chapters 5-7; and L.P. Singh, "Thai Foreign Policy: The Current Phase," *Asian Survey*, Vol. III, No. 11, November 1963, pp. 535-543.

42. See the press conference comments of Thanat on April 19, 1964, and the abovementioned interview of May 1 with Topping in *Foreign Affairs Bulletin*, Vol. III, No. 5, April-May 1964, pp. 536-538, 544-545.

43. Ibid., p. 533.

44. Dommen, p. 259.

45. See ibid., p. 260, and Parker, pp. 54-55.

46. Ibid., p. 55.

47. An editorial of April 9 in *Jen-min jih-pao* hailed Souvanna's visit as a significant token of Sino-Laotian friendship, of China's support for the neutralist government of national union in Vientiane, and of the mutuality of viewpoint between the two governments on Indochina problems. Translated in American Consulate-General, Hong Kong, *Survey of China Mainland Press (SCMP)*, No. 3198, April 14, 1964, pp. 32-33.

48. See, e.g., Ch'en Yi's letter to Souphanouvong of May 13 and to the co-chairmen of the Geneva Conference on the same day; ibid., No. 3221, May 19, 1964, pp. 20-22. See also Ch'en's reply to the British Foreign Secretary, in *Jen-min jih-pao*, May 27, 1964, pp. 1, 4.

49. See, in addition to the items cited in the preceding footnote, *Jen-min jih-pao*, May 13, 1964, in *SCMP*, No. 3221, pp. 22-26.

50. Editorial of June 15, 1964, in *Peking Review*, No. 25, June 19, 1964, p. 9.

51. CPR government statement of June 13, in ibid., p. 7.

52. *Jen-min jih-pao*, June 15, in ibid., p. 9.

53. See, e.g., the article by Commentator, "Aggression against Cambodia Cannot be Tolerated," *Jen-min jih-pao*, September 15, 1964, p. 4. As shall be discussed in greater detail in the context of Sino-Cambodian relations, this and other Chinese comments were primarily intended to deter open conflict involving Cambodia without committing the CPR to Cambodia's defense.

54. For example, Ch'ao Hai, "U.S. Imperialism Intensifies Control of Thailand," *Shih-chieh chih-shih*, No. 6, March 25, 1964, pp. 13-14; *Jen-min jih-pao*, August 11, 1964, p. 7 (article and map of bases in Thailand); ibid., August 28, 1964, p. 3 (a VTP broadcast concerning the American use of Thai bases "for aggression against Vietnam").

55. *Jen-min jih-pao*, March 12, 1965, p. 3; March 22, 1965, p. 5; April 6, 1965, p. 4; April 8, 1965, p. 4.

56. E.G., an April 1 statement by the TPF, published ibid., April 27, 1965, p. 1.

57. E.g., a VTP broadcast of May 25, 1965 on the northeast.

58. *Jen-min jih-pao*, April 28, 1965, p. 4.

59. Ibid., July 8, 1965, p. 3; italics supplied.

60. Ibid., October 7, 1965, p. 3.

61. The April 1965 Commentator article put American strength in Thailand at over 6,000 men. In his July article, American strength was said to be over 9,000 and in October, over 10,000. These figures are fairly accurate. The map that accompanied the October article pinpointed over thirty air bases in Thailand, over ten naval bases, four missile bases, and two radar stations.

62. "Thailand–Bridgehead of U.S. Aggression against Indo-China," *Peking Review*, No. 42, October 15, 1965, p. 9.

63. See the figures in *Los Angeles Times*, November 12, 1967, p. 1.

64. Interview in Bangkok, August 1968; statement by Premier Thanom Kittikachon, Bangkok domestic service radio, January 9, 1967.

65. See, e.g., the comments of Thanat Khoman in an interview with a *Newsweek* correspondent on January 6, 1966, in *Foreign Affairs Bulletin*, Vol. V, No. 3, December 1965-January 1966, pp. 309-310.

66. Speech of January 27, 1967, before the Bangkok South Rotary Club, in *Collected Statements*.

67. Ibid., p. 21, speech before the opening session of the 12th SEATO Council of Ministers meeting, April 18, 1967.

68. *New York Times*, March 10, 1967, p. 19.

69. Thai government announcement of March 24, 1967; Thai Permanent Mission, Press Release No. 5, same date.

70. The qualified enthusiasm of Thai government leaders over the presence of foreign troops in Thailand, whether under SEATO (as in the 1950s) or under the United States alone, is discussed in George Modelski, "The Asian States' Participation in SEATO," in Modelski, ed., *SEATO: Six Studies*, University of British Columbia, for the Australian National University, Vancouver, 1962, p. 98, and in Nuechterlein, *Thailand and the Struggle for Southeast Asia*, p. 240.

71. Interview with a correspondent of *Akahata (Red Flag)*, organ of the Japanese Communist Party, on December 30, 1965, as broadcast by NCNA (Peking) international service, January 4, 1966.

72. *Ta-kung pao* (Peking), February 25, 1966, p. 4.

73. Szu Mu, "The Advance of the Revolutionary Movement of the World's People is the Main Current of the Present Situation," *Shih-chieh chih-shih*, Nos. 2-3, February 10, 1966, p. 9.

74. The interpretations in this paragraph come from Harry Harding and Melvin Gurtov, *The Purge of Lo Jui-ch'ing: The Politics of Chinese Strategic Planning*, R-548-PR, The RAND Corporation, February 1971.

75. January 15, 1966, p. 4.

76. See, in particular, the commentary of January 28, 1966, p. 4.

77. *Jen-min jih-pao* commentary, April 27, 1966, p. 4. At this time, too, there were also strong though well-hedged warnings from Peking concerning Thai clashes with Cambodian forces. See Commentator's remarks, ibid., April 9, 1966, p. 4, and the citation (ibid., April 15, 1966, p. 4) of Sihanouk's statement that the Cambodians have Chinese friends just as the Thai have American friends in case of war.

78. Ibid., May 8, 1966, p. 5. Actually, the RTG had not announced a decision to increase its forces in South Vietnam, contrary to what was reported in *Jen-min jih-pao*. At that time there were only rumors in Bangkok of an

impending decision that was confirmed finally in November when Thanom stated that the RTG in fact had 300 troops in South Vietnam. Bangkok radio domestic service, November 7, 1966.

79. *Jen-min jih-pao*, May 14, 1966, p. 1.

80. Ibid., June 23, 1966, p. 5.

81. See, e.g., *Jen-min jih-pao*, March 26, 1966, p. 4.

82. For example, see the comments of Kulab Saipradit, the exiled writer, at a writers' conference in Peking, ibid., June 23, 1966, p. 6; Pridi's condemnation of revisionism in a letter to Chou, ibid., May 18, 1966, p. 5; and a VTP commentary on splittist tendencies in Soviet revisionism, as reprinted ibid., June 29, 1966, p. 6.

83. Radio Tirana domestic service broadcast of November 6, 1966.

84. See *Peking Review*, No. 20, May 13, 1966, p. 19.

85. VTP broadcast in Lao to northeast Thailand, January 7, 1967.

86. Broadcast of December 23, 1966.

87. The Chinese report on the December 1 message is in *Peking Review*, No. 7, February 10, 1967, pp. 26-28.

88. In *Jen-min jih-pao*, January 20, 1967, p. 5.

89. The only previous mention of Thai bases in the context of a threat to China apparently occurred in a Thai-language Radio Peking broadcast of December 23, 1966.

90. NCNA international service broadcast of April 3, 1967.

91. E.g., NCNA international service broadcasts of February 21 and August 8, 1967.

92. "The Victorious Road of the Thai People in their Fight for National Liberation," *Jen-min jih-pao*, October 8, 1967, p. 8.

Reference by Commentator to the direct participation of United States forces in the counterinsurgency effort of the RTG probably had in mind press reports that American helicopter pilots were ferrying Thai police and soldiers into combat, and that some American advisers had been accompanying Thai battalions on missions. *Los Angeles Times*, October 20, 1966, p. 1, and *New York Times*, November 27, 1966, p. 5.

93. *Jen-min jih-pao*, December 10, 1968, p. 6. The same theme has been repeated many times in Chinese commentaries since then, for example in a NCNA international service broadcast of March 27, 1970. On occasion, the CPT's own statements have admitted that numerous difficulties must be surmounted before the revolution can be successful. An example is the party central committee's statement of December 1, 1969, broadcast by VTP in Thai on that day.

94. Communiqué of the CPT central committee of December 1, 1967, broadcast by VTP in Thai, December 14, 1967.

95. General Praphat Charusathian, then Minister of Interior and presently deputy prime minister, expressed the opinion that factionalism had arisen in the Thai Communists' ranks over the Cultural Revolution. Some exiles, he said, had indicated their desire to return home and others had already left Peking for Macao. Reported in the Bangkok Chinese-language newspapers *Ch'ing-hua wan-pao, Shih-chieh wan-pao*, and others on May 17, 1967.

96. VTP broadcast of December 14, 1967.

97. Ibid., December 24, 1968.

98. *Senate Hearings on Thailand*, p. 628.

99. *Bangkok Post*, March 1, 1968; *Senate Hearings on Thailand*, p. 628.

100. Fistié, p. 320; Bernard K. Gordon, "Thailand: Its Meaning for the U.S.," *Current History*, Vol. LII, No. 305, January 1967, p. 53. General Praphat, on the other hand, denied any such connections. *Bangkok Post*, August 29, 1968.

101. *Bangkok Post*, March 1, 1968, *Bangkok World*, February 13 and June 29, 1968, and *Senate Hearings on Thailand*, p. 628 contain figures. For further analysis, see W.A. Standish, "Malay Moslem Mixtures," *Far Eastern Economic Review*, July 6, 1967, pp. 19-22, and Astri Suhrke, "The Thai Muslims: Some Aspects of Minority Integration," *Pacific Affairs*, Vol. XLIII, No. 4, Winter 1970-71, pp. 539-541.

102. *New York Times*, July 9, 1970, p. 8.

103. Speech by Thanat Khoman to a SEATO meeting on April 18, 1967, in Washington, D.C., in Thai Permanent Mission, Press Release No. 6, same date.

104. Cf. the remarks of Premier Thanom at a press conference (Bangkok domestic service broadcast, April 1, 1968), Praphat (*Bangkok Post*, Supplement, April 3, 1968), and Thanat (Bangkok domestic service broadcast, April 11, 1968).

105. *Los Angeles Times*, November 12, 1967, p. 8.

106. *New York Times*, January 19, 1967, p. 5 (announcement by Ambassador Graham Martin); *Le Monde*, January 21-22, 1968, citing a report by Ambassador Leonard Unger.

107. See the joint communiqué issued by Premier Thanom and President Johnson on May 9, 1968, following the Thai leader's visit to the United States (Thai Permanent Mission, Press Release No. 42, May 15, 1968), and Thanat's remarks before Senate Staffers, May 10, 1968, Press Release No. 44, May 31, 1968.

108. Thanat's statement in an interview with Terence Smith of the *New York Times*; see ibid., Press Release, No. 8, February 17, 1969.

109. See his article, "Which Road for Southeast Asia?" op. cit.

110. From Thanat's speech of August 3, 1966, to a meeting of the foreign ministers of the Association of Southeast Asia (ASA—Thailand, Malaysia,

Philippines), in *Foreign Affairs Bulletin*, Vol. VI, No. 1, August-September 1966, p. 3.

111. Speech in New York City on May 7, 1968; Thai Permanent Mission, Press Release No. 38, same date.

112. For documentation, see various issues of the official publication, *Foreign Affairs Bulletin*.

113. François Joyaux, "La politique étrangère de la Thailande en Asie," *Politique étrangère*, No. 4, 1966, pp. 340-343.

114. Address at the University of Minnesota; Thai Permanent Mission, Press Release No. 62, October 22, 1968.

115. Editorial of April 24, 1968. Thanat has also contended that the benefits of regional cooperation may eventually become apparent to Peking and bring China's leaders to the realization that participation in regional activities is the quickest path to the attainment of great-power status. Speech before the Asia Society in New York, February 24, 1970; Thai Permanent Mission, Press Release No. 11, same date.

116. Starner interview with Thanat, op. cit., p. 159.

117. Statement by Thanat in Tokyo, broadcast by Kyodo, May 17, 1968.

118. For example, see *Bangkok Post*, February 21, 1969.

119. See ibid., November 14, 26, 1970 and January 25, 1971, and *Bangkok World*, January 15, 1971.

120. Address before Senate staffers in Washington, May 10, 1968; text in Thai Permanent Mission, Press Release No. 44, May 31, 1968.

121. In the speech cited ibid., Thanat pointed out that Thailand's involvement in Vietnam was due not to an ideological affinity with the United States, but to Thailand's own interests. Although "it is suggested that we are committed to the western nations, to the United States in particular," he said, Thailand does not have *"a commitment to any one nation. It is a commitment to our freedom and our independence."* Italics in original.

122. For comments by Thai leaders on these alternatives, see ibid. and *Foreign Affairs Bulletin*, Vol. IV, No. 1, August-September 1964, pp. 729-730; and Vol. V, No. 2, October-November 1965, p. 199.

Notes to Chapter 3

1. For a similar listing of the major considerations in Cambodia's foreign policy, see Roger M. Smith, *Cambodia's Foreign Policy*, Cornell University Press, Ithaca, N.Y., 1965, p. 87.

2. The historic roots of the controversy are treated ibid., Chap. 2.

3. See Sihanouk's statement in *Cambodian News*, January 1963, cited in Michael Leifer, "Cambodia and China: Neutralism, 'Neutrality,' and National

Security," in A.M. Halpern ed., *Policies Toward China: Views from Six Continents*, McGraw-Hill, for the Council on Foreign Relations, New York, 1965, p. 346.

4. The Thai side of the controversy and its background may be found in the following publications of the Thai Ministry of Foreign Affairs: *Relations between Thailand and Cambodia*, Pranchandra Press, Bangkok, January 1959; *Facts about the Relations between Thailand and Cambodia*, Pranchandra Press, Bangkok, 1961; *Facts about the Relations between Thailand and Cambodia*, Vol. II, Pranchandra Press, Bangkok, February 28, 1962; *Facts about the Relations between Thailand and Cambodia*, Vol. III [Pranchandra Press?], Bangkok, March 1, 1963. Cambodia's case was made in such publications as Norodom Sihanouk, *Le Cambodge et ses relations avec ses voisins*, Ministère de l'Information, Phnom Penh, 1962, and Royaume du Cambodge, *Livre blanc sur la rupture des relations diplomatiques entre le Cambodge et la Thailand, le 23 octobre 1961*, Ministère de l'Information, Phnom Penh, February 1965.

5. Smith, p. 31. For background information on Son Ngoc Thanh and the Khmer Serai, see in addition Martin F. Herz, *A Short History of Cambodia: From the Days of Angkor to the Present*, Praeger, New York, 1958, pp. 73-76, 83-84.

6. See the letter to the United Nations Secretary-General by the Permanent Representative of Thailand, Yong Pholbun, February 18, 1966, in *Foreign Affairs Bulletin*, Vol. V, No. 4, February-March 1966, pp. 407-408.

7. See *Études cambodgiennes*, No. 10, April-June 1967, p. 15. The specific date was mentioned by Sihanouk in a speech of November 4, 1967, broadcast the following day over Phnom Penh domestic service.

8. See Chapter 12 of W. Howard Wriggins, *The Ruler's Imperative: Strategies for Political Survival in Asia and Africa*, Columbia University Press, New York, 1969.

9. Smith, pp. 190-199.

10. For the Thai view of Sihanouk's proposal, see *Foreign Affairs Bulletin*, Vol. III, No. 3, December 1963-January 1964, pp. 281-282.

11. Smith, p. 199.

12. The official reasons for the two announcements are given in a Royal Government statement published in *Études cambodgiennes*, No. 11, July-September 1967, p. 10.

13. E.g., in a press conference broadcast over Phnom Penh Radio, November 3, 1966.

14. Speeches of November 20 and 23, 1966, broadcast November 21 and 23, respectively, by Phnom Penh domestic service radio.

15. Quoted in Smith, p. 174.

16. Sihanouk, pp. 27-28.

17. Ibid., pp. 28-29, and Smith, p. 189.

18. Gordon, "Cambodia: Where Foreign Policy Counts," p. 444.

19. Smith, pp. 75-76.

20. For comments on the Sangkum's organization, membership, and "ideology," see Smith, "Cambodia," in George McT. Kahin, ed., *Governments and Politics of Southeast Asia*, 2d ed., Cornell University Press, Ithaca, N.Y., 1964, pp. 646-647; Steinberg, et al., p. 100; "Le Cambodge donne l'exemple," *Jeune afrique*, No. 320, February 26, 1966, p. 46.

21. Michael Leifer, *Cambodia: The Search for Security*, Praeger, New York, 1967, p. 118, quoting Sihanouk's remarks in *Cambodian News*, July 1961.

22. For precise distinctions among these types of policies, see Khalid I. Babaa and Cecil V. Crabb, Jr., "Nonalignment as a Diplomatic and Ideological Credo," *The Annals*, Vol. CCCLXII, November 1965, pp. 6-17.

23. The Neutrality Act is an adjunct to, but not an official part of, Cambodia's constitution. In effect, the act makes the declaration of the Cambodian delegation at the close of the 1954 Geneva Conference—that is, Articles 4 and 5 of the Final Declaration, in which Cambodia vows not to enter into military alliances except in self-defense—the policy of the state. See Smith, *Cambodia's Foreign Policy*, pp. 107-108.

24. Leifer, *Cambodia*, pp. 116-117.

25. *The Conference of Heads of State or Government of Non-aligned Countries: Belgrade, September 1-6, 1961*, Publicisticko-Izdavacki Zavod, Belgrade, 1961, pp. 183, 193.

26. See his article in *Jeune afrique*, No. 320, p. 32.

27. Leifer, "Cambodia and China," pp. 331-332.

28. See *Les paroles de Samdech Preach Norodom Sihanouk, 1967*, Ministry of Information, Phnom Penh, 1968, p. 755. (Hereafter cited as *Paroles, 1967*.)

29. For further discussion, see Smith, *Cambodia's Foreign Policy*, pp. 95-102. Later in 1956, Sihanouk made successful visits to the Soviet Union, Poland, and Czechoslovakia to establish diplomatic relations and to increase his aid "package" from the Communist nations. Ibid., p. 105.

30. In November 1963 Sihanouk had concluded that the implication of Diem's demise was for Cambodia to "com[e] to terms" with the Vietnamese and Chinese Communists before their "victory" in South Vietnam and Thailand. See his statement quoted in Leifer, *Cambodia*, p. 149.

31. In a letter to the *New York Times* in 1965 (June 4, p. 34), he quoted from a recently published article he had written: "I have never had the slightest illusion on the fate that awaits me at the hands of the Communists, as well as that which is reserved for 'my' government, after having removed from our region the influence, and especially the presence, of the 'free world,' and the U.S.A. in particular."

32. Writing in *Jeune afrique*, No. 320, p. 34.

33. Later, he wrote the *New York Times* correspondent, Harrison Salisbury: "If the West one day leaves Asia, China will stay eternally. By supporting us politically and diplomatically against our two traditional enemies, China until now has safeguarded our existence as an independent state." *New York Times*, August 4, 1966, p. 3.

34. Smith, *Cambodia's Foreign Policy*, p. 121.

35. On the conference and its recommendations, see G.H. Jansen, *Nonalignment and the Afro-Asian States*, Praeger, New York, 1966, pp. 334-342.

36. Ibid., Chap. 17. In November 1963, when Indonesia hosted the first Games of the New Emerging Forces (GANEFO) in Djakarta, Cambodia participated. This event followed a decision of the Cambodian Amateur Athletic Federation in April not to condemn Indonesia for having decided to exclude Israel and the Republic of China from the games. See Leifer, "Cambodia and China," p. 343.

37. Quoted ibid., p. 344.

38. Quoted in Leifer, *Cambodia*, p. 141.

39. Smith, *Cambodia's Foreign Policy*, pp. 108-109.

40. Ibid., p. 110, and Willmott, p. 80.

41. Ibid., p. 116.

42. Comments by Sihanouk on the nature and ambitions of the Pracheachon are contained in John P. Armstrong, *Sihanouk Speaks*, Walker and Co., New York, 1964, pp. 122 ff.

43. See Leifer, *Cambodia*, pp. 127-129.

44. The 1962 plot is discussed in Smith, *Cambodia's Foreign Policy*, pp. 121, 170.

45. See Sihanouk's remarks at the 1961 Belgrade Conference, in *The Conference of Heads of State . . .* , p. 182. A Yugoslav credit of $6 million for the construction of three small hydroelectric power plants was extended to Cambodia in 1963; it was the first of several credits Belgrade has granted Phnom Penh. Smith, *Cambodia's Foreign Policy*, p. 113.

46. Ibid., Table 1, p. 123.

47. Information on trade may be found in annual issues of the *Far Eastern Economic Review Yearbook* (Hong Kong).

48. The editorial said: "Obviously, if all countries in the world base their mutual relations on these [five] principles, then there would be no threat, intervention, or aggression by one country against another."

49. *Jen-min jih-pao*, November 22, 1963, p. 1.

50. André Tong, "Cambodia is Attracted to Communist China," *Est et Ouest*, No. 338, trans. in Joint Publications Research Service (JPRS), *Translations on South and Southeast Asia*, No. 81, April 7, 1965, pp. 7-8, 11.

51. *Jen-min jih-pao*, June 17, p. 1, and June 18, 1964, p. 4.

52. Ibid., July 5, 1964, p. 3.

53. Ibid., June 9, 1964, p. 3.

54. For further discussion, see Smith, *Cambodia's Foreign Policy*, pp. 200-202, 204-210.

55. See Jean-Pierre Simon, "Cambodia: Pursuit of Crisis," *Asian Survey*, Vol. V, No. 1, January 1965, p. 52.

56. *Jen-min jih-pao*, September 28, 1964, p. 1.

57. For the text of the Sihanouk-Liu communiqué, see ibid., October 6, 1964, pp. 1-2.

58. Ibid., October 10, 1964, p. 3.

59. In December 1964, a final round of United States-Cambodia discussions in New Delhi had failed to produce accord on a multilateral negotiation of the border dispute with South Vietnam and that government's claims to the offshore islands. The New Delhi talks were suspended by the United States on December 16. See Smith, *Cambodia's Foreign Policy*, pp. 211-215.

60. Text in NCNA (Peking) international service broadcast of October 21, 1964.

61. The communiqué of the last preparatory session of February 17 listed 40 organizations and parties that had been invited, including 4 from Cambodia, 5 from Laos, 11 from North Vietnam, and 20 from South Vietnam. Phnom Penh broadcast to Southeast Asia, February 18, 1965.

62. Text of the message is in *Jen-min jih-pao*, February 25, 1965, p. 1.

63. See Royaume du Cambodge, *Discours de S.P. Norodom Sihanouk Upayuvareach, chef de l'état du Cambodge, à l'occasion de l'ouverture de la conférence plenière des peuples indochinoises*, Ministry of Information, Phnom Penh, February 25, 1965.

64. Vietnam News Agency (Hanoi) broadcast of March 10, 1965.

65. *Jen-min jih-pao*, May 21, 1965, p. 1.

66. Ibid., August 15, 1965, p. 4.

67. From the final communiqué of October 3, 1965; published ibid., October 4, pp. 1, 4.

68. See ibid., October 22, 1965, p. 1. A Chinese spokesman at Algiers identified Cambodia, the DRV, North Korea, and Tanzania as supporters of China's recommendation for postponement. The previous June, when the first attempt to convene the Afro-Asian conference had been made, Cambodia was one of the countries that did not favor Soviet participation. See Jansen, pp. 397, 400, n. 1.

69. International service broadcast of October 19, 1965.

70. See, e.g., *Jen-min jih-pao*, October 22, p. 4; October 24, p. 4; and October 27, 1965, p. 1.

71. Phnom Penh domestic service broadcast of October 26, 1965.

72. Phnom Penh domestic service broadcast of June 24, 1965.

73. Speech of October 25, 1965, broadcast over Phnom Penh domestic radio, October 26.

74. Speech of November 27, 1965, broadcast the same day by Radio Phnom Penh. Further details were given by Sihanouk in a speech of November 29, broadcast the same day. But the aid figures cannot be confirmed from Chinese sources, which do not report them.

75. Speech of September 24, 1966, broadcast by Phnom Penh domestic service on the same day.

76. *Jen-min jih-pao*, May 1, 1966, p. 6.

77. Commentator, ibid., October 16, 1966, p. 4.

78. As reported by NCNA (Peking) international service, October 25, 1966.

79. Press conference remarks of November 3, 1966, as reported over Phnom Penh Radio to Southeast Asia, same date.

80. Phnom Penh domestic service, October 6, 1966.

81. A complete listing is provided in *Le Sangkum* (Phnom Penh), January 1967, trans. in JPRS, *Translations on Southeast Asia*, No. 146, February 21, 1967, pp. 39-40. See also the 1967 edition of *Far Eastern Economic Review Yearbook*, p. 135.

82. Phnom Penh domestic service broadcast of November 6, 1966.

83. Speech of November 20, 1966, broadcast by Phnom Penh domestic service November 21.

84. Comment at a press conference of November 3, 1966, broadcast by Phnom Penh radio to Southeast Asia the same day.

85. Phnom Penh domestic service broadcast of March 24, 1966.

86. Listings of Soviet assistance may be found in the *Le Sangkum* article, previously cited in JPRS (p. 40), and the 1967 *Far Eastern Economic Review Yearbook*.

87. Reported over Phnom Penh domestic service radio, December 11, 1966.

88. Nationwide speech of November 6, 1966, broadcast the same day by Phnom Penh domestic service. For discussions of the reasons behind Sihanouk's noninterference in the formation of the right-of-center cabinet, see Smith, "Cambodia: Between Scylla and Charybdis," *Asian Survey*, Vol. VIII, No. 1, January 1968, p. 72, and Robert Shaplen, "Letter from Cambodia," *The New Yorker*, January 13, 1968, pp. 78-79.

89. Message to the nation of April 3, 1967, in *Paroles, 1967*, pp. 107-108.

90. Ibid., pp. 189, 213 ff.

91. Speeches by Sihanouk of May 9 and 15, 1967. Ibid., pp. 328-329, 360-363; also, Phnom Penh Radio domestic service broadcasts of those dates.

92. *Paroles, 1967*, p. 362.

93. Speech before a special congress of the National Assembly, Phnom Penh domestic service, same date. A far more guarded version of the speech was published in *Paroles, 1967*, p. 22.

94. *Paroles, 1967*, p. 33.

95. Text in *SCMP*, No. 3961, June 16, 1967, pp. 28-29.

96. VNA (Hanoi) international service broadcast of June 12, 1967. The broadcast sought to make it appear that the NLF's recognition preceded that of the Soviet Union by stating that the NLF's statement was dated May 31. In fact, though, the announcement did not come until June 8.

97. Correspondence between Sihanouk and Pham Van Dong was made public by VNA (Hanoi) international service broadcast of June 22, 1967.

98. May 6, 1967, broadcast, Phnom Penh to Southeast Asia.

99. Broadcast to Southeast Asia, May 14, 1967.

100. Message broadcast by NCNA (Peking) international service, May 11, 1967.

101. Further detail on the contents of the *Ts'an-k'ao hsiao-hsi* during this period is available in *The Washington Post*, August 28, 1967, article by Stanley Karnow.

102. *Paroles, 1967*, p. 758. Sihanouk's message was, however, broadcast by NCNA (Peking) international service, June 21, 1967.

Notes to Chapter 4

1. Ibid., and Charles B. McLane, *Soviet Strategies in Southeast Asia: An Exploration of Eastern Policy under Lenin and Stalin*, Princeton University Press, Princeton, N.J., 1966, p. 317.

2. Thomson, pp. 19-20. From 1944 to 1946, the CPB was part of the AFPFL.

3. "Communism and Nationalism in Burma," *Far Eastern Survey*, Vol. XVIII, No. 17, August 24, 1949, p. 196.

4. Donald E. Smith, *Religion and Politics in Burma*, Princeton University Press, Princeton, N.J., 1965, pp. 132 ff. On U Nu's religious and political values, see also E. Sarkisyanz, *Buddhist Backgrounds of the Burmese Revolution*, Martinus Nijhoff, The Hague, 1965, pp. 211-220.

5. On the philosophic differences between leaders of the Revolutionary Council and the AFPFL, see John H. Badgley, "Burma: The Nexus of Socialism and Two Political Traditions," *Asian Survey*, Vol. III, No. 2, February 1963, pp. 89-95.

6. The Council's commitment to an essentially Buddhist doctrine of change and its rejection of Communist social credos was early made clear in two publications of the BSPP: the "Philosophy," entitled "The System of Correla-

tion of Man and Environment" (discussed ibid., p. 202), and "Specific Characteristics of the BSPP," *Working People's Daily* (Rangoon), September 6, 1964.

7. "The Communist Parties of Burma," in Robert A. Scalapino, ed., *The Communist Revolution in Asia: Tactics, Goals, and Achievements*, Prentice-Hall, Englewood Cliffs, N.J., 1965, p. 306.

8. See Trager, *Burma*, p. 217.

9. Quoted ibid., p. 218.

10. Ibid., pp. 218-219.

11. Ibid., pp. 220-227. Trager thus rejects an alternative hypothesis that neutralism was decided upon mainly as a mid-path between opposing pro-East and pro-West sentiment among the existing political parties.

12. Ibid., p. 227.

13. In U Nu, *Burma Looks Ahead*, Ministry of Information, Rangoon, 1953, pp. 98-101.

14. On these last points, see William C. Johnstone, *Burma's Foreign Policy: A Study in Neutralism*, Harvard University Press, Cambridge, Mass., 1963, pp. 74-75, and Trager, *Burma*, p. 220.

15. Speech before the National Press Club in Washington, D.C., July 1, 1955, in U Nu, *An Asian Speaks*, Embassy of the Union of Burma, Washington, D.C., 1955.

16. Trager, et al., *Burma's Role in the United Nations, 1948-1955*, Institute of Pacific Relations, New York, 1956, p. 7.

17. The fullest account of Burma's response to events in Korea is by Isabelle Crocker, *Burma's Foreign Policy and the Korean War: A Case Study*, P-1576-RC, The RAND Corporation, Santa Monica, Calif., December 12, 1958.

18. On these and related events, see Oliver E. Clubb, Jr., *The Effect of Chinese Nationalist Military Activities in Burma on Burmese Foreign Policy*, P-1595-RC, The RAND Corporation, Santa Monica, Calif., January 20, 1959, especially Chap. 3.

19. Communiqué of December 12, 1954, in Chinese People's Institute of Foreign Affairs, ed., *A Victory for the Five Principles of Peaceful Co-existence*, Foreign Language Press, Peking, 1960, pp. 3-5. Hereafter cited as *A Victory for the Five Principles*.

20. Lea E. Williams, *The Future of the Overseas Chinese in Southeast Asia*, McGraw-Hill, New York, 1966, p. 11.

21. See the communiqué of November 9, 1956; ibid., pp. 6-7.

22. For background, see Trager, *Burma*, pp. 243-245, and Daphne E. Whittam, "The Sino-Burmese Boundary Treaty," *Pacific Affairs*, Vol. XXXIV, No. 2, Summer 1961, pp. 174-179.

23. *The Nation* (Rangoon), December 24, 1954; quoted in Johnstone, p. 171.

24. Quoted ibid., p. 176.

25. The figures on the Communist forces are in Hugh Tinker, *The Union of Burma: A Study of the First Years of Independence*, Oxford University Press, London, 1957 (1st ed.), p. 35. On the Communists' military gains, see the map and list of captured towns, ibid., pp. 44-45.

26. Ibid., p. 49.

27. See Badgley, "Burma's Radical Left," p. 51.

28. Based on Burmese newspaper accounts of that time, cited in Johnstone, pp. 181-182, and the testimony of a Communist military commander who surrendered in 1968, in *Guardian* (Rangoon), October 21, 1968.

29. Johnstone, p. 171.

30. Badgley, "Burma's Radical Left," pp. 51-52.

31. Tinker, p. 58.

32. Aleksandr Kaznacheev, who defected from the Soviet Embassy in Rangoon in 1959, has testified that the embassy was under instructions by 1957 to convey to the Chinese Communists, who admittedly were the dominant influence over the CPB, that the rebellion had to be called off and the party made to enter into peaceful political competition. See his *Inside a Soviet Embassy: Experiences of a Russian Diplomat in Burma*, J.B. Lippincott, Philadelphia, 1962, pp. 138-139, 214-215.

33. On the 1960 agreements, see Whittam, pp. 180 ff.; *A Victory for the Five Principles*, pp. 28-41; and Maung Maung, "The Burma-China Border Settlement," *Asian Survey*, Vol. I, No. 1, March 1961, pp. 38-43.

34. Article III of the treaty; text in *A Victory for the Five Principles*, pp. 30-32.

35. See, e.g., Johnstone, pp. 196, 199. Johnstone argues that the treaty not only "gives to the Peking regime a veto over Burma's future foreign relations in respect to military defense," but also "has given to Communist China an open door to the world through a friendly country and has enabled Chinese Communist influence to reach the shores of the Bay of Bengal."

36. For a fuller discussion of the China-India dispute and its place in Peking's diplomacy, see John Rowland, *A History of Sino-Indian Relations: Hostile Co-existence*, Van Nostrand, Princeton, N.J., 1967, Chap. 10.

37. For documentation, see *Jen-min jih-pao*, October 16 and 29, 1961, p. 1.

38. See the editorial, ibid., October 14, 1961, p. 1, in which the Sino-Burmese border treaty is spoken of as a "shining example," and a statement of the CPR Foreign Ministry on December 6, 1961 (ibid., December 7, p. 1), responding to Indian charges of Chinese aggression.

39. *The Nation*, December 30, 1962.

40. Article by the editorial departments of *Wen-hui pao, Chieh-fang jih-pao*, and *Life of the Party Branch*, August 10, 1967, reprinted in *Peking Review*, No. 36, September 1, 1967, p. 11.

41. See, for instance, an article in *Wai-shih hung-ch'i* (*Foreign Affairs Red Flag*, Peking), No. 6, June 14, 1967, p. 1, by the Proletarian Cultural Revolution Foreign Affairs Section Liaison Committee.

42. *Kuan-yü kuo-chi kung-ch'an chu-yi yün-tung* . . . , p. 22.

43. Text of the final communiqué from Rangoon on April 25 is in *Jen-min jih-pao*, April 27, 1963, p. 1.

44. Chieh Li-fu, "*Paukphaw* Sentiment Runs Deep," *Shih-chieh chih-shih*, No. 9, May 10, 1963, p. 15.

45. Badgley ("The Communist Parties of Burma," p. 305) suggests that such a trade-off may in fact have taken place. One piece of circumstantial evidence he offers is that after Liu's visit, Ne Win "flew to [New] Delhi apparently to act as an intermediary between Nehru and Chou En-lai after the latter's return from Africa. . . ."

46. NCNA (Peking) broadcast of September 3, 1963.

47. November 19, 1963, p. 4.

48. Robert A. Holmes, "Burmese Domestic Policy: The Politics of Burmanization," *Asian Survey*, Vol. VII, No. 3, March 1967, p. 194.

49. Communiqués from these visits may be found in *Jen-min jih-pao*, February 19, 1964, p. 1, and July 13, 1964, p. 1.

50. For example, ibid., August 4, p. 5, and August 7, 1964, p. 3.

51. Ibid., September 27, 1964, p. 4, and November 18, 1964, p. 4.

52. Rather than criticize Burma directly, however, NCNA, in a broadcast from Peking of September 10, 1963, cited the proleft *Mandalay Times* in support of China's antitreaty position.

53. See Badgley, "Burma's Zealot Wungyis: Maoists or St. Simonists," *Asian Survey*, Vol. V, No. 1, January 1965, p. 60.

54. Ne Win's letter of December 3, 1964, was published in *Jen-min jih-pao*, December 15, 1964, p. 1. In the letter, Ne Win also mentioned that Burma had been participating in UN disarmament talks—a point not calculated to impress Peking.

55. Holmes, p. 193.

56. Ibid., p. 192. For an evaluation of the impact of nationalization and other more direct "anti-Chinese" measures on the local Chinese, as seen from the Nationalist side, see *Chung-yang jih-pao* (*Central Daily News*, Taipei), April 17, 1968, p. 1.

57. Badgley, "Burma's Zealot Wungyis," op. cit.

58. *Vanguard Daily* (Rangoon), May 26, 1968.

59. *Guardian*, May 11, 1968.

60. See, for instance, the review of the CPB's history by Ba Thein Tin, a politburo member resident in Peking, in *Peking Review*, No. 35, August 25, 1967, pp. 12-16, and No. 36, September 1, 1967, pp. 19-24. Thein Tin

attempted to show how, after September 1964, the CPB consistently followed Maoist guidelines on violent struggle from rural bases, proletarian party leadership of a peasant war, formation of "an antifeudal united front," and self-reliance.

61. Text of the message is in New China News Agency, Daily Bulletin No. 2434, October 2, 1964. The fact that the message wholeheartedly endorsed China's position in the rift with Moscow may also help explain why it was published.

62. *Guardian*, May 26, 1968; *Vanguard Daily*, same date.

63. Testimony of a member of the Toungoo District Party Committee who surrendered to the government in the summer of 1967. Rangoon domestic service broadcast of August 18, 1967; also, *Vanguard Daily*, May 26, 1968.

64. According to a district party committee member, as reported in a broadcast from Rangoon on November 14, 1967.

65. *Botataung* (Rangoon), May 19, 1968. According to this report, the "life forum movement" began in early 1966, with Tharrawaddy District selected as the year's model area. Of the first 78 trainees, 73 were under 21 years of age.

66. *Guardian*, April 27, 1968.

67. *Guardian*, April 27, 1968.

68. Ibid., May 11, 1968. See also M. Aleksandrov, "The 'Burmese Experiment,'" *Literaturnaya gazeta*, translated in *The Current Digest of the Soviet Press*, Vol. XXI, No. 18, May 21, 1969, p. 20.

69. The executions were reported in a Rangoon domestic service broadcast of April 18, 1968.

70. Trager, *Burma*, p. 265.

71. The communiqué appears in *Jen-min jih-pao*, August 2, 1965, pp. 1 and 3. Other aspects of Ne Win's trip are covered ibid., July 24-August 1.

72. Ibid., August 24, 1965, p. 1. The news report did not mention the subject of the discussions. During the same month, incidentally, the North Vietnamese foreign minister and vice premier, Nguyen Duy Trinh, also spent a day in Rangoon; but his talks were likewise private and unpublicized.

73. Ibid., March 27, 1966, p. 3.

74. Ibid., April 16, 1966, p. 1.

75. For the text of the final communiqué, see ibid., April 20, 1966, p. 1.

76. Badgley, "Burma's China Crisis: The Choices Ahead," *Asian Survey*, Vol. VII, No. 11, November 1967, p. 756. *After* the summer 1967 crisis, an NCNA broadcast, looking back over Ne Win's conduct toward China during previous years, concluded that the GUB-India agreement "actually carved out 90,000 square kilometers of Chinese territory at the presumptuous demand of the Indian expansionists."

77. Trager, "Sino-Burmese Relations: The End of the Pauk Phaw Era," *Orbis*, Vol. XI, No. 4, Winter 1968, pp. 1039-1040. Trager maintains that the

CPR agencies kept about 500 small private schools going, with an estimated enrollment of roughly 10,000 students. See also Holmes, p. 193.

78. Trager, "Sino-Burmese Relations," p. 1039.

79. See, in particular, Yi Ta, "Sino-Burmese Cultural Intercourse," *Jen-min jih-pao*, April 18, 1966, pp. 3-4.

80. For examples in China's relations not only with Burma but also with Ceylon, Nepal, and Cambodia—all countries that would experience the "backlash" of the Cultural Revolution later in 1967—see Melvin Gurtov, "The Foreign Ministry and Foreign Affairs in the Chinese Cultural Revolution," in Thomas W. Robinson et al., *The Cultural Revolution in China*, University of California Press, Berkeley, 1971.

81. The previously cited *Jen-min jih-pao* editorial of April 20, 1966, which gave the significance of Liu's trip to Burma, dwelled on the points of agreement between Burma and China and ended by saying: "As Chairman Liu Shao-ch'i concludes his visit to Burma, we wish wholeheartedly that the people of China and Burma will forever coexist in friendship."

82. Ibid., April 21, 1966, p. 1.

83. See, for example, ibid., July 8, 1966, p. 4, and July 14, 1966, p. 6; also, NCNA (Peking) international service broadcast of October 29, 1966.

84. Interview with a reporter for the Swedish Communist Party organ, *Clarté*, in *Ch'en Yi yen-lun hsüan (Selected Speeches of Ch'en Yi)*, Tz'u-lien ch'u-pan she, Hong Kong, 1967, p. 24. The book is an unofficial publication put out during the Cultural Revolution in an attempt to discredit the foreign minister's foreign policy views.

Notes to Chapter 5

1. See Trager, "Sino-Burmese Relations," p. 1040. The Red Guards may actually have been overseas Chinese who had left Burma for China some months earlier.

2. Trager, "Sino-Burmese Relations," pp. 1040 ff.

3. Reported in an article in *Peking Review*, No. 28, July 7, 1967, p. 20.

4. Rangoon domestic service broadcasts of June 26 and 27, 1967.

5. For an account of these and other events from the Chinese viewpoint, see *Peking Review*, No. 28, July 7, 1967.

6. NCNA (Peking), June 28, 1967, in *SCMP*, No. 3971, June 30, 1967, pp. 28-29; *SCMP*, No. 3972, July 1, 1967, pp. 37-38.

7. An international service broadcast of June 28 said the wearing of badges was fully justified. It declared that the anti-China fever in Burma was "not accidental," but reflected Burma's inability "to cope with its problems in its domestic and foreign policy." A later broadcast the same day by NCNA ended by saying: "The Chinese government and people are following closely the moves

of the Burmese government." A third broadcast in late evening expressed renewed outrage at the alleged deaths of "over 50 Chinese residents and students." The GUB was labeled "reactionary" and warned of the "blood debt" it would have to pay.

8. Rangoon domestic service broadcast of June 29; *Le Monde*, June 30, 1967.

9. Rangoon domestic service broadcast, June 28, 1967.

10. NCNA (Peking) international service broadcast of June 29, 1967; *Peking Review*, No. 28, July 7, 1967, p. 17.

11. NCNA (Peking) international service broadcast of June 29.

12. Excerpts from the memorandum and a report of China's reply were broadcast by NCNA (Peking) on July 1, 1967. The demonstration in question was reported by NCNA on June 29 to have involved 200,000 people and to have taken place in front of the GUB Embassy in Peking.

13. Alleging the death of over 50 Chinese and the incarceration of another 600, Hsiao demanded, among other things, that the Burmese offenders be punished, the Chinese families compensated, and permission granted him to examine the corpses. NCNA (Peking) international service, June 29, 1967.

14. By contrast, when NCNA announced on June 23 that the CPB Central Committee had sent the CCP Central Committee a message of congratulations on the explosion of China's first hydrogen bomb (June 18), the message made no allusion to events in Burma and no derogatory remarks about the GUB.

15. As broadcast by NCNA (Peking), June 30, 1967.

16. NCNA (Peking) broadcast, July 1, 1967. See also *Peking Review*, No. 28, July 7, 1967, p. 22.

17. NCNA (Peking) international service, July 6, 1967; *New York Times*, July 8, 1967, pp. 1, 3.

18. At a memorial rally for the dead aid technician, who had risen to the status of a martyr, Ba Thein Tin claimed that the Communist-led armed forces controlled 60 percent of Burma's territory. He also said Burma might become another Vietnam in a few years; that the party had survived because it had adhered to Marxism-Leninism and Mao's thoughts; and that the White Flags would pursue a protracted war strategy, encircling the cities from the countryside. *Peking Review*, No. 29, July 14, 1967, pp. 10-15.

19. *New York Times*, July 10, 1967, p. 6.

20. Rangoon domestic service broadcast of July 17, 1967.

21. Thomas W. Robinson, "Chou En-lai's Role in the Cultural Revolution in China," in Robinson et al.

22. *Hung-wei-pao* (*Red Guard Daily*, Peking), October 18, 1967.

23. Ibid., September 15, 1967. The alleged details of the occupation of the Foreign Ministry by Red Guards groups under Wang Li and Yao Teng-shan in

defiance of Chou are contained in *Yeh-chan pao* (*Field Combat*, Canton), March 1968; trans. in *SCMP*, No. 4158, April 16, 1968, pp. 5-6.

24. According to a Phnom Penh domestic service broadcast of August 7, 1967, Sihanouk was reported to have sharply criticized the KCFA for issuing a pro-Chinese statement on events in Indonesia and Burma when the Cambodian government had chosen to remain silent.

25. Based on interviews in Phnom Penh, August 1968.

26. *Paroles, 1967*, p. 758. Phurissara's visit was not reported in the Chinese press or domestic service radio broadcasts. When he departed, he was seen off by a vice-minister of foreign affairs, Han Nien-lung, not Ch'en Yi.

27. Interview in Phnom Penh.

28. Speech of September 12, 1967, in *Paroles, 1967*, pp. 695-696.

29. Interview in Phnom Penh.

30. *Paroles, 1967*, pp. 649-650. According to a Phnom Penh domestic service broadcast of September 4, 1967, two days later, a relatively moderate leadership was installed in the new National Committee for Sino-Khmer Friendship; Penn Nouth, Sihanouk's personal adviser, was named chairman.

31. *Paroles, 1967*, pp. 653-654.

32. Ibid., pp. 655-656. Sihanouk struck another blow at the left when he declared that the *Khmer Ekreach*, arch foe of the Chinese Embassy, would be indemnified by the government for losses suffered when its offices were ransacked by leftist demonstrators. Ibid.

33. At the same time—Sihanouk's press conference of September 11—Chau Seng and So Nem, who had been brought into the May 1 administration, were ordered to leave the government, and all newspapers except those directly under Sihanouk were suspended. Ibid., pp. 675-676; 677, 680.

34. Ibid., p. 677.

35. Ibid., p. 707. The genuineness of Sihanouk's intention to remove his officials from Peking may be gauged by his announcement that the ambassador, Truong Cang, would be returning to replace Chau Seng on the High Council of the Throne. Phnom Penh broadcast to Southeast Asia, September 14, 1967.

36. Telegram from Truong Cang to Sihanouk, September 14, 1967. Reported in Sihanouk's press conference of September 18; *Paroles, 1967*, pp. 711-712.

37. Telegram from Truong Cang of September 15, 1967; ibid., pp. 712-715.

38. *Asahi Evening News* (Tokyo), September 5, 1967.

39. *Paroles, 1967*, p. 715.

40. Reported in *Le Monde*, September 20, 1967.

41. The Cambodian government announced it was withdrawing on September 7, 1967. The reasons given were that the Bank was linked to organizations such as the Asian and Pacific Council (ASPAC) and the Association of Southeast Asian Nations (ASEAN), whose "essential aims are to serve American imperi-

alism in all its forms." *Etudes cambodgiennes*, No. 11, July-September 1967, p. 9.

42. As it happened, the NCNA's 2-year permit to publish bulletins expired on September 16, 1967. See ibid., pp. 718-719, 721. In a speech of September 19, Sihanouk specified that NCNA had violated the terms of the Cambodia-CPR agreement of September 1965 by distributing subversive tracts that called for insurrection. Ibid., p. 732.

43. Quoted in *Le Monde*, October 1-2, 1967.

44. For substance of the decisions and their impact on the ministry, see Gurtov, "The Foreign Ministry and Foreign Affairs in the Chinese Cultural Revolution."

45. "U.S. Imperialism is the Deadly Enemy of the Cambodian People," p. 5.

Notes to Chapter 6

1. *Paroles, 1967*, p. 860.

2. For an overly dramatized account of Mrs. Kennedy's purposes in traveling to Cambodia, but one correct in its essentials, see Bernard and Marvin Kalb, "Jacqueline Kennedy's Secret Mission in Asia," *McCall's*, Vol. XCV, No. 9, June 1968, pp. 61, 107-113.

3. In a press conference of October 5, for instance, Sihanouk reminded listeners that several of his officials preferred close ties with the United States to a pro-China policy. If he were to fall, he said, the pro-American group might take his place. Phnom Penh domestic service, same date.

4. Message broadcast over Phnom Penh domestic service, November 10, 1967.

5. Phnom Penh broadcast to Southeast Asia, December 1, 1967.

6. E.g., Commentator's remarks in *Jen-min jih-pao*, November 17, 1967, p. 6, and a statement of the Ministry of Foreign Affairs of November 26, 1967, broadcast by NCNA (Peking) domestic service, same date.

7. *Jen-min jih-pao*, December 28, 1967, p. 3.

8. *Christian Science Monitor*, October 27, 1967.

9. Dispatch by George McArthur and Horst Faas, in *New York Times*, November 21, 1967, p. 3. Nearly a month after their report, the ICC went to the Mimot region and, not surprisingly, found "no proof to justify the allegations of journalists of the United States on the subject of the existence of an alleged Viet Cong camp...." Report of December 29, 1967, in Mission Permanente du Cambodge auprès des Nations Unies, Bulletin de Presse, No. 4/68.

10. Speech of December 27 to the National Congress, as broadcast over Phnom Penh domestic service, same date.

11. *Washington Post*, December 29, 1967, p. A4.

12. Speech of January 6, 1968, in *Paroles, 1968*, pp. 9 ff.

13. Broadcast the same day over Phnom Penh service to Southeast Asia.

14. Phnom Penh broadcast to Southeast Asia, January 13, 1968.

15. Soon after that statement, the Soviet Embassy in Washington transmitted a note of the Soviet government concerning Cambodia. In the note, "profound anxiety" about American intentions was expressed, and a warning was given that the USSR would "not remain indifferent" to violations of Cambodia's territorial integrity. On the ICC, the Soviet statement considered that strengthening the Commission would only provide another "pretext for hostile actions against" Cambodia. Text in Tass international service broadcast, January 18, 1968.

16. For example, see his press conference comments of November 26, 1967, and January 7, 1968, reported in Mission du Cambodge, Bulletin de Presse, No. 7/68.

17. The communiqué was broadcast by VNA international service on January 12, 1968. Previously, in December, the NLF had issued several statements through the clandestine Liberation Radio supporting Sihanouk's tough stance against "United States aggression" and promising "to stand beside" the Cambodian army in case of an expansion of the war across the border. Broadcasts of December 13 and 25, 1967.

18. Tito's visit led to a communiqué that omitted reference to American policy in Vietnam. The generally aggressive policies of imperialism were cited, however, and "support" was registered for the DRV and the NLF. China was not mentioned in the document. Phnom Penh broadcast to Southeast Asia, January 22, 1968.

19. See Sihanouk's interview with William Attwood, "Sihanouk Talks," *Look*, April 2, 1968, p. 66.

20. These themes were contained, for example, in his press conference of January 27, in *Paroles, 1968*, pp. 59 ff.; a news conference to February 11, ibid., pp. 106-107; and in a letter to *Le Monde*, published March 7, 1968.

21. *Paroles, 1968*, pp. 87-88 and 107.

22. Press conference of February 28; ibid., p. 158.

23. Ibid., p. 178.

24. Ibid., p. 200 (speech of March 13).

25. On the Pathet Lao: Sihanouk's special message to the nation of April 22, broadcast over Phnom Penh domestic service, April 23, 1968; press conference of May 23, broadcast the next day by Phnom Penh domestic service; and speech of August 17, broadcast by Phnom Penh domestic service, same date. Sihanouk noted during these statements that the Pathet Lao had yet to recognize Cambodia's borders and that, inasmuch as they were backed by the North Vietnamese, their failure to do so limited the significance of Hanoi's promises. On the Viet Cong: speech of August 21, broadcast the same day over Phnom Penh domestic service; press conference of August 31, broadcast by Phnom Penh domestic service the same day.

26. *Réalités cambodgiennes*, June 21, 1968, p. 16.

27. From Sihanouk's interview in April 1968 with a correspondent of *Mainichi Shimbun* (Tokyo), in *Kambuja* (Phnom Penh), No. 38, May 15, 1968, p. 15.

28. Editorial in *Réalités cambodgiennes*, January 24, 1969, pp. 3-6.

29. Phnom Penh domestic service, on December 14, 1968, broadcast an undated message from Prince Souphanouvong to Sihanouk announcing the Pathet Lao's policy shift. It is likely that North Vietnam influenced the decision, perhaps in the belief that her image at the Paris peace talks could be improved thereby at little cost.

30. Text of the general's report is in *Neak Cheat Niyum*, March 24-30, 1969. Periodically thereafter, Radio Phnom Penh and other Cambodian sources reported on Viet Cong activities in the border provinces and on clashes between Cambodian and Viet Cong military units.

31. Ibid., March 21, 1969, p. 18.

32. E.g., in press conference remarks of April 16, 1969, as broadcast by Phnom Penh domestic service, same date.

33. See *Réalités cambodgiennes*, September 19, 1969, pp. 6-7. Again, however, these pledges meant nothing. On October 18, Sihanouk reported that there were 40,000 Communist troops in Cambodia's border provinces. A report by Lon Nol for the second half of September confirmed the figure and said it represented an increase over the first half of the month of several thousand troops. (*Le Sangkum*, October 1969.)

34. Editorial, July 26, 1968, pp. 3-5.

35. Leifer, *Cambodia*, p. 188.

36. Sihanouk's views on U.S. policy on Vietnam were offered in an interview with a *Mainichi* correspondent, previously cited from *Kambuja*, No. 38.

37. See, e.g., Sihanouk's speech of September 30, 1967, in which he contrasted China's rigorous adherence to her proclamations of friendship in the decade after the first CPR aid was received (1956-1965) with China's change of attitude toward Cambodia once the Cultural Revolution began. In *Paroles, 1967*, pp. 754-755.

38. *Réalités cambodgiennes*, December 19, 1969, p. 45.

39. See T.D. Allman, "Anatomy of a Coup," *Far Eastern Economic Review*, April 9, 1970, p. 19.

40. From Paris, Sihanouk said he understood the motivations behind the demonstrations but considered them an army-instigated plot to gain United States military aid. He warned that Cambodia in the end would become "a second Laos." *New York Times*, March 12, 1970, p. 3 and his message to the queen, broadcast by Phnom Penh domestic service, March 12.

41. Remarks on French television, March 12, 1970, as reported by Agence France Presse.

42. *New York Times*, March 17, 1970, p. 14.

43. Text in *Peking Review*, No. 13, March 27, 1970, pp. 15-17.

44. Ibid., statement of March 21, 1970, p. 19.

45. Radio Peking broadcast (in Cambodian) to Cambodia, March 23, 1970. Published in *Jen-min jih-pao*, March 25, 1970, p. 5.

46. Ibid., March 24, 1970, p. 5. Kuo Mo-jo, greeting a Japanese delegation in his capacity of honorary president of the China-Japan Friendship Association, was more specific. He said on March 24: "The recent coup d'etat in Cambodia . . . is a component part of the U.S. imperialist plot to expand war in Indo-China and carry out aggression against the countries in Indo-China." *Peking Review*, No. 13, March 27, 1970, p. 7.

47. Radio Hanoi domestic service, March 21, 1970.

48. "Commentator" article in *Nhan Dan*, March 22, 1970, as broadcast by Radio Hanoi to South Vietnam, same date.

49. Broadcast by VNA (Hanoi) international service, March 25, 1970.

50. See *Los Angeles Times*, March 26, 1970, p. 22.

51. *New York Times*, March 21, 1970, p. 1; March 26, p. 1.

52. Ibid., March 28 and 29, 1970, p. 1.

53. *Jen-min jih-pao*, March 27, 1970, p. 6.

54. See articles ibid., March 28, 29, 31, 1970, p. 5.

55. Articles ibid., March 31 and April 2, 1970, p. 6.

56. Ibid., April 6, 1970, p. 2.

57. See *Los Angeles Times*, April 16, 1970, p. 1 and *New York Times*, April 23, 1970, p. 1.

58. *Los Angeles Times*, April 16, 1970, p. 8.

59. According to the Chinese report of the meeting, it was held "at a certain place in the border area of Laos, Vietnam, and China." The report and the joint communiqué of the conference are ibid., April 28, 1970, pp. 1, 5.

60. See, for example, the articles in *Jen-min jih-pao* of April 7-8, 1970, p. 5, and the editorial of April 30 in which American "self-defense" forays into Cambodia are characterized as the prelude to "large-scale armed intervention."

61. Chou's speech was made at a banquet on April 25 at the Indochinese "summit" meeting. But *Jen-min jih-pao*'s news summary of the conference on April 28 had not mentioned a speech by Chou. The text appears ibid., May 3, 1970, p. 2.

62. Probably because of the Sino-Soviet border talks, Peking only occasionally and indirectly criticized Soviet policy in post-Sihanouk Cambodia. The harshest anti-Soviet language came from the Albanians. Radio Tirana domestic service, May 12, 1970.

63. For an excellent comparative picture of the pre- and post-Sihanouk Cambodian economic situation, see Donald Kirk, "Cambodia's Economic Crisis," *Asian Survey*, Vol. XI, No. 3, March 1971, pp. 238-255.

64. See, e.g., the articles by John Hughes in *Christian Science Monitor*, November 22, 1967, and by Peter Boog, "The People's War," *Far Eastern Economic Review*, November 16, 1967, p. 320. The reports regarded new American military aid deliveries as dramatic; in fact, they seem to have been the same end-items and training services the United States had been providing Burma for ten years.

65. Boog (ibid., p. 323) writes that after the Burma-China rupture, Soviet Premier Kosygin "sent a message to General Ne Win . . . pledging full support and sympathy for Burma in its troubles with China. This was followed almost immediately by a top-level seven-man economic mission which spent over a month in Rangoon discussing the possibility of Soviet aid to help stabilize the Burmese economy. . . ."

66. Quoted in *Le Monde*, July 4, 1967.

67. Burmese violations of China's land and air space were protested August 11 in a Foreign Ministry note that also referred to past CPR protests dating as far back as January 1965. "Severe punishment" was promised by "the Chinese people and the Chinese People's Liberation Army." (*Peking Review*, No. 34, August 18, 1967, p. 36.) The slaying of Chinese border inhabitants by Burmese troops was said to have occurred in February, April, and July 1967. NCNA (Peking) international service broadcast of August 10, 1967.

68. Note of the CPR Foreign Ministry of October 4, 1967; broadcast the same day over NCNA (Peking) international service.

69. *Forward* (Rangoon), Vol. VI, No. 8, December 1, 1967, p. 24.

70. *Far Eastern Economic Review*, February 15, 1968, p. 257.

71. NCNA (Peking) broadcast of May 30, 1968; *Yomiuri Shimbun* (Tokyo), October 26, 1968; NCNA (Peking) broadcast of August 5, 1968.

72. Radio Peking in Burmese to Burma, August 15, 1968.

73. NCNA international service, September 26 and December 17, 1968.

74. E.g., NCNA broadcasts of December 26, 1968, February 8, 1969, and April 27, 1969; and an article in the army newspaper, *Liberation Army Daily*, March 28, 1969, broadcast by NCNA the same day (in *SCMP*, No. 4389, April 3, 1969, pp. 25-26).

75. *Loktha Pyeithu Nezin* (Rangoon), November 7, 1969. Several Western newspapers, including the *New York Times* on November 8, 1969, incorrectly reported that Ne Win had charged Chinese Communist involvement in these clashes.

76. Rangoon domestic service, April 6, 1970.

77. *Guardian*, May 26, 1968, reprints part of that directive.

78. An undated issue of the White Flag organ, *People's Power*, republished by *Peking Review* (No. 34, August 18, 1967, p. 34), said: "China's great proletarian cultural revolution tells us unequivocally and clearly that the struggle

against Right opportunism [and] revisionism will be a protracted, arduous and complicated one."

79. Rangoon domestic service broadcast, April 18, 1968; *Vanguard Daily*, May 11, 1968.

80. Article by Win Aung in *Jen-min jih-pao*, September 1, 1967; broadcast by NCNA (Peking) international service, same date. Similar statements may be found in an article by Ba Thein Tin (in *Peking Review*, No. 48, November 24, 1967, pp. 19-21) and in a resolution of the CPB Central Committee Politburo (ibid., No. 51, December 15, 1967, pp. 5-6).

81. Reported via Rangoon domestic service, November 28, 1968. See the documentary collection in *Peking Review*, No. 13, March 28, 1969.

82. Rangoon domestic service, May 17, 1968; *Guardian*, May 26, 1968; *Vanguard Daily*, May 26, 1968.

83. Trager, "Burma: 1967–A Better Ending than Beginning," *Asian Survey*, Vol. VIII, No. 2, February 1968, p. 115.

84. Robert Dickson Crane, "Revolutionary Regionalism in Southeast Asia," *The Reporter*, May 2, 1968, p. 15. The Karens belonging to the KNDO claim about 7000 supporters, but this figure seems far too high and probably includes many part-time villagers and sympathizers. See *Washington Post*, September 5, 1967, p. 22, article by John Stirling.

85. Captured weapons of Chinese manufacture have reportedly included grenades, light machine guns, carbines, rifles, and grenade launchers. See, for instance, *Working People's Daily*, June 4 and 13, 1968; *Botataung*, July 17, 1968, and *New York Times*, August 31, 1970, p. 5.

86. In *Peking Review*, No. 36, September 1, 1967, p. 21.

87. NCNA broadcast of March 28, 1968.

88. For example, an NCNA broadcast of April 27, 1969; *Jen-min jih-pao*, March 28, 1970, p. 6, and an NCNA broadcast of September 4, 1970.

89. On the North-East Command, see Anthony Polsky, "Threatening Command," *Far Eastern Economic Review*, September 26, 1968, pp. 605-606, and *New York Times*, August 31, 1970, pp. 1, 5.

90. Based on aid figures in the Ellender Report, p. 9, and Trager, *Burma*, p. 336. If only disbursed aid is counted, the percentage given above would be still lower (about 12 percent). (In calculating aid to Burma from the non-Communist countries, loans and grants from various international organizations are not included.)

91. For a statement of Burma's official position, see *New York Times*, May 2, 1967, p. 13.

92. On Burma's relations with the ASEAN members, see Kathryn E. Rafferty, *Burma and Southeast Asian Regionalism*, RAC-TP-363, Research Analysis Corporation, McLean, Virginia, May 1969, especially pp. 8-16, 29.

Notes to Chapter 7

1. On the application of Mao's "theory of contradictions" to international affairs, see "Apologists of Neo-Colonialism"—Comment on the Open Letter of the Central Committee of the CPSU (4), by the Editorial Departments of *Jen-min jih-pao* and *Hung-ch'i (Red Flag)*, in *Peking Review*, No. 43, October 25, 1963, p. 7; Szu Mu, "The Advance of the Revolutionary Movement of the World's People is the Main Current of the Present Situation," *Shih-chieh chih-shih*, Nos. 2-3, February 10, 1966, p. 9.

2. See Editors of *Jen-min jih-pao*, "Forward Along the Road of the Great Lenin," in *Lieh-ning chu-yi wan sui (Long Live Leninism)*, San-lien Bookstore, Hong Kong, 1960, p. 61.

3. See the discussion in Franz Schurmann, *Ideology and Organization in Communist China*, University of California Press, Berkeley, 1966, pp. 44-45.

4. *Ta-kung pao* (Peking), February 24, 1966, p. 4 (reproducing an undated article by the army newspaper *Chieh-fang chün-pao (Liberation Army Daily)*.

5. Ibid. An editorial in *Shih-chieh chih-shih* (No. 18, September 25, 1964, p. 8) proclaimed that the attacks of imperialism and its followers on China "can only expose their evil face as enemies of all oppressed peoples and nations; they can only prove that we are doing right and doing well, that from this day on we must continue working in this way, until the revolutionary struggles of all the world's people achieve final victory."

6. For related comments, see Richard H. Solomon, "Parochialism and Paradox in Sino-American Relations," *Asian Survey*, Vol. VII, No. 12, December 1967, pp. 831-850.

7. See, for instance, "Observer," "Disputing Bundy," *Jen-min jih-pao*, February 20, 1966, p. 4.

8. "The proletarian party must be high-principled and should also be flexible. At times it must also carry out necessary compromises advantageous to the revolution. But it cannot, in the name of flexibility and necessary compromises, basically abandon principled policies and revolutionary goals." From the previously cited CCP letter to the Soviet party, *Kuan-yü kuo-chi kung-ch'an chu-yi yün-tung tsung lu-hsien ti chien-yi*, p. 22.

9. Ibid., p. 21: "Whoever considers a revolution can be made only if everything is smooth sailing, only if there is an advance guarantee against sacrifices and failure, is certainly no revolutionary." Revolutionaries must accept that "victory and defeat in struggle, the advance and retreat of movements, are often intertwined." By continuing the struggle under adverse circumstances, revolutionaries broaden their experience, consolidate their ranks, and gain new adherents. Hsiang Tung-hui, "The Big Agitation is a Good Thing," *Jen-min jih-pao*, March 1, 1966, p. 4.

10. Mao is quoted (ibid.) as having said: "Big wind and big waves are not to be feared. The society of man developed precisely from big wind and waves." Speaking at the Lushan Conference (July 23, 1959), Mao also related anxiety to

progress: "When one does not worry and does not have zest, nothing can be achieved." (Text in *Chinese Law and Government*, Vol. I, No. 4, Winter 1968-69, p. 40.) Ch'en Yi, speaking of the Laotian situation in August 1961, said that so long as it did not escalate dramatically, "it is good for the international situation to be a little tense. If the situation softens, the national liberation movement may slacken. We will walk on two legs: if the United States wants to relax, we will make the situation tense." Modified version of a speech to graduating students of the Peking Higher Academy, in *Ch'en Yi yen-lun hsüan*, p. 12.

11. The best historical exposition of the united front is Lyman P. Van Slyke, *Enemies and Friends: The United Front in Chinese Communist History*, Stanford University Press, Stanford, Calif., 1967. See also A.M. Halpern, "The Influence of Revolutionary Experience on Communist China's Foreign Outlook," in Werner Klatt, ed., *The Chinese Model: A Political, Economic and Social Survey*, Hong Kong University Press, Hong Kong, 1965, pp. 144-145.

12. Schurmann, p. 37.

13. See Li Wei-han, "The Chinese People's Democratic United Front: Its Special Features" (part 2), *Peking Review*, No. 35, September 1, 1961, p. 13, and Lin Piao, "Long Live the Victory of People's War!" ibid., No. 36, September 3, 1965, p. 22.

14. When Ch'en Yi visited Burma in January 1961, for example, he composed a poem that he recited two years later during another visit: "I live at the head of the [Irrawaddy] river; You [the Burmese] live at its base; Our mutual sentiment is unlimited; We both drink the same water." In *Shih-chieh chih-shih*, No. 9, May 10, 1963, p. 15.

15. Schelling, *The Strategy of Conflict*, Oxford University Press, New York, 1963, p. 22.

16. See, e.g., Gordon, *Toward Disengagement in Asia*, pp. 75-76; and Werner Levi, *The Challenge of World Politics in South and Southeast Asia*, Prentice-Hall, Englewood Cliffs, N.J., 1968, pp. 105-106, 120-121.

17. For one view of the institutional and political bases of revolutions, see the discussion in Samuel P. Huntington, *Political Order in Changing Societies*, Yale University Press, New Haven, Conn., 1968, pp. 275 ff.

18. Ibid., pp. 304-307.

19. E.g., see Gordon, *Toward Disengagement in Asia*, pp. 76, 166-168, 176; Greene, p. 37 ff.

20. See Edward Vose Gulick, *Europe's Classical Balance of Power*, W.W. Norton Co., New York, 1966; John H. Herz, pp. 66-67.

21. These considerations undercut the workability of an all-Asian balance of power such as Alastair Buchan ("An Asian Balance of Power?" *Encounter*, Vol. XXVII, No. 6, December 1966, pp. 62-71) has proposed—one based mainly on political cooperation and special responsibilities for India, Japan, and Australia.

22. Greene, pp. 40-41.

Bibliography[a]

China

Books and Monographs

Barnett, A. Doak, *Communist China and Asia: Challenge to American Policy*, Random House, Inc., New York, 1960.

Ch'en Yi yen-lun hsüan (Selected Speeches of Ch'en Yi), Tz'u-lien ch'u-pan she, Hong Kong, 1967.

China and the Asian-African Conference (Documents), Foreign Language Press, Peking, 1955.

Dutt, Vidya Prakash, *China and the World: An Analysis of Communist China's Foreign Policy*, Frederick A. Praeger, Inc., New York, 1964.

Halpern, A.M., ed., *Policies Toward China: Views from Six Continents* McGraw-Hill Book Co., for the Council on Foreign Relations, New York, 1965.

Harding, Harry and Melvin Gurtov, *The Purge of Lo Jui-ch'ing: The Politics of Chinese Strategic Planning*, Report R-548-PR, The RAND Corporation, Santa Monica, California, February 1971.

Hinton, Harold C., *Communist China in World Politics*, Houghton Mifflin Co., Boston, Massachusetts, 1966.

Hudson, G.F., Richard Lowenthal, and Roderick MacFarquhar, eds., *The Sino-Soviet Dispute*, Frederick A. Praeger, Inc., New York, 1961.

Inoki, Masamichi, ed., *Japan's Future in Southeast Asia*, Symposium Series II, Kyoto University, Center for Southeast Asian Studies, Kyoto, 1966.

Johnston, Douglas M. and Hungdah Chiu, *Agreements of the People's Republic of China, 1949-1967: A Calendar*, Harvard University Press, Cambridge, Massachusetts, 1969.

Klatt, Werner, ed., *The Chinese Model: A Political, Economic and Social Survey*, Hong Kong University Press, Hong Kong, 1965.

Lee, Chae-Jin, "Chinese Communist Policy in Laos, 1954-1965," unpublished Ph.D. dissertation, University of California, Los Angeles, 1966.

---

[a]Note: Although some sources have been used for more than one country, these have only been listed once. Sources mentioned in the footnotes but that do not appear in the bibliography—such as radio broadcasts and certain non-English language newspapers—were obtained from translations in the Foreign Broadcast Information Service *Daily Reports*.

Mao Tse-tung, *The Selected Works of Mao Tse-tung*, 5 vols., International Publishers Co., Inc., New York, 1954.

Mozingo, David, *China's Foreign Policy and the Cultural Revolution*, Interim Report No. 1, IREA Project, Cornell University, Ithaca, New York, March 1970.

Purcell, Victor, *The Chinese in Southeast Asia*, 2nd ed., Oxford University Press, London, 1965.

Robinson, Thomas W. et al., *The Cultural Revolution in China*, University of California Press, Berkeley, 1971.

Schurmann, Franz, *Ideology and Organization in Communist China*, University of California Press, Berkeley, 1966.

Ten Glorious Years, Foreign Language Press, Peking, 1960.

Van Slyke, Lyman P., *Enemies and Friends: The United Front in Chinese Communist History*, Stanford University Press, Stanford, California, 1967.

Williams, Lea E., *The Future of the Overseas Chinese in Southeast Asia*, McGraw-Hill Book Co., for the Council on Foreign Relations, New York, 1966.

Source Materials (in Chinese and in translation)

American Consulate-General, Hong Kong, *Current Background*, 1962-1968.

————, *Selections from China Mainland Magazines, 1968.*

————, *Survey of China Mainland Press*, 1953, 1956, 1960-1970.

Ch'iao-wu cheng-ts'e wen-chi (*Collected Documents on Overseas Chinese Affairs Policy*), Jen-min ch'u-pan she, Peking, 1957.

Chinese People's Institute of Foreign Affairs, ed., *A Victory for the Five Principles of People's Co-existence*, Foreign Languages Press, Peking, 1960.

Jen-min jih-pao (People's Daily), Peking, 1960-1971.

Jen-min shou-ts'e (People's Handbook), Ta-kung pao she, Tientsin, 1962-1965.

Kuan-yü kuo-chi kung-ch'an chu-yi yün-tung tsung lu-hsien ti chien-yi (A Proposal Concerning the General Line of the International Communist Movement), Jen-min ch'u-pan she, Peking, 1963.

Lieh-ning chu-yi wan sui (Long Live Leninism), San-lien shu-tien, Hong Kong, 1960.

New China News Agency Daily Bulletin, 1959, 1964-1965.

Peking Review, 1963-1971.

Red Guard newspapers by various organizations in and outside Peking, 1966-1967.

Shih-chieh chih-shih (World Knowledge), 1962-1966.

Ta-kung pao, Peking, 1966.

Articles and Miscellaneous Publications

Adie, W.A.C., "China and the Bandung Spirit," *Mizan*, Vol. VIII, No. 1, January-February 1966, pp. 2-13.

———;"Vagaries of Chinese Policy," *Mizan*, Vol. IX, No. 6, November-December 1967, pp. 231-244.

Bridgham, Philip, "Mao's Cultural Revolution in 1967: The Struggle to Seize Power," *The China Quarterly*, No. 34, April-June 1968, pp. 6-37.

Chung-yang jih-pao (Central Daily News, Taipei), 1967-1968.

Fei-ch'ing yen-chiu (Studies of Chinese Communism, Taipei), 1967-1968.

FitzGerald, Stephen, "China and the Overseas Chinese: Perceptions and Policies," *The China Quarterly*, No. 44, October-December 1970, pp. 1-37.

Halpern, A.M., "The Chinese Communist Line on Neutralism," *The China Quarterly*, No. 5, January-March 1961, pp. 90-115.

———, "The Foreign Policy Uses of the Chinese Revolutionary Model," *The China Quarterly*, No. 7, July-September 1961, pp. 1-16.

Hsing-tao jih-pao, Hong Kong, 1967.

Solomon, Richard H., "Parochialism and Paradox in Sino-American Relations," *Asian Survey*, Vol. VII, No. 12, December 1967, pp. 831-850.

Tsou, Tang and Morton H. Halperin, "Mao Tse-tung's Revolutionary Strategy and Peking's International Behavior," *American Political Science Review*, Vol. LIX, No. 1, March 1965, pp. 80-99.

Thailand

Books and Monographs

Black, Cyril E. and Thomas P. Thornton, eds., *Communism and Revolution: The Strategic Uses of Political Violence*. Princeton University Press, Princeton, N.J., 1964.

Brimmell, J.S., *Communism in South East Asia: A Political Analysis*, Oxford University Press, London, 1959.

Centre d'Étude des Relations Internationales,. *Régime Interne et Politique Extérieure dans les Pays d'Asie*, Cahiers de la Fondation Nationale des Sciences Politiques, No. 146, Armand Colin, Paris, 1966.

214

The Communist Threat to Thailand, Thai Sambhand Press, Bangkok, August 1967.

Darling, Frank C., *Thailand and the United States*, Public Affairs Press, Washington, D.C., 1965.

Dommen, Arthur J., *Conflict in Laos: The Politics of Neutralization*, Pall Mall Press, London, 1964.

Insor, D., *Thailand: A Political, Social, and Economic Analysis*, Frederick A. Praeger, Inc., New York, 1963.

Keyes, Charles F., *Isan: Regionalism in Northeastern Thailand*, Cornell University, Dept. of Asian Studies, Ithaca, New York, 1967.

Lamb, Alastair, *Asian Frontiers: Studies in a Continuing Problem*, Frederick A. Praeger, Inc., New York, 1968.

McCabe, Robert Karr, *Storm Over Asia: China and Southeast Asia, Thrust and Response*, New American Library of World Literature, Inc., New York, 1967.

Modelski, George, ed., *SEATO: Six Studies*, University of British Columbia, for the Australian National University, Vancouver, 1962.

Nuechterlein, Donald E., *Thailand and the Struggle for Southeast Asia*, Cornell University Press, Ithaca, New York, 1965.

Skinner, G. William, *Chinese Society in Thailand: An Analytical History*, Cornell University Press, Ithaca, New York, 1957.

————, *Leadership and Power in the Chinese Community of Thailand*, Cornell University Press, Ithaca, New York, 1958.

Smith, Harvey H., et al., *Area Handbook for Thailand*, 2nd rev. ed., U.S. Government Printing Office, Washington, D.C., 1968.

Thompson, Virginia and Richard Adloff, *The Left Wing in Southeast Asia*, Wm. Sloane Associates, under the auspices of the International Secretariat, Institute of Pacific Relations, New York, 1950.

Toye, Hugh, *Laos: Buffer State or Battleground*, Oxford University Press, London, 1968.

Trager, Frank N., ed., *Marxism in Southeast Asia: A Study of Four Countries*, Stanford University Press, Stanford, California, 1959.

U.S. Senate, Committee on Foreign Relations, Subcommittee on United States Security Agreements and Commitments Abroad, *Hearings: Kingdom of Laos*, Pt. 2, October 20-22, 28, 1969, 91st Congress, 1st Session, Government Printing Office, Washington, D.C., 1970.

————, *Hearings: Kingdom of Thailand*, Pt. 3, November 10-17, 1969, 91st Congress, 1st Session, Government Printing Office, Washington, D.C., 1970.

Wilson, David A., *Politics in Thailand*, Cornell University Press, Ithaca, New York, 1962.

Official Sources

Foreign Affairs Bulletin, Department of Information, Ministry of Foreign Affairs, Bangkok, 1962-1968.

"Statement by Mr. Thanat Khoman, Minister of Foreign Affairs of Thailand, at the opening session of the Ninth Meeting of the Council of Ministers of the South-East Asia Treaty Organization, Manila, April 13, 1964," n.p., n.d.

Thailand at the Geneva Conference on Laos, Department of Information, Ministry of Foreign Affairs, Bangkok, 1961.

Thailand, Ministry of Foreign Affairs, *Collected Statements of Foreign Minister Thanat Khoman*, Vol. III, November 1966-October 1967, Department of Information, Bangkok, 1967.

———, *Facts About the Relations Between Thailand and Cambodia*, Prachandra Press, Bangkok, 1961.

———, *Facts About the Relations Between Thailand and Cambodia II*, Prachanda Press, Bangkok, February 28, 1962.

———, *Facts About the Relations Between Thailand and Cambodia III*, [Prachandra Press?], Bangkok, March 1, 1963.

———, *Relations Between Thailand and Cambodia*, Prachandra Press, Bangkok, January 1959.

Thailand, Permanent Mission to the United Nations, Press Releases, 1966-1970.

Articles and Miscellaneous Publications

Couret, Bernard, "Negative Neutrals? Never," *Far Eastern Economic Review*, April 11, 1968, pp. 65-66.

Fistié, Pierre, "Minorités ethniques, opposition et subversion en Thailande," *Politique étrangère*, No. 3, 1967, pp. 295-324.

Girling, J.L.S., "Northeast Thailand: Tomorrow's Viet Nam?" *Foreign Affairs*, Vol. XLVI, No. 2, January 1968, pp. 388-397.

Gordon, Bernard K., "Thailand: Its Meaning for the U.S.," *Current History*, Vol. LII, No. 305, January 1967, pp. 16-21.

Hanna, Willard A., "Thailand's Strategic Northeast: Defense and Development," *American Universities Field Staff Reports*, Southeast Asia Series, Vol. XIV, No. 1, January 1966.

Joyaux, François, "La politique étrangère de la Thailande en Asie," *Politique étrangère*, No. 4, 1966, pp. 335-343.

Karnow, Stanley, "The Looking Glass War," *Far Eastern Economic Review*, December 21, 1967, pp. 539-547.

Keyes, Charles F., "Ethnic Identity and Loyalty of Villagers in Northeastern Thailand," *Asian Survey*, Vol. VI, No. 7, July 1966, pp. 362-369.

Long, Millard F., "Economic Development in Northeast Thailand: Problems and Prospects," *Asian Survey*, Vol. VI, No. 7, July 1966, pp. 355-361.

National Broadcasting Company, "Meet the Press" Interview with Thai Foreign Minister Thanat Khoman, Vol. IX, No. 17, May 9, 1965.

Nuechterlein, Donald E., "Thailand after Sarit," *Asian Survey*, Vol. IV, No. 5, May 1964, pp. 842-850.

———, "Thailand: Another Vietnam?" *Asian Survey*, Vol. VII, No. 2, February 1967, pp. 126-130.

Parker, Maynard, "The Americans in Thailand," *The Atlantic*, Vol. CCXVIII, No. 6, December 1966, pp. 51-58.

Poole, Peter A., "Thailand's Vietnamese Minority," *Asian Survey*, Vol. VII, No. 12, December 1967, pp. 886-895.

Santosh, A.B., "The First Round," *Far Eastern Economic Review*, April 6, 1967, pp. 23-25.

Singh, L.P., "Thai Foreign Policy: The Current Phase," *Asian Survey*, Vol. III, No. 11, November 1963, pp. 535-543.

Standish, W.A., "Malay Moslem Mixtures," *Far Eastern Economic Review*, July 6, 1967, pp. 19-22.

Stanton, Edwin F., "Communist Pressures in Thailand," *Current History*, Vol. XXXVIII, No. 22, February 1960, pp. 102-109.

Starner, Frances L., "No 'Camouflage Surrender,'" *Far Eastern Economic Review*, October 17, 1968, pp. 155-159.

Suhrke, Astri, "The Thai Muslims: Some Aspects of Minority Integration," *Pacific Affairs*, Vol. XLIII, No. 4, Winter 1970-71, pp. 531-547.

"Thailand: The Northeast," *Asia*, No. 6, Autumn 1966, pp. 1-27.

Thanat Khoman, "Which Road for Southeast Asia?" *Foreign Affairs*, Vol. XLII, No. 4, July 1964, pp. 628-639.

Warner, Denis, "Underground in the Northeast," *The New Republic*, April 6, 1963, pp. 8-9.

Wilson, David A., *China, Thailand and the Spirit of Bandung*, Paper P-2607, The RAND Corporation, July 1962.

———, "Introductory Comment on Politics and the Northeast," *Asian Survey*, Vol. VI, No. 7, July 1966, pp. 349-352.

———, "Thailand: A New Leader," *Asian Survey*, Vol. IV, No. 2, February 1964, pp. 711-715.

Newspapers (also applicable to Burma and Cambodia)

Bangkok Post, 1967-1971.

Bangkok World, 1967-1971.

Christian Science Monitor, Boston, 1967-1968.

Izvestiia, Moscow, 1967.

Krasnaia zvezda (Red Star), Moscow, 1964.

Le Monde, Paris, 1966-1969.

Los Angeles Times, 1965-1971.

New York Times, 1965-1971.

Washington Post, 1967-1971.

Cambodia

Books and Monographs

Armstrong, John P., *Sihanouk Speaks*, Walker and Co., New York, 1964.

Coedès, George, *The Making of South East Asia*, Trans. from the French by H.M. Wright, University of California Press, Berkeley, California, 1966.

Decornoy, Jacques, *L'Asie du Sud-Est: Vingt ans à la recherche d'un avenir*, Casterman, Paris, 1967.

Field, Michael, *The Prevailing Wind: Witness in Indo-China*, Metheun and Co., London, 1965.

Gordon, Bernard K., *The Dimensions of Conflict in Southeast Asia*, Prentice-Hall, Inc., Englewood Cliffs, New Jersey, 1966.

_____, and Anne V. Cyr, *Cambodia and Southeast Asian Regionalism*, Report RAC-R-73, Research Analysis Corporation, McLean, Virginia, July 1969.

Herz, Martin F., *A Short History of Cambodia: From the Days of Angkor to the Present*, Frederick A. Praeger, Inc., New York, 1958.

Leifer, Michael, *Cambodia: The Search for Security*, Frederick A. Praeger, Inc., New York, 1967.

Noel, Don O., Jr., Reports from Cambodia, sponsored by the Alicia Patterson Fund of New York City, November 1966-April 1967.

Poole, Peter A., *Cambodia's Quest for Survival*, American-Asian Educational Exchange, New York, 1969.

SarDesai, D.R., *Indian Foreign Policy in Cambodia, Laos, and Vietnam, 1947-1964*, University of California Press, Berkeley, California, 1968.

Shaplen, Robert, *Time Out of Hand: Revolution and Reaction in Southeast Asia*, Harper and Row, New York, 1969.

Smith, Roger M., *Cambodia's Foreign Policy*, Cornell University Press, Ithaca, New York, 1965.

Steinberg, David J. et al, *Cambodia: Its People Its Society Its Culture*, Rev. by Herbert H. Vreeland, Human Relations Area Files Press, New Haven, Connecticut, 1959.

Willmott, William E., *The Chinese in Cambodia*, University of British Columbia Press, Vancouver, 1967.

Official and Semi-Official Sources

Documents

Cambodge, Mission Permanente du, auprès des Nations Unies, Bulletin de Presse, 1968.

Cambodge, Royaume du, *Battambang et son passé*, Ministry of Information, Phnom Penh, 1968.

———, *Biographie de S.A.R. le Prince Norodom Sihanouk chef de l'état du Cambodge*, Ministry of Information, Phnom Penh, November 1965.

———, *Discours de S.P. Norodom Sihanouk Upayuvareach, chef de l'état du Cambodge, à l'occasion de l'ouverture de la conférence plenière des peuples indochinoises*, Ministry of Information, Phnom Penh, February 25, 1965.

———, *Livre blanc sur la rupture des relations diplomatiques entre le Cambodge et la Thailande, le 23 octobre 1961*, Imprimerie du Ministère de l'Information, Phnom Penh, February 1965.

———, *Les paroles de Samdech Preah Norodom Sihanouk, 1967, 1968*, Ministry of Information, Phnom Penh, 1968.

———, *Principaux discours, messages, déclarations et allocutions de Son Altesse Royale Le Prince Norodom Sihanouk en 1962*. Ministry of Information, Phnom Penh, October 1963.

———, *Principaux discours, messages, allocutions, déclarations, conférences de presse et interview de Son Altesse Royale le Prince Norodom Sihanouk, année 1963*, Ministry of Information, Phnom Penh, July 1964.

———, *Le retour de l'indépendance nationale, 9 novembre 1953: textes et documents*, Ministry of Information, Phnom Penh, n.d.

Sihanouk, Norodom, *Le Cambodge et ses relations avec ses voisins*, Imprimerie du Ministère de l'Information, Phnom Penh, 1962.

_____, *Notre socialisme buddhique*, Ministry of Information, Phnom Penh, December 1965.

_____, *La monarchie cambodigienne et la croisade pour l'indépendance*, Imprimerie Rasmey, Phnom Penh, 1961.

Journals

Études cambodgiennes, Ministry of Information, Phnom Penh, 1967.

Kambuja, Phnom Penh; director: S.A.R. Prince Norodom Sihanouk; 1968.

Réalités cambodgiennes, Phnom Penh, 1967-1969.

Le Sangkum, Phnom Penh, 1968.

Special Papers and Reports

British Information Services, "Cambodia: Text of a Statement by the Secretary of State for Foreign Affairs, the Rt. Hon. Michael Stewart, M.P., presenting a White Paper on Cambodia to the House of Commons, June 3, 1965 and Text of the Preface to the White Paper," New York, 1965.

Conference of Heads of State or Government of Non-aligned Countries, The: Belgrade, September 1-6, 1961, Publicisticko-Izdavacki Zavod, Belgrade, 1961.

Great Britain, Interim and Progress Reports of the International Commission for Supervision and Control in Cambodia, 1955-1959. Cmd. 9458 (No. 1, 1955), 9534 (No. 2, 1955), 9579 (No. 3, 1955), 9671 (No. 4, 1956), 253 (No. 1, 1957), 526 (No. 1, 1958), 887 (No. 1, 1959). H.M. Stationery Office, London, 1955 *et sqq.*

_____, *Recent Diplomatic Exchanges concerning the Proposal for an International Conference on the Neutrality and Territorial Integrity of Cambodia*, Cambodia No. 1 (1965), Cmd. 2678, H.M. Stationery Office, London, June 1965.

U.S. Department of State, Bureau of Intelligence and Research, *World Strength of the Communist Party Organizations*, 21st ed., Department of State Publication 8455, Washington D.C., 1969.

Articles and Miscellaneous Publications

Allman, T.D., "Anatomy of a Coup," *Far Eastern Economic Review*, April 9, 1970, pp. 17-21.

Attwood, William, "Sihanouk Talks," *Look*, April 2, 1968, pp. 64-68.

Babaa, Khalid I. and Cecil V. Crabb, Jr., "Nonalignment as a Diplomatic and Ideological Credo," *The Annals*, Vol. CCCLXII, November 1965, pp. 6-17.

"Le Cambodge donne l'exemple," *Jeune afrique*, No. 320, February 26, 1966.

Gordon, Bernard K., "Cambodia: Where Foreign Policy Counts," *Asian Survey*, Vol. V, No. 9, September 1965, pp. 433-448.

Joint Publications Research Service (U.S. Department of Commerce), *Translations on South and Southeast Asia*, 1965-1969.

Kalb, Bernard and Marvin, "Jacqueline Kennedy's Secret Mission in Asia," *McCall's*, Vol. XCV, No. 9, June 1968, pp. 61, 107-113.

Kirk, Donald, "Cambodia's Economic Crisis," *Asian Survey*, Vol. XI, No. 3, March 1971, pp. 238-255.

Leifer, Michael, "Cambodia: The Limits of Diplomacy," *Asian Survey*, Vol. VII, No. 1, January 1967, pp. 69-73.

————, "Cambodia: The Politics of Accommodation," *Asian Survey*, Vol. IV, No. 1, January 1964, pp. 674-679.

————, "The Failure of Political Institutionalization in Cambodia," *Modern Asian Studies*, Vol. II, No. 2, April 1968, pp. 125-140.

————, "Rebellion or Subversion in Cambodia?" *Current History*, Vol. LVI, No. 330, February 1969, pp. 88-93.

New Times, Moscow, 1967-1968.

Shaplen, Robert, "Letter from Cambodia," *The New Yorker*, January 13, 1968, pp. 66-89.

Sihanouk, Norodom, "Cambodia Neutral: The Dictate of Necessity," *Foreign Affairs*, Vol. XXXVI, No. 4, July 1958, pp. 582-586.

Simon, Jean-Pierre, "Cambodia: Pursuit of Crisis," *Asian Survey*, Vol. V, No. 1, January 1965, pp. 49-54.

Smith, Roger M., "Cambodia: Between Scylla and Charybdis," *Asian Survey*, Vol. VIII, No. 1, January 1968, pp. 72-79.

Usvatov, A., "Cambodia: Between Two Fires," *New Times*, No. 41, October 11, 1967, p. 17.

Willmott, William E., "Cambodian Neutrality," *Current History*, Vol. LII, No. 305, January 1967, pp. 36-40.

Burma

Books and Monographs

Byliniak, S.A., *Gosudarstvennye finansy nezavisimoi Birmy (The National Finances of Independent Burma)*, "Nauka," Moscow, 1968.

Ellender, Senator Allen J., *Review of United States Government Operations in South Asia*, Senate Doc. No. 77, 90th Cong., 2d Sess., Government Printing Office, Washington, D.C., 1968.

Furnivall, John S., *Colonial Policy and Practice: A Comparative Study of Burma and Netherlands India*, New York University Press, New York, 1956.

Hinton, Harold C., *China's Relations with Burma and Vietnam*, Institute of Pacific Relations, New York, 1958.

Johnstone, William C., *Burma's Foreign Policy: A Study in Neutralism*, Harvard University Press, Cambridge, Massachusetts, 1963.

Kaznacheev, Aleksandr, *Inside a Soviet Embassy: Experiences of a Russian Diplomat in Burma*, J.B. Lippincott Co., Philadelphia, 1962.

Kunstadter, Peter, ed., *Southeast Asian Tribes, Minorities, and Nations*, 2 vols., Princeton University Press, Princeton, New Jersey, 1967.

Leach, E.R., *Political Systems of Highland Burma: A Study of Kachin Social Structure*, Harvard University Press, Cambridge, Massachusetts, 1954.

Maung Maung, *Burma in the Family of Nations*, Djambatan and the Institute of Pacific Relations, Amsterdam and New York, 1956.

Ne Win, *Birma na novom puty (Burma on the New Road)*, "Nauka," Moscow, 1965.

Pye, Lucian W., *Politics, Personality, and Nation Building: Burma's Search for Identity*, Yale University Press, New Haven, Connecticut, 1962.

Rafferty, Kathryn E., *Burma and Southeast Asian Regionalism*, Technical Paper RAC-TP-363, Research Analysis Corporation, McLean, Virginia, May 1969.

Rowland, John, *A History of Sino-Indian Relations: Hostile Co-Existence*, D. Van Nostrand and Co., Princeton, New Jersey, 1967.

Sarkisyanz, E., *Buddhist Backgrounds of the Burmese Revolution*, Martinus Nijhoff, The Hague, 1965.

Smith, Donald Eugene, *Religion and Politics in Burma*, Princeton University Press, Princeton, New Jersey, 1965.

Tinker, Hugh, *The Union of Burma: A Study of the First Years of Independence*, Oxford University Press, London, 1957.

Trager, Frank N., *Burma—From Kingdom to Republic: A Historical and Political Analysis*, Frederick A. Praeger, Inc., New York, 1966.

_____, Patricia Wohlgemuth, and Lu-yu Kiang, *Burma's Role in the United Nations 1948-55*, Institute of Pacific Relations, New York, 1956.

Zhukov, E.M., ed., *Sovremennye teorii sotsializma "natsional'nogo tipa" (Modern Theories of "National-type" Socialism)*, "Mysl'," Moscow, 1967.

Official Sources (including Newspapers)

Forward, Directorate of Information, Rangoon, 1967-1970.

Guardian, Rangoon, 1968.

The Nation, Rangoon, 1962, 1968.

Nu, U., *An Asian Speaks*, Embassy of the Union of Burma, Washington, D.C., 1955.

———, *Burma Looks Ahead*, Ministry of Information of the GUB, Rangoon, 1955.

———, *Forward With the People*, Ministry of Information of the GUB, Rangoon, 1955.

Articles and Miscellaneous Publications

Badgley, John H., "Burma: The Nexus of Socialism and Two Political Traditions," *Asian Survey*, Vol. III, No. 2, February 1963, pp. 89-95.

———, "Burma's China Crisis: The Choices Ahead," *Asian Survey*, Vol. VII, No. 11, November 1967, pp. 753-761.

———, "Burma's Radical Left," *Problems of Communism*, Vol. X, No. 2, March-April 1961, pp. 47-55.

———, "Burma's Zealot Wungyis: Maoists or St. Simonists," *Asian Survey*, Vol. V, No. 1, January 1965, pp. 55-62.

Boog, Peter, "The People's War," *Far Eastern Economic Review*, November 16, 1967, pp. 314-323.

Cady, John F., "Burma's Military Regime," *Current History*, Vol. XXXVIII, No. 222, February 1960, pp. 75-81.

Clubb, Oliver E., Jr., *The Effect of Chinese Nationalist Military Activities in Burma on Burmese Foreign Policy*, Paper P-1595-RC, The RAND Corporation, January 20, 1959.

Crane, Robert Dickson, "Revolutionary Regionalism in Southeast Asia," *The Reporter*, May 2, 1968, pp. 11-16.

Crocker, Isabelle, *Burma's Foreign Policy and the Korean War: A Case Study*, Paper P-1576-RC, The RAND Corporation, December 12, 1958.

Current Digest of the Soviet Press, 1967-1968.

Far Eastern Economic Review Yearbook, 1963, 1967-1970.

Furnivall, J.S. "Communism and Nationalism in Burma," *Far Eastern Survey*, Vol. XVIII, No. 17, August 24, 1949, pp. 193-197.

Holmes, Robert A., "Burmese Domestic Policy: The Politics of Burmanization," *Asian Survey*, Vol. VII, No. 3, March 1967, pp. 188-197.

Law, Edward M. Yone and David G. Mandelbaum, "Pacification in Burma," *Far Eastern Survey*, Vol. XIX, No. 17, October 11, 1950, pp. 182-186.

Maung Maung, "The Burma-China Border Settlement," *Asian Survey*, Vol. I, No. 1, March 1961, pp. 38-43.

Polsky, Anthony, "Threatening Command," *Far Eastern Economic Review*, September 26, 1968, pp. 605-606.

Silverstein, Josef, "Burma: Ne Win's Revolution Reconsidered," *Asian Survey*, Vol. VI, No. 2, February 1966, pp. 95-102.

Theodorson, George A., "Minority Peoples in the Union of Burma," *Journal of Southeast Asian History*, Vol. V, No. 1, March 1964, pp. 1-16.

Trager, Frank N., "Burma and China," *Journal of Southeast Asian History*, Vol. V, No. 1, March 1964, pp. 29-61.

_____, "Sino-Burmese Relations: The End of the Pauk Phaw Era," *Orbis*, Vol. XI, No. 4, Winter 1968, pp. 1034-1054.

_____, "Burma: 1967–A Better Ending than Beginning," *Asian Survey*, Vol. VIII, No. 2, February 1968, pp. 110-119.

_____, "Burma: 1968–A New Beginning?" *Asian Survey*, Vol. IX, No. 2, February 1969, pp. 104-114.

Whittam, Daphne E., "The Sino-Burmese Boundary Treaty," *Pacific Affairs*, Vol. XXXIV, No. 2, Summer 1961, pp. 174-183.

Southeast Asia and International Politics

Bachrach, Peter and Morton S. Baratz, "Decisions and Nondecisions: An Analytical Framework," *American Political Science Review*, Vol. LVII, No. 3, September 1963, pp. 632-642.

Brecher, Michael, *The New States of Asia: A Political Analysis*, Oxford University Press, New York, 1963.

Buchan, Alastair, "An Asian Balance of Power?" *Encounter*, Vol. XXVII, No. 6, December 1966, pp. 62-71.

Cady, John F., *Southeast Asia: Its Historical Development*, McGraw-Hill Book Co., New York, 1964.

Claude, Inis L., Jr., *Power and International Relations*, Random House, New York, 1962.

Gordon, Bernard K., *Toward Disengagement in Asia: A Strategy for American Foreign Policy*, Prentice-Hall, Englewood Cliffs, New Jersey, 1969.

Greene, Fred, *U.S. Policy and the Security of Asia*, McGraw-Hill Book Co., New York, 1968.

Gulick, Edward Vose, *Europe's Classical Balance of Power*, W.W. Norton Co., New York, 1955.

Gurtov, Melvin, *Southeast Asia Tomorrow: Problems and Prospects for U.S. Policy*, John Hopkins Press, Baltimore, 1970.

Herz, John H., *International Politics in the Atomic Age*, Columbia University Press, New York, 1959.

Huntington, Samuel P., *Political Order in Changing Societies*, Yale University Press, New Haven, Connecticut, 1968.

Jansen, G.H., *Nonalignment and the Afro-Asian States*, Frederick A. Praeger, Inc., New York, 1966.

Johnson, John J., ed., *The Role of the Military in Underdeveloped Countries*, Princeton University Press, Princeton, New Jersey, 1962.

Kahin, George McT., ed., *Governments and Politics of Southeast Asia*, 2d ed., Cornell University Press, Ithaca, New York, 1964.

Kautsky, John H., ed., *Political Change in Underdeveloped Countries: Nationalism and Communism*, John Wiley, New York, 1962.

Levi, Werner, *The Challenge of World Politics in South and Southeast Asia*, Prentice-Hall, Englewood Cliffs, New Jersey, 1968.

McLane, Charles B., *Soviet Strategies in Southeast Asia: An Exploration of Eastern Policy under Lenin and Stalin*, Princeton University Press, Princeton, New Jersey, 1966.

Miller, J.D.B., *The Politics of the Third World*, Oxford University Press, for the Royal Institute of International Affairs, London, 1967.

Rosenau, James N., ed., *Linkage Politics: Essays on the Convergence of National and International Systems*, Free Press, New York, 1969.

Scalapino, Robert A., ed., *The Communist Revolution in Asia: Tactics, Goals, and Achievements*, Prentice-Hall, Englewood Cliffs, New Jersey, 1965 and 1969.

Schelling, Thomas C., *The Strategy of Conflict*, Oxford University Press, New York, 1963.

van der Kroef, Justus M., "Interpretations of the 1965 Indonesian Coup: A Review of the Literature," *Pacific Affairs*, Vol. XLIII, No. 4, Winter 1970-71, pp. 557-577.

Wriggins, W. Howard, *The Ruler's Imperative: Strategies for Political Survival in Asia and Africa*, Columbia University Press, New York, 1969.

About the Author

Melvin Gurtov is associate professor of political science at the University of California, Riverside. He was born in Brooklyn, New York, on September 2, 1941. Dr. Gurtov did undergraduate and graduate work at Columbia University, had advanced Chinese language training at the Stanford University center on Taiwan, and received his doctorate from the University of California, Los Angeles, in 1970. He was a staff member of the Social Science Department of The Rand Corporation for five years. He is the author of *The First Vietnam Crisis: Chinese Communist Strategy and United States Involvement, 1953-1954* (New York, 1967) and *Southeast Asia Tomorrow: Problems and Prospects for U.S. Policy* (Baltimore, 1970), and coauthor of *The Cultural Revolution in China* (Berkeley, 1971). He has contributed essays on China, Taiwan, and Southeast Asia to a number of books and periodicals. Dr. Gurtov, with his wife, Rochelle, and daughter, Ellene, makes his home in Pacific Palisades, California.

Index